KEROUAC
AND THE **B**EATS

D1571187

Front row, left to right: Robert LaVigne, Shig of City Lights, poets Larry Fagin, Lew Welch, Peter Orlovsky, Leland Meyerzove (lying down); second row, left to right: poets David Meltzer, Michael McClure, Allen Ginsberg, Daniel Langton, a friend of Ginsberg's, Richard Brautigan, Gary Goodrow of the committee, and painter Nemi Frost; in back: Stella Levy, Lawrence Ferlinghetti. The last gathering of the Beat Generation. North Beach gathering of Poets/Artists. City Lights Book Store, San Francisco, 1965. Photograph by Larry Keenan.

KEROUAC
AND THE BEATS

A PRIMARY SOURCEBOOK

EDITED BY

Arthur and Kit Knight

Foreword by John Tytell

PARAGON HOUSE

NEW YORK

First edition, 1988

Second printing

Published in the United States by

Paragon House
90 Fifth Avenue
New York, NY 10011

Library of Congress Cataloging-in-Publication Data
Main entry under title:

Kerouac and the Beats.

   Bibliography: p.
   1. American literature—20th century—History and
criticism.   2. Bohemianism—United States—History—
Sources.   3. Kerouac, Jack, 1922–1969.   4. Authors,
American—20th century—Biography—Sources.   5. Authors,
American—20th century—Interviews.   I. Knight, Arthur
Winfield, 1937– .   II. Knight, Kit.
PS228.B6K48   1988   810'.9'0054   87-35716
ISBN 1-55778-067-6
ISBN 1-55778-095-1 (pbk.)

Manufactured in the United States of America

For John Clellon Holmes
IN MEMORIAM

CONTENTS

Idiosyncratic phrasings, spellings, and punctuation have been faithfully preserved throughout this book, for reasons of historical/ literary continuity.

FOREWORD

THE BEAT BROTHERHOOD

Literary reputation can be a treacherous matter, and fame, as Jack Kerouac once observed ruefully, can be as transient as dirty newspaper blowing down a city street. The Beat Generation is still a recent phenomenon in American literature; a number of its members are still writing, and its permanent reputation is still in the process of being formed. The literary reputation of the Beats has changed remarkably in the eighties, and they are no longer treated with the grinning condescension we reserve for bohemians whom we refuse to take seriously. Kerouac's *On the Road* has practically achieved the status of an American classic, a book that portrays the ethos of a generation in the way that *Huckleberry Finn* or *The Sun Also Rises* did in earlier eras. William Burroughs has produced a considerable body of work and *Naked Lunch* has long been regarded as the seminal expression of post-modernist fiction. Allen Ginsberg's "Howl" is in all the anthologies; it has had an enormous effect on American poetry, and has become the best-selling work by an American poet in our time, the most influential long poem since "The Waste Land." The Beat movement covers a broad geographical spectrum, from New York City to San Francisco, and it includes a range of other writers who have won large followings, such as Gary Snyder, Lawrence Ferlinghetti and Gregory Corso.

The key figure in this movement is still Jack Kerouac. Every so often a writer appears who so aptly captures the music of his moment, the attitudes and aspirations of his time, that he becomes the voice of a generation. Kerouac was such a writer and *Kerouac and the Beats* is a reflection of his centrality. Kerouac's story is one of the more anomalous in the history of American letters. Like Poe, Melville, or Faulkner, he did much of his early work in anonymity, under adverse conditions, and with little encouragement. When the book for which he is best known, *On the Road,* appeared in 1957, it aroused consternation and controversy among the book reviewers and literary critics who helped to shape popular taste. They deplored the delirious manners and reckless mores of head-strong characters who seemed able to sacrifice conventional bonds and obligations for the sake of excitement. The critics labeled it hedonistic, nihilistic, and blatantly onanistic.

The uproar caused by Kerouac's novel and by other Beat writings, such as Ginsberg's *Howl* and Burroughs's *Naked Lunch,* now seems out of proportion, but in the late 1950s the conflict cut across the literary standards of a culture, just as it heralded the conflict of generations that would occur in the United States in the 1960s. Apparently some taboo had been threatened, some nerve in the cultural nexus had been exposed, some tacit agreement between artist and audience had been spurned. Kerouac's critics saw him as the leader of a group of young barbarians storming the literary citadel.

Part of the difficulty in assessing the Beat movement is that excess is often mistrusted and usually feared. During the fifties, a time of many silent omissions, the Beat polemic was release. Their politics were not leftist as much as libertarian and the purpose was to rouse, to challenge, to question the changes caused by the new technologies, to help Americans remember that this too was once a place where men could dream of a better future. Such visions as they managed occurred as the consequence of a struggle with their own conditioning, at great psychic cost. In Kerouac's case, the struggle burned him out before he was fifty. The value of such suffering for the community, however, is whatever spiritual insight may ensue, particularly if the sufferer seeks to record the changes along the way. In this sense Burroughs, Kerouac, and Ginsberg share a communion of perception.

When I began my work on the writers of the Beat Generation, as a young scholar who had previously written about Henry James and Ford Madox Ford, about Baron Corvo and Richard Crashaw, there was virtually no useful material on the subject. My interest began when I was asked, during the time of troubles in American universities at the end of the sixties, to deliver a lecture as if it were my last opportunity to address a university audience. I felt my own literary interests might not be immediate enough for the concerns of students and faculty anguished over our involvement in Southeast Asia. The Beats were political and engaged; their work had power, though it was then unappreciated and misunderstood.

I began with some of the novels and poems, only intending to speak my piece and move on to other areas of literary endeavor. But when I realized how maligned and patronized the Beats had been throughout the various controversies concerning them, I decided to write an essay on their origins and importance. This appeared in *The American Scholar* and provoked interest. Before I knew it, I was reading all the available literature and embarked on *Naked Angels,* the first comprehensive account of the Beats.

I was fortunate in living in New York City, since Allen Ginsberg had deposited his letters and papers at Columbia University, but the collection was a chaotic quagmire without collation or chronology, a disorder of undated notes and fading letters stuffed in shoeboxes. The awful state of the Ginsberg papers seemed to be an index of how the Beats were then regarded. After a year of reading this material, making several trips to other university collections, particularly the one at the Humanities Research Center in Austin, Texas, and using private collections like the one owned by Kerouac's friend John Clellon Holmes, I knew enough to begin interviewing various Beat writers. What I had to learn was how to ask the questions (often despite the feeling that I was just blundering into the trivial) that could serve to break through the surface of events as they inevitably become fogged in time and memory—a distance compounded by the mistrust of the man asking the questions.

I sent the *American Scholar* essay to Ginsberg and to Burroughs, and they each liked it enough to make themselves available. Ginsberg was full of articulated memory and valuable assistance; Burroughs was much more removed, having the fear of biographical treachery that may be instinctive with certain writers. I used my tape recorder and I remember the way Burroughs would stiffly rise and walk twelve feet away from my machine so that it could not possibly pick up his murmured reply to a question that might have been too personal, too close to the bone of past suffering. But I regarded whatever I got as an advantage, for no one had previously been permitted even to sketch the details of his life, and the result is happily included in this volume. I suppose my greatest luck, however, was in locating and interviewing the lesser figures in the Beat group: men like Huncke (whom I reached only through a fluke of friendship and after enough negotiation to end a small war); Lucien Carr (who tried to get me drunk when I met him in a bar near the Daily News building, and who only began to trust me after a former student, a New York City fireman in uniform, came over to greet me); John Clellon Holmes, Kerouac's novelist friend, who offered me grace and hospitality; and Carl Solomon, whom Ginsberg had met at New York Psychiatric Institute and who then spent eight years in other institutions, still afflicted and still on tranquilizers, and still asking the same unanswerable questions one would expect to read only in a novel by Dostoevski.

A formidable barrier in terms of literary reputation was a general disdain for the Beats among the academic critics. The Beats had so violated the idea of literary decorum that seemed so important in the fifties by their personal appearances (Ginsberg undressing after reading "Howl" in answer to a questioning professor who wanted to know what he meant by nakedness; Kerouac, who wore open-necked checked shirts and presented himself more as woodsman than wordsman) and by what they set down in print that few critics (even the more rebellious ones like Leslie Fiedler) had the courage to take them seriously. There was little sympathy for the sheer absurdity causing the improvised playfulness evident in Robert Frank's film, "Pull My Daisy," which allowed the inspired antics of Ginsberg and Corso to the music of Kerouac's narration. At that time, there was little precedent on these shores for writers who psychoanalyzed each other or who so openly used their experiences with drugs or homosexuality as subject matter—that Verlaine had once shot and seriously wounded Rimbaud in Belgium was the sort of scandal that seemed unmentionable in American art, as if the critics believed that the passions of life were somehow separated from what writers wrote about. The late fifties, when *Howl, On the Road,* and *Naked Lunch* appeared, have been characterized by Ginsberg as a time vexed by the "syndrome of shutdown," but it was apparent that the genteel strictures which had governed public taste and publishing for so long were ready to be challenged. In 1960, when I was still an eager undergraduate, two events signaled that change: the public confrontation of the House Un-American Activities Committee in San Francisco by an unruly mob, and the publication of *Tropic of Cancer* (to the accompaniment of sixty local legal contentions).

What was interesting to me was that the established critics seemed threatened by the quality and character of Beat writing, appalled as Allen Tate was by Burroughs's scatological sexuality, his scenes of sadistic terror presented in a scary moral vacuum with what must have seemed gratuitous shocks like the following line from *Naked Lunch*: "We see God through our assholes in the flashbulb of orgasm." Others, like Norman Podhoretz in his piece "The Know Nothing Bohemians," impugned Kerouac's ebullience, his romantic declaration that the writer should accept his original notation, that revision was a subtle form of censorship, an accommodation to satisfy an editor or public taste. Since revision is a writer's shibboleth, a sacred cow of literary enterprise, we can retrospectively understand why Kerouac caused such an uproar, why he was so suspected and outcast by both the critics and some of his fellow craftsmen, like Truman Capote, who quipped that Kerouac's writing was really only typing, or Randall Jarrell, who castigated Kerouac, arguing that the quality of personal revelation in *On the Road* was more suitable to successful psychoanalysis than to fiction.

As a graduate student, reading Northrup Frye or R.P. Blackmur on James, schooled in the fastidious euphonics of the New Criticism, I was taught to believe that literary credibility was in large part a function of critical authority. But the Beat writers were almost universally deplored and, by some, clearly despised. The early reviews of *Howl,* the first major publication by a Beat writer and a book that changed the direction of American poetry in the mid-fifties, document this. John Hollander, writing about his own Columbia classmate in a spirit of evident distrust for what he saw as modish avant-garde posturing, complained in *Partisan Review* of the "utter lack of decorum of any kind in this dreadful little volume." James Dickey, in *Sewanee Review,* established Ginsberg as the tower of contemporary Babel, finding the poem full of meaningless utterance. Ginsberg's own self-assumed role of media clown in the sixties did little to redeem or improve this reputation. For some time, the critics could not fathom the poetic precedents for his long lines, just as they were put off by his blatant message of apocalypse, and his hysterically strident condemnation of the very institutions that fostered their efforts.

I suppose it was partly a response to the nearly unanimous

rejection of Beat writing by the critics, the view that they were philistines without a viable literary past, some species of distasteful and aberrant contemporary anomaly, that caused me to discover their lineage. Also, given the tempest of the late sixties, my own radical sympathies may have subsumed the more genteel aspects of my academic calling. In Ginsberg's case that lineage included Blake, Whitman, eastern Buddhism, and the French Surrealism that also affected Burroughs and Kerouac. Burroughs, perhaps because of his post-modernist experimentalism, had received some intelligent criticism from the British critic Tony Tanner, and from Mary McCarthy and Marshall McLuhan. With Kerouac, who had tried so hard to create an authentically American voice (but who in *On the Road* had also written a book with deep layers of picaresque convention), what was central was the romantic legacy of spontaneity, the rhythms of jazz, an evocation of natural speech as opposed to literary inflection that finds antecedents in Twain and William Carlos Williams, especially in a novel only published posthumously, *Visions of Cody,* which I regard as a neglected masterpiece in the Joycean mode.

Kerouac's reputation is changing in the literary community, and some of those who formerly disparaged him are now out of print, while most of his work has been brought back. There has been considerable critical interest in his work lately; several plays, two films and a half-dozen books have been written about him, and others are projected. Burroughs and Ginsberg are still writing, as are Snyder, Ferlinghetti, and Corso, so the Beat phenomenon is now entering its fifth decade and much of the enormous change in small press and alternative publishing is a testament to its continuing presence.

In its way, *Kerouac and the Beats* is a reflection of such publishing changes, since most of the material originally appeared in the *unspeakable visions of the individual,* an alternative magazine organized by Arthur and Glee and later Kit Knight. The title for the magazine was Kerouac's, and many of the memoirs, interviews and journals collected here relate to Kerouac, man and legend. Herbert Huncke's initial impression was that Kerouac was an "arrow-collar" type, a clean-cut college kid. To Kerouac's daughter Jan, he was a baby who needed protection. To his friend John Clellon Holmes, the first person to read *On the Road,* Kerouac was a writer poisoned by instant celebrity, a man who had weathered his anonymity with Buddhism and by working as a solitary fire lookout in the northwest mountains and "who no longer knew what the hell he was supposed to be." Holmes was attracted to Kerouac's enormous capacity for human empathy in an alienated age, and that empathy is the bond between Kerouac and his friend Neal Cassady, the subject of the memoirs by Carolyn Cassady and Edie Parker (Kerouac's first wife). Other astonishing instances of this empathy are found in the letters Kerouac wrote to his friends, some of which are included in this collection. The most vital of these letters is the one to Allen Ginsberg describing Mexico where he remembers Enrique, a Mexican hipster who helped him find marijuana. They eat tortillas in jungle huts in a place "beyond Darwin's chain" and the human connection becomes very powerful. The lyricism, as in the epiphanous section on Mazatlan, is balanced by a sad awareness of his own misfortune. Near the end of the letter, he finds William Burroughs in Mexico City wildly writing, "looking like a mad genius in littered rooms," and the observation is a sign of how the lives of so many of the Beats filter through the experiences recorded here.

JOHN TYTELL

Neal Cassady shaving. Allen Ginsberg's apartment, San Francisco, 1965. Photograph by Larry Keenan.

1

POOR GOD

Carolyn Cassady

W hat is there to do? There must be something to *do*. I have heard the sentence, that clanging final sentence, clapping from the mouth of that old man who *dared* to presume to judge Neal. What does *he* know? And Neal standing there so quiet and polite and defenseless, while that apoplectic bigot screams "I don't *care* if there's no evidence, I DON'T LIKE HIS ATTITUDE!" Just because Neal wouldn't admit he smoked pot. I sit, I pace, I stand, I look up into the hills from whence has come so much help before . . . no good.

So I do what I always do and write to Jack and Allen . . . the only family I can share this with. As expected, they reply with distress, sympathy and encouragement. In addition here is a letter from Gregory Corso, totally unexpected . . . an act of Grace that not only corrects my negative impressions of him but provides a comforting anecdote to my anger and despair. Especially the last page:

> . . . This is hard to say yet I feel I have the earthly journey that is miles and miles of vision and sorrow and awakening to say: Neal's walk in life has always been pyloned by roses; and if a great old sick rose blocks his walk, he'd certainly not sidestep. That's what is so true and lovely in the man. When you see him please tell him for me that I well know that all things render themselves; I never knew this before, because when I used to come upon that obstructive rose I'd sidestep, yet would I continue on, venture on, but stand there and complain; well, I learned enough this last year in Europe to dispense

with the complaints; how absurd I realized to complain that which is life. I hope this makes sense. I want it to, because I am very unhappy about what has happened to Neal. I'm almost apt to say, Poor God and not Poor Neal.

> my love,
> Gregory

Ironically, Neal begins officially serving his "time" on Independence Day, 1958, three months after his arrest. The sentence is five years to life on two counts, and the degrading three months doesn't count. I naively suppose he will be locked up for at least five more years, so Neal must explain to me that sentences don't mean what they say. Five years means two and life means around seven, though there are always possible variables. I don't understand again. It seems some sort of code or game they play, and it infuriates me. Why not say it like it is? Why have to study the rules, must you get a score-card? Where does one get an education for this sort of experience in life? I am ranting a lot, as I have for three months, and there is a good deal more to come, especially when I have to consider their plan for survival of the prisoner's family while the breadwinner is safely being sustained by the taxpayers. Dear Gregory, I will learn the futility of complaining "that which is life," but I bitterly resent the senselessness.

At first, Neal is sent to a medical facility at Vacaville, where prisoners undergo psychological testing supposedly to determine the most appropriate means and circumstances for their "correction." As far as we ever discover, this purpose is a carefully guarded secret, or a myth perpetrated, like so many others, to soothe the conscience of society. Perhaps, to be charitable, it is an attempt to soften the initial blow and shock of the real punishment to come.

At any rate, it is a fairly humane institution, and Neal lives in relative decency. His letters show him to be less bitter than when I'd seen him in the San Francisco City Jail, and there is a revival of his sense of humor, understandably sarcastic in tone. He has been at Vacaville a week, and I've received only one letter when he arrived. I assume he is kept busy adjusting to his new environment, his skull bristling with electrodes while he ponders a multiple-choice. I am wrong.

Dearest Carolyn:

~~Unbelevable~~ (no eraser) Unbelievable as it may seem, I've written you half a doz. letters since being here. Oh, I know you've received only one, the second I wrote (the first was rejected for writing above lines) besides this, the sixth. So here's the abridged story of my 3rd, 4th and 5th:

Wed. last, after devouring you 6-page beauty, proving more than mere Karma-spouse devotion, began preparing what I considered an equally uplifting missive manifesting mutual matehood. By writing every spare moment that day & the next, I managed to get it mailed Thru. night, but, because trying to cover everything at once, I had conserved space by crowding lines on back of unruled page (just as I had on the letter your received, right?). It was rejected.

Expecting to be "pampered," like a fool, I proposed to sgt. in charge that it be allowed to pass "just this once," and, of course, I'd not write tiny again. After consulting with Capt, the hour I cooled my soon-to-be-subservient heels in the horseshoe pit, he recalled me to tell me the letter seemed full of "double-talk" . . . secret answers to your secret questions, and thus couldn't be sent; so ended letter #3.

All day Friday, with natural resentment tempered only by what I thought was the humor of it all, I composed an awkward, biting satire on "double-talk" and tried mailing this farce to you. But no go. Instead my supposed wit proved a bad mistake in judgement when Sat AM I was called in and chewed on for openly insulting the Capt. So this letter, the 4th and the funniest, I thought, was the most sternly rejected, as well as being, quite probably, put in my central file to show I disrespect authority.

Anyway, Sat. nite I mailed another, the 5th attempt to get thru a "message to Garcia"; this new one was a most sorry affair, reflecting much of my deep disgust over the whole sad hassel in which I'd stupidly involved myself. So desparingly blah was it that, altho already 5 days late answering you, I quickly regretted having written at all . . . but, hurray, my prayers working via a bum memory, it was returned this morning for forgetting to put my number, etc. on flap of envelope.

Well, now that I've wasted nearly a page by explaining somewhat my delay in writing . . . (tho have been scribbling so furiously all week I have writer's cramp) I'll began anew this long-retarded reply to your #1.

As I read this detailed description, disbelief grows into awe. Here he is reviewing all the things that had been rejected by the censors, yet they allowed the retelling to pass. I can only suppose they bought this avowed contrition. Perhaps he is learning the game, albeit the hard way, but I abandon the hope of ever being able to outguess the probable behavior of those in control.

He now pushed his "unworried pencil . . . still minus eraser . . ." to the new answer telling me not to try and do any more

Arthur Knight and Carolyn Cassady. Los Gatos, California, January 16, 1979. Photograph by Kit Knight.

toward his release and explaining the idiocies of the penal system and his speculations on his fate.

> ". . . you see, all first-time 5-to-lifers, no matter the charge, go before the 3-man prison board in 18 months and THEN get their time set, & this is usually 2½ in 2½ out on parole. Despite this more or less standard policy, God's Grace crowning our humble efforts, I'm still sure of being home to start our personal 'Easter of New Beginnings' at least by the exact date in 1960 . . ."

As evidenced in his prison letters, Neal had always been fascinated with the writing of Proust. He used to delight in reading aloud to Jack, marvelling at the non-stop sentences and the intricate dissection of thoughts. Not only does he play with these methods in his letters, but sometimes he'll write an entire page of alliteration. Doubtless these exercises are his only creative outlet, and although I enjoy them, I am aware that the therapy involved for him in searching for the right word is more important than the sentiments wrung from his labors. The *mot juste* in this case is not its meaning but its initial letter.

He is ever conscious of the censors and indulges in frequent gushes of conscience and remorse for their benefit . . . this his only avenue of conning in such a profitless environment. I do not begrudge him these rare moments.

For my part, the only joy I know during these two years is to find that small crumpled envelope in the mail box. One thanks I give the system is the absence of descriptive return address. My chief concern, of course, is for the children (now aged 10, 9 & 7) who do not know their father is in prison. They are usually in school when the mail arrives, and if not, I'm really the only one interested in it.

As the reader will appreciate, I think, I wait until I can settle down alone with coffee and cigarette to concentrate on these elaborate epistles, pencil-written on 5″ × 7″ ruled paper in as small a hand as he can get by with.

From the beginning Neal shows an increasing absorption in religion. I certainly pray for a higher power to intervene, and that Neal may accept this test as an enforced monastic interlude. It has happened to others; Starr Daily, for one, whom Neal idolizes and had once sought out for advice. So much depends on attitude, and Neal knows it; his Cayce obsession had convinced him. When first arrested, he had managed a remarkable acceptance and eagerly and reverently told me of the "miracles" that had taken place that time, including his release. When he was re-arrested, his faith did not suffice to surmount the injustice. His bitterness was so intense it blinded him to not only the remembrance of the recent testimonials but to common sense as well. In both cases the higher law was aptly demonstrated, maddeningly clear to him, and his failure to overcome only increased his self-condemnation.

His sudden reversion to Catholicism saddens me at first. It seems nothing more than rote and dogma, surface declarations accomplishing nothing toward a basic change within. So the disappointment is the more acute when we learn Hugh Lynn Cayce has been refused the right to correspond with Neal; he had been a close friend and valued counsellor for many years. (Not too surprising, then, both Luanne and Jackie, two secret lovers, are granted this permission as well as that of visiting.)

By the time Neal is settled in Vacaville, he has made considerable progress already toward his religious routine:

. . . Amid other actions, disregarding my damning letter skit, to aid this happy Sunday happening & amongst other reasons for attempting even minimal valid repayment to Him, such as the *in*valid one of injury to callow pride by shallow shame suffered in ever-increasing recognition of weak sloth reinforcing strong lust, I've begun seriously composing prayers.

Most appropriate here, did not modesty (false, of course) & space (limited, yet unreal, you know) forbid quoting, would be the one to Apostle St. Paul that is based on his Epistle for the Easter Mass from Cor. 4:7–8; I would quote this ex-Saul hoping to soon reenact his splendid rebirth . . . should I be called "Kneel"? No room for quote; you read it with Johnny.

To accompany my regular evening and morning prayers, I've made up several others, to St. Michael esp. who, remember, while not the Way, is Lord of the Way. I'm most proud . . . oops, that nemesis word again . . . of one of these that calls on (thru Holy Ghost, of course, who controls, nay, *is* all positive prayer power) every one of the 262 Popes, Peter to Pius XII, to help hasten my growth as well as all mankind. The better to emulate these leaders, I am memorizing their names & add a new one each day to the prayer, i.e., today's Pope . . . the 21st in order (I began July 1st) is St. Carnelius, who reigned from 251–263. Next week will get back to your wonderful 1st letter, the first paragraph of which is all I've managed to answer so far . . .

When I try to be subtle about my concern for his fervor, which I fear is bordering on fanaticism, he sees through me, as usual, and, not sidestepping, as usual, faces me with my own fears:

Dear Dynamo & Sweet Scrivner of Pretty Pages 99&100% pure Carolyn:

As it allows of no tergiversation to concede that much worth in a picture depends on where the artist chooses to sit . . . or stand, as you usually do . . . so, too, a felon must admit that whatever value is gained by confinement rests largely on (a seeming paradox) his physical position.

While, of course, accentuating the all-important mental attitude, most attention, despite every effort contrariwise, is still naturally centered, being over ½ animal (you know . . . 4 glands to 3, or less, because one of those upper trio, the pineal, is partially fossilized by lime salts at puberty in practically everyone) on the restricted bodily activity which, tho in itself a small thing, when experienced without break over an extended length of time, considerably exaggerates the already tightly repressed emotional reaction until, if uncheckable by rational means, rubbed-raw nerves explode into a "stir-craziness."

Hence, such expressions among the "con-wise" as, "do your own time," meaning stay clear of another's tension; "keep your mind off the streets," meaning women, etc. Happily, thanks to you and God, as well as this State's enlightened penal system, there's little chance I could become seriously subject to unhingement thru any of these material fixations. No, if anything unbalanced me . . . further, that is . . . it would have the reverse type cause, i.e., inordinate dwelling on immaterial objects.

Actually, were there possible such an one nowadays, I *am* a "religious nut" and pray to become more so . . . and will! . . . for aren't we to be moderate in all things *except* love of God? (By its very definition and 1st principles there can't be any conscious moderation, i.e., holding back, in religion.) In fact, besides being poor slang & an incorrect term, there is no such person as a "religious nut," but only "nutty religion" (& not even that) which is really what I meant to say, or warn myself especially against all along. But enuf line-consuming verbosity; back to realities of relationship . . .

. . . One last bit on the religion "kick" (& indeed it is this, whether in or out; it's really the only "kick" left, true?) I read that Postulant in Cisterian monastary spends 90 days at least as such; this corresponds to my 3 months in SF jail; 2 years as novice, equalling my term inside pen; 3 years under "simple" vows, my period of outside parole. So, just as they take over 5 years in all before being finally accepted, I'll be completely discharged & accepted back into society only after a similar passage of time. Interesting, what?

Here he is instructing me that he has lost none of his knowledge of metaphysics in spite of his new passion, but it would not be wise to reassure me too directly and thus enlighten his censors by the same means.

Neal is in Vacaville for three months. Although his keepers are obviously mad, the institution in general is not as deliberately degrading to the inmates as are the other prisons he passes through. There are psychological games to play, which Neal loves (as can be guessed from his letters) as well as more balanced and rewarding physical regimes.

I look out cell window and watch trains meeting and passing a half mile away and within few 100 years there daily comes creeping a local freight over Sacramento Northern branch line. Ho hum, let 'um work; I'm on vacation.

Took gym test today. Ran 250 yards back & forth in 53 seconds, chin-ups 15, sit-ups 37 . . . all in "very good" category. Took 900-question quiz on "attitude & comprehension," then spelling, I.Q., mech. apt., scholastic, math, vocab. voc. skills, etc. Now all tests over & am in 2 week "Group Behavior Adjustment" class. Our ball team (tell Johnny I'm a Giant, too, just like on his cap) won 2 of last 3 & now in second place in league. Each Sat. go to confession to receive on Sun. the Holy Euchurist from fine German priest here. Gained 10 lbs! Feeling increasingly purged of all old desires, especially of flesh.

If the good doctors read his repeated insistence that he is through forever of any former associates or habits, they can well believe they have a sure-fire system of reform. In spite of the accusations that Vacaville is a "country club," I do so wish he may stay there . . . or why isn't that sort of imprisonment sufficient punishment? A chance for increased self-respect to find a foothold in a crack of the confining wall.

Neal hopes to be sent to Soledad, where he says "the kissing facilities are better," but instead he draws San Quentin. I suppose the policy is consistent with that of the Armed Forces whereby given choices for stations, the only ones you may be sure you won't get are the ones you request.

His vacation is over. Quite a different tone now permeates his letters from San Quentin:

Dearest Dear Carolyn, Wonder Wife:

Even as they were striking my leg irons, that had, along with two sidearm-carrying officers, locked door, barred windows & snow-white pajamas (minus the half-expected bright red or yellow bulls-eye on the back) most adequately subdued any wild urge to disembark during the short bus ride from Vacaville, I began experiencing the generation of a not inconsiderable self-pity, soon to become, while the procedure progressed, almost overpowering by virtue of those repeated shocks every new dismal view bordering sheer disbelief administered in separate but accumulative blow to my so-sorry-for-myself-sharpened conception as, now buffeted from both within and without into a bewildering numbness, I at last encountered, when first stumbling across the "Big Yard," as the "cons" call it . . . in that characteristic state it seems to engender, a paradoxical one of hazelike concentration, the main source of what gloomy eminations my all-too-sympathetic mood had rendered it recipient; that psychical wall each convict's despair-ridden tension made to exist inside the, high and wide though they be, far weaker stone walls of this infamous old . . . 1859 is chiseled atop the facade of one still-used building . . . prison, at which, accompanying 23 more, I finally arrived last week.

After a troubled sleep, in sagging bunk beneath one of a thug who'd escaped 8 times, much disturbed by an anxiety dream concerning some just-right blonde, fatty-cheeked both above and below (Presumably you, since I personally know no other) & myself at a drive-in movie . . . remember the one in Kansas we attended so long ago? . . . Along this line, the next day another shared sadness, but in a far lighter vein of thought than the Pope's death, served for further perception into my always too weak realization of excessive self-centeredness, the demise, real enuf, tho figuratively and collectively, of the Milwaukee Braves in the World Series.

Much more, however, responsibility for lifting me from that blue funk of depression this place must naturally impress on "fish" (new convicts) can be attributed to an increasing awareness over this last week of the balancing factor it equally imposes: compassion. Truly, I've never seen, nor is there elsewhere in this noble country concentrated, surely not even in Sing Sing, such an assorted assemblage of absolutely pitiful misfits as are the 5,042 felons . . . latest count, which Radio KROW announced on 6 PM news as largest number here since 1942 . . . in whose routine I am daily . . . & nightly, ugh . . . immured until at least Easter of 1960.

Neal's first "job" in this grim new home is sweeping the floor of the textile mill.

. . . which reminds me how I've been using prayer lately, or how this ex-beatster beats a beat bastille: Rule: blank mind-desire proportionately to each bodily nullification. Example: Hearing. To overcome eardrum-bursting racket made by the cotton textile mill's 4-million-dollars worth of 1745 R.P.M. $68 \times 72''$ hi-speed looms, whose constantly collecting flug is my weary job to sweep all day from beside & beneath, I, thus noisely assured safeguard from eavesdropping, deadening surfaced thought to equate the deafness, incessantly shout into that accompanying roar every prayer known & since . . . saying them hurriedly it takes just one hour to complete their entirety. Each minute, after the first 60, finds me repeating the very one said on that very moment last hour. Don't demurmer, it at least eliminates clock-watching.

Near the end of his first year, on our wedding anniversay, he tries to give me an idea of his living conditions, if living it is.

My dear wife, sweet April fool, laden doubly with toil because I did soil and foil the precious bloom of your tender love—bestowed in all its fresh entirety that glorious and (judge) Golden [We were married April 1, 1948 by Judge Joseph Golden, subsequently impeached to

Neal's delight. He thought he overcharged us.] moment 11 years and 11 hours ago when we blew your practically last sawbuck to officially cinch that truly meant-to-be union which each day I, despite causing its previous & current adversity, sincerely thank Divine Providence for even permitting, as I mull it during those 16 of every 24 hours locked behind these 13 tan (to me) [Neal was color-blind.] colored bars fronting my $4\frac{1}{2} \times 7\frac{1}{2} \times 9\frac{1}{2}$ foot cell:

To get some better idea of what lying so encaged is like, you might put car mattress in the bathtub, thereby making it softer, and if not as long at least much cleaner than is my bug-ridden bunk; then bring in your 200 lb. friend, Edna, or the more negatively aggressive, Pam. Lock the door, &, after dragging 11 rowdy kids into our bedroom to parallel the 1,100 noisy ones housed in this particular cell block; of course, in the bathroom, you must remove the toilet seat, towel racks, cabinet . . . anything other than a small mirror & $4\frac{1}{2}''$ shelf . . . remain almost motionless so as not to inadvertently irritate armed-robber-Edna, ponder past mistakes, present agonies & future defeats in the light of whatever insights your thus disturbed condition allows . . .

About now I'm wondering if there are no censors at "Q." Perhaps they believe Neal sincere in an outburst like the following, but, yes, they are still with us, their objections tuned to a different wave-length than those at Vacaville:

. . . April 2 got a heartrending Easter card from John & Jamie . . . what no Cathy? . . . Tell John how pleased I was he got right number of humps (sand containers) on top of engine. Don't tell Jamie how tragically ironic I found it that she (guided by what mysterious hand beneath the surfactual ignorance?) spelled "Hey, Hey" as "Hay, Hay" to innocently twist deeper in firmer-fix the sharp memory-knife cutting my remorse anew by her unwittingly giving such appropriate name to the vile weed used in that selfish habit of vice putting me here where everything once possessed, from job to joy, has gone irrevocably up the felon flu in a black smoke the more Hellishly felt for burning, conversely from Hay, so steel and concretely real . . . seared by the heat of which my reaction momentarily fanned resentment from still smoldering ember to blazing open flame in a self-piteous whale of a wail to my Godfather, which was so filled with frail whine, the censor wisely rejected & returned it with the curt command, "Write a *letter*." So, submerged under this further funk of having wounded pride pricked, the bubble of Literary smugness burst as well, for the comment implied nonacceptance more for style than complaint, since slip giving reason for letter's return had no other mark whatsoever on it, not even a check in the space where it should logically be . . .

*Neal Cassady and Anne Murphy. Oakland, California, 1966. Photograph by
Larry Keenan.*

Neal Cassady, waiting for Ken Kesey. Oakland, California, 1966. Photograph by Larry Keenan.

In the early years, Neal had enjoyed letter-writing and was encouraged to consider style and technique by Jack and Allen. [It was their urging that started him on *The First Third*.] Letters to them are energized with a thrust of action, directed inward or outward and often frustrated but nonetheless moving toward some progression. It seemed to me his prison letters illustrated his own stymied condition. With his intense and tortured efforts to create disciplined phrases and choose exact words, I visualized his total Mind, lacking means of expansion or broader forms of expression, trapped within the intricate convolutions of his physical brain . . . turned, twisted, folded back upon itself . . . like his driving . . . ever wary of the cops, opening up on dangerous curves and risking a few dexterous maneuvers to outwit and baffle them.

He was very much of this earth as well as in it; he grasped and manipulated and developed incredibly perfected skills in the use of his physical instrument, pitted mainly against himself rather than other people even in sports. But he must master the requisite imposed by any particular activity or object . . . whether railroad cars, tire-recapping equipment or automobile driving. He was equally intrigued with the manipulation of people.

Within, his intense energy raged the battle between exhuberant Life and love and the destructive daemon: hostility toward women, stupid authority and, most notably, himself. Before he died, this Devil appeared in the form Neal had created, and "I talk to him all the time," he told me.

The seeds of his later "raps" can be found in his letters. When he was no longer capable of writing, except for a few times when in some local jail, he was compelled to express his Aquarian insights in talk, his agile intellect now struggling with the emotional whip of self-hatred and the physical disintegration of drug-induced destruction.

Complex though the maze of thoughts is in his prison letters, the ideas can, with effort, be followed. When he could only manage verbalizing, the labyrinth becomes tangled, and increasingly are there gaps and dead-end passages.

I pleaded with him to go to Mexico in 1968, knowing there were so many traffic warrants out against him, that if he were caught I feared he'd be returned to San Quentin for good. Gavin Arthur, who had been his teacher there, was furious with me. "Why did you do that?" he fumed. "Neal was at his very best in prison; it's the only place he could stay healthy and use that magnificent mind."

A lot could be said about that point of view.

2

AN INTERVIEW WITH WILLIAM S. BURROUGHS

John Tytell

This interview was recorded in Burrough's New York City loft on March 24, 1974.

JOHN TYTELL: *In 1950 you were studying in Mexico City College. What kind of school was that?*

WILLIAM BURROUGHS: It was organized for people on the G.I. Bill and classes were in English. I studied archeology, mostly Mexican, and Mayan and Aztec. Aztec is very difficult, Mayan very easy.

JT: *Where did you do your undergraduate work?*

WB: 1936. Harvard. English lit.

JT: *Did you take any courses in modern literature?*

WB: Not formally.

JT: *Did you read Joyce or Eliot then?*

William Burroughs. Kerouac Conference, Boulder, Colorado, 1982. Photograph by Sharon Gwynup.

WB: Eliot was there as a visiting professor. I went to one of his lectures, he gave lectures and seminars. Eliot was very much something that people were into at that time.

JT: What modern writers most moved you at that time?

WB: I wasn't really in modern literature, but Eliot, Joyce, Kafka, Fitzgerald, of course.

JT: They are making a movie of The Great Gatsby.

WB: I'm sure it will be a real mess.

JT: But not at the box office.

WB: I'm not even sure of that. Generally speaking they know what they're doing, but they don't always. They will go all out on these spectaculars that don't work at all. I was just looking the book over myself with the idea of making a film, and there just is no film there—everything's in the prose, you take that away and you've got wooden dialogue and creaky action.

JT: The prose does have an elusive quality so that it appears easy, but underneath the surface is that astonishingly intricate imagery and richness. I think you are right, this will just be a stageshow.

WB: It isn't cinematic.

JT: What did you do after you left Harvard? I'd like to establish a chronology.

WB: A year in Europe studying medicine at the University of Vienna. After that I returned to America and studied psychology briefly at Columbia, then back at Harvard doing graduate work in anthropology. Then a year in New York with an advertising agency. In the army briefly, out again, Chicago where I worked as an exterminator and at various other jobs. Back to New York in 1943. Left in about '46 for Texas, then New Orleans.

JT: When did you leave for Mexico?

WB: 1949. I stayed in Mexico until 1952, South America in 1953, back in New York, in 1953. Then I went to Europe, first to Italy and then Tangiers from about 1954 to 1958. Then Paris. Then between Paris and London during the early sixties. In 1964 I was in Tangiers, in 1965 I was here for a year, and from then on mostly in London.

JT: I would like to ask you specific questions about certain of these years. When you were in New York 1943, where did you live?

WB: Uptown, downtown, all over, around the Village, Columbia.

JT: I heard that you worked as a bartender.

Anne Waldman and William Burroughs. Boulder, Colorado, July 30, 1982.
Photograph by Arthur Knight.

WB: For about three weeks on Bedford Street.

JT: It was at that time you first met Kerouac and Ginsberg. Ann Charters says that Dave Kammarer introduced you. Where had you known Kammarer?

WB: St. Louis: we were brought up together. I'd known him all my life.

JT: I heard that when you first visited Kerouac you were interested in learning how to get seaman's papers?

WB: Vaguely. I did get seaman's papers years later but never used them.

JT: I read in your correspondence that you did what might be termed a "lay analysis" or psychoanalysis of Allen Ginsberg? What was that like?

WB: That's true. It was a very sketchy procedure.

JT: Had you been analyzed?

WB: Oh yes. Waste of time and money.

JT: How did Allen take your analysis?

WB: Well, now he was interested—people like to talk about themselves.

JT: At one time did you share an apartment with Edie Parker, Joan Adams and Kerouac?

WB: Yes. It was a big apartment and I had a room there for about four or five months in '44.

JT: Do you feel that in any way you influenced Kerouac and Ginsberg at that time?

WB: Influenced in what way?

JT: You've written that certain figures leave their impression in terms of speech and language.

WB: Well I should say that Kerouac influenced me much more than I influenced him because I wasn't at all interested in writing at that time, and he was one of several people who told me that I should write. The title of *Naked Lunch* was his, not mine.

JT: Kerouac would later type portions of that novel for you in Tangiers.

WB: That was many years later.

JT: I wanted to ask how that book finally came together, and what role others may have had in helping you assemble it.

WB: One of the key figures was Sinclair Beiles who was working for Girodias at that time. Girodias had seen the novel, not the version that finally appeared but a version that I had before, remember that there were about a thousand pages to this from which the final material was selected, and some of the overflow went into *The Soft Machine, The Ticket That Exploded, Nova Epxress* and some of it is still unpublished, and in the archives.

JT: Was any of the original material part of Queer?

WB: No. That was a separate thing and way back.

JT: Carl Solomon told me of reading it and feeling that it wasn't the right time to bring it out.

WB: Ace had no intention of bringing it out. Wyn said I'd be in jail if it was published. But it has very little to do with the subsequent material from which *Naked Lunch* was assembled.

JT: How did you first meet Huncke?

WB: Through Bob Brandenberg who was a sort of marginal hoodlum who used to hang around the West End in 1944.

JT: Huncke told me the story about the morphine syrettes and was it a sawed off shotgun or a pistol?

WB: No, it was a submachine gun.

JT: But that's a fairly large weapon?

WB: This guy stole it and carried it out under his coat.

JT: Was it an army weapon?

WB: Yes. He had smuggled this thing out and nobody wanted to touch it. I finally sort of gave it away to somebody.

JT: Could one get ammunition for that?

WB: Sure, standard 45.

JT: Huncke told me that you maintained an apartment on Henry Street on the lower East Side then.

William Burroughs, Jr. Boulder, Colorado, July 6, 1976. Photograph by Arthur Knight.

WB: That's right, I had that apartment for fifteen dollars a month. A walk-in kitchen and a few small rooms.

JT: How did you start with morphine?

WB: Well the syrettes were the beginning. I met this guy named Phil White who bought some of the syrettes from me, and he turned me onto the morphine. Then I started going around with him to doctors.

JT: Getting script, as you call it in Junkie. *When had opium become illegal?*

WB: Since the Harrison Narcotics Act around 1914. But you could still get preparations like paregoric.

JT: Was Huncke a new kind of person for you to have met, or had you met people like him before?

WB: No, I'd not met anyone like Huncke before.

JT: What attracted you to him?

WB: Well, you know, he had some interesting stories. Also, he was associated with Phil White and we would get junk together.

JT: Didn't Huncke introduce you to Bill Garver?

WB: He did. He had been in jail, and then he brought Garver around to Joan's apartment.

JT: Garver was a notorious coat-thief, wasn't he?

WB: That's true. He also had a small income of twenty-five dollars a week friom his father which was not enough for his habit. So he had to supplement that by stealing overcoats. When his father died, he came into about three to four hundred dollars a month, that's when he moved to Mexico. Later we lived in the same building. He is Bill Gains in *Junkie.*

JT: Huncke told me that he introduced you to Dr. Kinsey when Kinsey began his research around Times Square.

WB: He did indeed. Kinsey and Ward Pomeroy. We met at a place called The Angler, that was on Eighth avenue between 42nd and 43rd.

JT: Did Kinsey interview you?

WB: No, Pomeroy did.

JT: Did you know Bill Cannastra?

WB: I never met him. I heard a lot about him from Allen Ginsberg, but more particularly from Allen Ansen.

JT: I asked you earlier whether you thought you had in any way influenced Ginsberg or Kerouac, and you said that Kerouac had influenced you more, because he made you aware of writing, but Allen Ginsberg told me that one way that you definitely influenced both of them was with books that you suggested that they read, that he had no introduction to modern literature and that you gave him Hart Crane and Auden and Eliot and other books, Kafka, that you gave Kerouac Spengler.

WB: And perhaps Celine.

JT: Were you reading Wilhelm Reich at the time?

WB: Either then or later.

JT: What about Lucien Carr? Was he part of your circle then?

WB: Yes. I'd known Lucien from St. Louis, introduced to him by David Krammar. I saw Lucien subsequently in Chicago when I was there.

JT: Did you meet frequently with Kerouac, Ginsberg, Carr, or were your encounters sporadic?

WB: Sporadic. I saw a lot of Dave because I had known him for a long time and he lived right around the corner of Morton Street when I lived in the Village. The others lived uptown, and I saw more of them when I moved there.

JT: When you shared the apartment with Ginsberg, Joan Adams and Edie Parker?

WB: That's right. Edie Parker who married Jack Kerouac.

JT: After Jack had been apprehended as an accessory to Carr's murder of Kammarer?

WB: Not as an accessory but a material witness.

JT: How did that happen? I've heard so many different versions, and that Kammarer had been Carr's scoutmaster.

WB: There was some such connection. Then they took a trip to Mexico, and there was trouble between Kammarer and Lucien's mother.

JT: I read in your correspondence that you and Kerouac wrote a novel based on the friendship and subsequent murder.

WB: We did write such a novel—*The Hippoes Were Boiled in Their Tank.*

Brion Gysin and William Burroughs. London, 1972. Photograph by Gerard Malanga.

JT: How did you get that title?

WB: It was in a news broadcast about a circus fire, so we used that.

JT: Is the book in your archives?

WB: No, we can't get hold of it. It's with Sterling Lord. Richard Aaron was supposed to come over here to try and recover it.

JT: What led you to leave New York?

WB: Well, there was a definite likelihood of legal difficulties. When I left I went to Texas.

JT: That's when you began farming?

WB: No, it wasn't. I forgot, I first left, and then I came back to New York, and then left again, so it was two times that I left.

JT: Huncke told me that after the New Waverly scene you, Neal Cassady and Huncke returned to New York in a jeep from New Waverly.

WB: That was later.

JT: From reading your letters I could tell that you were hassled by bureaucrats at the time you were farming, or at least that you resented their controls a great deal.

WB: Well, there were cotton allotments and all kinds of rules. We were okay on that, but not always, and then there was a matter of loans that had to be negotiated. It's really no operation for people who are operating with small capital. If anything goes wrong you're wiped out.

JT: So you're totally at the mercy of credit?

WB: Completely.

JT: In the letters you describe that the relativity of the law had never been clearer to you because of your experience with farming. In particular because of the wetbacks, the way they would be encouraged to come in by the state and at the same time there could be penalties, selectively applied.

WB: Very selectively applied. You got in wrong with the authorities and a truck would drive up and take all your wetbacks away, and you'd be left in cotton picking season with no help.

JT: At the same time, any wetback would be earning five times what he could get in Mexico.

WB: But this didn't happen to the big farmers.

JT: Because they had protection?

WB: Yes. In the big ranches the wetbacks were herded all over the place. They had guards with machine guns. They tried to pull a strike once and the guards shot three of them, so they all went back to work. They had no rights.

JT: In New Waverly you also grew grass? Were you farming anything else?

WB: Couldn't farm anything else.

JT: Was the soil bad?

WB: The problem was how were you going to farm, with what? I mean you could get a horse and plow and do subsistence farming.

JT: Cassady and Ginsberg visited you in New Waverly? What was your impression of Cassady?

WB: I thought he was a very pleasant, easy-going person.

JT: I've heard that he was very intense, capable of long monologues. Was that true then?

WB: I always felt his capacity for silence. I've been with him for eight hours and never exchanged a word.

JT: What kind of driver was he?

WB: Brilliant, a fantastic driver. I had a jeep and the clutch and brakes were out, and he could brake it by putting it into reverse.

JT: I heard that he drove Kesey's bus at high speeds around curves knowing somehow that there was nothing coming the other way.

WB: He was capable of unbelievable feats of instant calculation.

JT: How did you spend your days in New Waverly? Were you writing at that time?

WB: No, no, no. I didn't write anything, hardly, until I was thirty-five. Anyway, I wasn't writing. But there were always things to do, like put a fence around the place, cut wood, walk around.

JT: Was the country beautiful?

WB: It was heavy timber. Oak and persimmon, not too much pine. The kind of country that starts in southern Missouri and goes all the way down to east Texas. There were raccoons and foxes and squirrels and armadilloes.

JT: What led you to invite Huncke to the New Waverly place?

WB: I don't remember.

JT: How long was he there?

WB: Quite a while, four or five months.

JT: Did Kerouac visit you there?

WB: No, he didn't.

JT: He visited you on several other occasions, though?

WB: He lived with me in New Orleans, then later in Mexico.

JT: Had he written The Town And The City *then?*

WB: Yes.

JT: Had you seen any of it? Did you know you were a character in it?

WB: I hadn't seen any of it at that time, but he told me I appeared in it.

JT: What was his mood like then?

WB: It was very good.

JT: In one of the letters you mention that on a later visit in Mexico, I think in 1952, he was depressed, uncooperative and unhappy.

WB: He was moody and a little bit paranoid.

JT: Do you think the difficulty he was having getting On The Road *accepted had anything to do with his attitude?*

William Burroughs. London, 1972. Photograph by Gerard Malanga.

WB: Possibly. But then he seemed to take that rather philosophically. The book was literally years kicking around. Malcolm Cowley like it, but the editor-in-chief didn't at all, and so there were all those delays which might have been just as well because the timing of the book was good, had it been published earlier, it might not have received the same attention.

JT: That's an interesting point. And he did a lot of writing during the six years between finishing On The Road *and its publication in 1957.*

WB: Oh yes. He was always writing.

JT: Can you tell me more about the history of Naked Lunch?

WB: I had this great amorphous manuscript. Girodias had seen some of it and had rejected it. I was living in Paris. This was 1958. Allen Ginsberg was also there and he sent selections off to Irving Rosenthal for *The Chicago Review,* and then *The Chicago Review* folded in protest after having difficulty with the university over the issue because of my material and something by Kerouac as well, and then Rosenthal published it in *Big Table.* That was what called it to Girodias' attention. He saw *Big Table* and said now I want the book. So he sent Sinclair Beiles over to my room who said Girodias wants to publish the book, and he wants it in two weeks. So I got busy, and Brion Gysin helped with typing—Allen had gone—and Sinclair Beiles was most helpful. I was just typing it out and giving it to Beiles with the idea that when we got galley proofs I could decide the final order. But he took one look at it and said leave it the way it is. So it was just really an accidental juxtaposition. And the book was out a month later.

JT: That's a kind of "automatic" structuring—without any wilfull control. How does that approach Kerouac's ideal of spontaneity?

WB: Kerouac was not thinking of an accidental procedure but of spontaneity in writing. He was always very opposed to writing with "cut-ups" which is, in a sense, an accidental procedure. Kerouac believed the first version was the best, and I have never found this to be true. I work over things and edit them very carefully.

JT: When Girodas took Naked Lunch *you were living at the "Beat hotel," 9 rue Git le Couer?*

WB: And Olympia Press was around the corner. Girodias had inherited the press from his father, it was then called The Dial Press, and they had originally come from Manchester. Girodias' brother later translated *Naked Lunch* into French, and Gallimard took it a year after it had been published in English.

JT: Wasn't there an obscenity trial in the States?

WB: Two, the first was in Boston where we won on appeal, then in Los Angeles we won in the lower courts. By that time it was pretty well established that there was no censorship on the written word.

JT: Has Henry Miller been a writer who in any way influenced you?

WB: No.

JT: Had you read de Sade?

WB: I looked at de Sade when I was in Paris. Girodias had some translations, but I found it heavy going.

JT: Did you have any interest in Gertrude Stein when you were at Harvard?

WB: I read *Three Lives* there.

JT: Later, did Brion Gysin try to interest you in her work?

WB: No, but he knew her. She was the one who told Paul Bowles that he shouldn't stay in Paris but should find some other place.

JT: What were your lodgings like at 9 Rue Git le Couer?

WB: A single room. I had an alcohol stove in the room. There was no phone, but I had red tile floors. It was very cheap.

JT: Judging from the letters, Ginsberg, Kerouac, everyone seems to have stayed there.

WB: At different times.

JT: Where was the Villa Delirium?

WB: That was the Muniria in Tangiers where I lived for a number of years.

JT: I read in your letters that when you first went to Tangiers you lived in a whorehouse. What was that like? Faulkner once said in an interview that a whorehouse was the ideal place for a writer to live.

WB: It was not that kind of a whorehouse at all. It was just a small place where Tony Dutch who ran it rented out rooms. Tony was a great cook and if you wanted to take meals there you could. After that I moved into the Muniria where I stayed off and on for many years. It's changed hands many times. First it was owned by a Belgian whose son was involved with smuggling, then it was run by an ex-madam from Indochina. She had an "in" with the authorities and ran it for many years without trouble. She sold out and a retired British civil servant took it over.

JT: I have some other miscellaneous questions. What about the story that your first wife was a Hungarian countess?

WB: She wasn't. Her name was Ilse Herzfeld Klapper, they were solid, wealthy bourgeois Jewish people in Hamburg. She had to get out because of Hitler and went to Yugoslavia, and I married her in Athens to get her into the States. She supported herself by working in a travel agency and various jobs. She was very efficient. She was secretary for Ernst Toller, a leftist playwright who tried to commit suicide several times. But he always arranged it so that someone would come and prevent him. And she was a very punctual person. If she went to lunch at twelve she would be back at twelve-thirty. It just so happened that she ran into an old acquaintance in the street and was ten minutes late, and when she returned he was dead in the bathroom. At his funeral she met Kurt Kaszner, a famous Austrian actor who had married a very rich American girl.

She became his secretary. Then Mrs. Kaszner died, and the servants said he had poisoned her and she was dug up again, but there was nothing in it, she died of natural causes. Then she worked for John le Touche as his secretary until he died under mysterious circumstances.

JT: I've heard that you had applied to the O.S.S. during the war?

WB: I did and was not accepted. I went down and saw Bill Donovan with a letter of introduction from an uncle, but he referred me to somebody else and nothing happened.

JT: You mentioned that you were in the army?

WB: For a short time, five months. I was stationed in St. Louis.

JT: When was that?

WB: During the war, in 1942, I think.

JT: Do you record your dreams?

WB: I write them down.

JT: How do you do it?

WB: I wake up six times in the course of the average night. I'll just make a few notes. If it's of interest, I transcribe it in the morning. I get at least half, perhaps more, of my material from dreams, characters, sets, etc.

JT: Can you tell me about the Dutch Schultz filmscript?

WB: I had been interested in Dutch Schultz for a long time, having read his famous last words. There were about 2,000 of them since he was shot on October 23rd at 10 PM and he died about 24 hours later, and they had a police stenographer at his bedside. Anyway, he presumably wrote all his words down, though he was delirious and the stenographer may have missed words. Then David Budd came over with quite a bit of research material, that is to say, a series of articles that had appeared in *Colliers* by his lawyer, Dixie Davis. I became interested and wrote a film treatment which was about fifteen pages, this was published in *Harper's*. Then someone named Harrison Starr wanted to produce this as a movie so he paid a sum of money—ten thousand dollars or something like that—for me to write a film play which I wrote, and that was published by Grollier Press as *The Last Words of Dutch Schultz*. There were other negotiations and I went on to write a full length film script, a shooting script in 1971.

JT: Wasn't part of Naked Lunch *written like that, as a film script?*

WB: No, in play form, but I'm talking about a shooting script, like indoors, medium shot, or close-up. So that was 195 pages. Richard Seaver is publishing that with a lot of stills. But the film was never made.

JT: How come?

WB: Well, the people were interested, but it was expensive, all gangster films are expensive to make.

JT: Is anyone trying to film Naked Lunch?

WB: Brion Gysin did a script, but it seems to be up in the air.

JT: Years ago you said you were writing a Zen western novel about a gunfighter.

WB: I never actually wrote it.

JT: Can you tell me about Kells Elvins?

WB: I met him at the age of twelve at the John Burroughs school. He was at Harvard in 1938 when we wrote the story called "Twilights Last Gleaming" which was published almost verbatim in *Nova Express*. That story was the beginning of Dr. Benway.

JT: What was the John Burroughs school?

WB: Just a private day school in Clayton, Missouri. We moved out to Clayton which was a suburb of St. Louis, the school was right down the road and Kells lived up the road.

JT: *So you knew him since childhood.*

WB: And I wrote to him in 1961 saying that the story would appear in *Nova Express* which does mention that he is the co-author, and found out from his mother that he had died about four months before that.

JT: *In your last books you seem to be using cut-ups more selectively than previously.*

WB: I use them very selectively now. You see, *Minutes To Go* was experimental, now I may make a cut-up of a page and only use a sentence or two.

JT: *They seem to be more deliberately used in* The Wild Boys, *and the result is greater impact jarring you into a dream or different reality.*

WB: Just cut up something, and suddenly you'll get a sentence that's right. Like the technology of writing that I'm going into in this course. This sentence came out of a cut-up; "Technology requires a why." You have to know what you're doing to figure everything out while you're doing it.

JT: *That's an odd word choice, technology rather than technique.*

WB: But it's the same thing, technology or technique, it's a way of doing something.

JT: *How do you find teaching at CCNY? Have you taught before?*

WB: I just gave two lectures at the University of the New World in Switzerland in 1972, I think. I do enjoy teaching at CCNY, I don't know whether my pupils are learning anything, but I'm learning a great deal, and making my own ideas explicit. I'm considering the question of whether there is a technology for writing as there is for learning how to fly, or for learning physics, or engineering. Now how many of those who fly have taken courses in flying, or how many physicists have taken courses in physics—well, obviously all of them—but how many writers have taken courses in writing?

JT: You never took courses in writing.

WB: More haven't than have.

JT: One wonders whether it is a craft that can be taught—I can see how you can be helped by a critic sensitive to your own strengths and weaknesses.

WB: Well, following it right through, take learning to fly or physics, you're wasting your time unless you meet certain qualifications. If you're going to be a flier you've got to have coordination, a certain degree of intelligence, or you're wasting your time. Given that, these things can be taught. But given all the qualifications for writing, whatever those may be, like some ability to empathize with other people's minds—well a writer like, Beckett doesn't need that because he's on his own, going inside, so it may not always apply. Another factor may be the physical discipline, spending long hours writing. For example, if you are learning something like skiing or karate, you have to have an instructor, and if you do it and don't do it right your performance is going to decline—this is not true of writing. Writing is learned by writing. Kerouac, when I first met him, had already written a million words, and that was when he was twenty-three. And lots of it was very bad.

JT: There was this early novel called The Sea Is My Brother.

WB: He had many different manuscripts, and I read most of it, and thought it was pretty bad. But writers learn from bad writing, but a skier does not learn from bad skiing.

JT: There is a more direct relationship between experience and practical act with writing than most of us imagine. I guess good writers reach a point when they can finally do it, as with Kerouac, when he could become, as it were, spontaneous.

WB: At any rate I've learned about writing and the technology of writing by teaching this course.

JT: *Do you plan to write about that?*

WB: I'm having all the lectures transcribed. Naturally I have extensive notes, but there's always extemporizing, questions.

JT: *Do you have good students?*

WB: They are quite a receptive group.

JT: *I wanted to tell you that a number of my students seem to be sexually excited by a book like* The Wild Boys, *especially by the association of violence and sexuality, even in* Naked Lunch *they admit to being turned on despite the elements of comedy or parody.*

WB: I find that sexual passages are the most difficult to write. I don't mean the pornographic novels, the ones Girodias was publishing, because they're not sexy at all. They're very easy to write. People write them as fast as they can type. That pornographic style derives from *Fanny Hill*, which is about as unsexy as you can get. Actually, most of those books are written by junkies, and they have no sexual feeling for what they are writing.

JT: *There are sections of your work that play with pornographic situations very successfully, like "Seeing Red" in* The Wild Boys *where a man comes through customs with a dirty picture that is left undescribed but which causes paroxysms for the officials.*

WB: I think description of any sort is difficult, but sexual passages have to be written and rewritten.

JT: *Does this have to do with a basic repression we all have, a fear to describe sex?*

WB: No, it's just as hard to describe anything. Straight narrative is easy. If I attend to a narrative I can write it almost as fast as I can type.

JT: *There seems to be a return to narrative elements in your recent books,* The Wild Boys *and* Exterminator! *You seem to be using experimental devices more sparingly.*

WB: With more deliberate intent, I think.

JT: *Could you define obscenity in literature?*

WB: I don't think it means anything. What they mean is explicit sex scenes, but that's all soft-core now, there's virtually no censorship left on the written word. Where it might occur is if you have something out of the hard-core circuit. There has been some trouble with "Last Tango."

JT: *If that's true, will shame and fear be less an agency of control in this society?*

WB: Undoubtedly. But of course it is confined to certain areas. I think a very healthy degree of liberation has occurred. You read the Presidential Report in which they said that 50% of people who saw sex on film found that they were sexually freer. Just the impact of seeing people doing these things on the screen makes people realize "Well, why in the hell should anyone worry about it?" If the actor is willing to get up there without any mask on, how can you be ashamed of it?

JT: *Michael McClure once wrote that his intention was "to free the word fuck from its chains." Has that happened?*

WB: It has: there are no chains there.

JT: *And no future possibility of chains?*

WB: I doubt it, unless something drastic happens.

JT: *You seem, more than most writers, to have been occupied with kinds of scientific inquiry, and this is reflected in your story situations, for example the character in* The Wild Boys *who stores electricity during shock therapy and then releases it through his eyes as a death ray. At the same time, I don't feel that you can be seen as a science fiction writer.*

WB: I've talked to a lot of science fiction writers about this. The younger and more progressive ones maintain that the old categories are breaking down, and science fact has overtaken science fiction. In books like *The Terminal Man* the subject is not what's going to happen in three hundred years, but things that can and have been done right now. So the ideas about science fiction are changing as science overtakes it.

JT: Do you read science fiction?

WB: When I have time, but only when I can find any that's good. I'll get a stack and most of it is terrible though there are some good ideas, but there are very few that can convince you that it ever could have happened anywhere.

JT: Have you read anything by Rudolph Wurlitzer?

WB: I read *Nog* and liked it.

JT: What about someone like Robbe-Grillet?

WB: Haven't read him. I saw an excellent movie based on his work.

JT: What about Beckett?

WB: Well, yes. I would think of Beckett in the same way as Genet, as a writer that I admire very much. I've read practically everything Genet has written. He's a very great writer and not writing anymore.

JT: You met him in Chicago, didn't you, in 1968?

WB: Genet said there were two things: me and the French language, I've put one into the other et c'est faites. With Beckett I like the early novels best, like *Watt* and *Malone Dies*. Now he's getting too hermetic.

JT: Rather than simply informing us of a vision of the future, as in The Wild Boys, *I feel the ultimate end of your fiction is a kind of alchemy—magic based on precise and incantatory arrangement* of language to create particular effects, such as the violation of Western conditioning.

WB: I would say that that was accurate, but I would also say that I am creating a character. And my characters are often a composite: Say I have a dream of a character who looks like this, then I'll find a picture or a person, and then maybe a character in someone's else's story. One tries to create a vision of a living being. Of course the beginning of writing, and perhaps of all art, was related to the magical. Cave painting, which is the beginning of writing—after all, remember that the written word is an image, we forget this but we don't have a pictorial writing but the written word is an image and painting and writing were originally one and the same. The purpose of those paintings was magical, that is to produce the effect that is depicted.

JT: Is your intention shamanistic, to ward off disaster?

WB: Not necessarily disaster, but certainly to produce effects. For example, all primitive sculpture is magical, but as soon as these things are sold to tourists, they have no vitality. The saying is that painting, writing and sculpture are traditionally magic, and that it is intended to produce certain effects.

JT: Like the sense of transformation implicit in the rate of change in all of your writing?

WB: There is also the question of the actual relations between formal ritual magic and writing. People who are into ritual magic like Aleister Crowley—he may have been a competent black magician but he is not a good writer, in fact he's not readable.

JT: Have you studied magic formally or involved yourself in any kind of cult systems?

WB: Well, the whole content of the Mayan books is obviously magical, but we can't understand very much of it because Bishop Landa burned so much of the writing.

JT: Have you studied any other non-Western procedural maps like The Book of the Dead? Or gnostic texts like the Cabala?

WB: Not very deeply. I've looked at *The Book of the Dead*. I've read a lot of the literature of magic, but never involved myself very deeply.

JT: Is there any practical accommodation of magic in your work as a writer?

WB: Well, I simply feel that all magic *is* magic. That is if you get a very subtle evocation of the 1920s in Fitzgerald. . . .

JT: Yes. But that's "magic" in a romantic sense, the idea of evoking a memory onto a page and while that's beautiful, I was thinking of weaving a spell.

WB: But "weaving a spell" is magic. Now you've got the kind of magic that newspapers are involved in, people like Luce who were quite consciously capable of creating events. There is a very definite technique for doing that, and some of it is very much like magic—they stick someone full of pins and then show the picture to millions of people and they will get an effect. Do you realize to what extent being on the front cover of *Time* is a kiss of death? The Nobel Prize is another one. Hearst used to say that he didn't write the news, he made it. But that is all negative magic which has very little to do with the writer's work.

3

AN INTERVIEW WITH PHILIP WHALEN

Anne Waldman

This conversation is from a longer interview that took place with Philip Whalen in September 1971 in Bolinas, California. It was later in the afternoon and various neighboring & visiting poets dropped by to see how the event was progressing & ended up participating as well. Tom Clark, Lewis MacAdams, Lewis Warsh & Michael Brownstein and I were all present.

Anne Waldman

ANNE WALDMAN: *When was the movie or video of you made for National Educational TV?*

PHILIP WHALEN: Late 1965, they made it. It was . . . I think it took two days. They came over to my place in Beaver Street and they photographed for awhile in the room there and then they shot. They had another shot of me coming out of the house and another one walking up the hill and we took a shot of the, up on the very top of the, hill, ah, I can't think of the name of that little tiny park up there, it's supposed to be the geographical center of the San Francisco peninsula, and another day we were out at the Palace of the Legion of Honor and they photographed me around there . . .

AW: Moving around? I never saw it . . .

PW: No, standing in one place, but they took forever you know setting up shots and fooling around doing it all around and about. There were long waits you know between everything while all this technical work was done, it was very tiresome.

AW: Did they have you reading at all?

PW: Oh yeah, yeah, they had me reading, they recorded both indoors and outdoors, I think. At least the sound man was with them all the time with his tape recorder . . . I never saw the finished print, I only saw rushes of the film. I never saw what it looked like, they cut it down after all that shooting. They cut it down to ten minutes or something like that and then the other ten minutes was Gary.

AW: Was it shown out here?

PW: Yeah, well it's been shown all over, I guess, it's part of that National Educational TV series on "Poetry USA." We saw the one on Creeley the other night down here in Bolinas, which had been made at Placitas, at the adobe house in Placitas, it's very beautiful.

AW: How and when did you first meet Bob Creeley?

PW: Creeley? Oh, he showed up one day when I was living on Milvia Street in 1956, and he came in and I was living in Milvia Street and I think Allen Ginsberg was staying temporarily at Orlovsky's place in San Francisco, and anyway, he just showed up at the door and said who he was and I had seen the *Black Mountain Review,* or Allen had told me about it or something, and anyway, he just showed up and said that he needed a place to rest or something about how he was unhappy and we had a nice long talk. Then there was another day when I can remember when he and Allen and I were in San Francisco and we were in the Portsmouth Plaza which at one time used to be a hillside of grass and trees, now all messed up with that brick pedestrian overpass and the garage underneath it, and one thing and another. It really is a trap now but in those days it was simply a big open square with grass, so we sat over

Philip Whalen, holding portrait of himself, drip painted by Michael McClure. San Francisco, California, 1965. Photograph by Larry Keenan.

Allen Ginsberg and Anne Waldman. Naropa Institute, Boulder, Colorado, July 7, 1976. Photograph by Arthur Knight.

there looking at poems and talking about poetry. We sort of wandered all around North Beach and San Francisco, it was a very nice afternoon. Anyway, that was the first couple of times I saw him, and then he took, he gathered up stuff from us at that point and printed it all in the *Black Mountain Review No. 7,* right? All right, ask a question.

AW: What about this quote they have here on your book "the continuous nerve movie"? Could you expound on that?

PW: That's a quote out of the little preface poem to "Every Day."

AW: They asked you to write the blurb?

PW: No, no.

AW: Oh, they did that?

PW: Yeah, I think that copy was written either by Don Carpenter or maybe at the Harcourt office back east, I don't know . . .

AW: Well, do you think it sums up something?

PW: No. (Laugh) No, I was opposed to the idea of "collected poems"—in the first place I'm too young, I'm still writing lots of poems and, ah, they wanted to call this thing the collected poems and that's why I wouldn't do it, and they called it whatever other title would come up because it's just not, it's really not, "collected poems." It doesn't include the, that book called *The Calendar* that I wrote when I was at Reed and a whole lot of other odds and ends that I decided not to print and that are still in among those manuscripts at Columbia and in among the manuscripts that I have in my own files and what not.

AW: Did Jim Koller edit the entire book?

PW: Well, he looked at it, but then I'm the one who put it all together and he advised me at one point about the order.

LEWIS WARSH: I'm on. I've always wondered about your various jobs . . .

PW: . . . got a job in the North American aircraft plant on Imperial Boulevard and I stayed there about, oh, not more than two months I suppose and I got money enough to go back to San Francisco, and then I was in San Francisco awhile looking for a job and rushing around and finally I got a job for a little while in an advertising and typography place as an apprentice printer, and what I did was distribute type, actually, but anyway I got fired from that job because the boss in the place had hired me and he hadn't cleared the deal with the union shop steward there, although I had gone through the formality at the union hall of being registered as the proper apprentice and passed all the examinations and interviews and so on, but the other guy didn't like the whole scene so I was asked to go away after about a month or so, but it was all right because I was absolutely broke and starving at that point . . .

AW: Were you writing next?

PW: Oh yeah, off and on, and then seems like the next thing that happened was that I went and stayed with some other friends of mine, some old Reed friends in L.A. and I was there for several months and then I got a refund on the income tax and came back to San Francisco and at that time Gary Snyder had an apartment in Russian Hill, or rather Telegraph Hill, right at the corner of Green and Montgomery Street, and he said come on up and stay with me and so I did, and then that was late in '52 and then early in, let's see, in the summer of '53 we both went to work for the Forest Service up in Washington at Mt. Baker National Forest and then in the winter of '53 I was in San Francisco and in L.A. again and then I came back up in '54 and we went off to the mountains again and worked that summer.

LW: Were you involved in Buddhism at that point?

PW: Oh, I started getting interested in that when I was about 18, I suppose—17, 18, 19 years old, books I found in the Portland Public Library—A.P. Sinnet's *Esoteric Buddhism* and Lin Yutang's *Wisdom of China and India,* and a whole lot of other stuff. Madame Blavatsky's books.

AW: Who are these people that, it says "a very great number of people . . . if I should perish . . . would be ecstatically happy if I should kill myself by whatever means . . . but I refuse to give them that satisfaction . . ."

PW: I just simply mean that the entire capitalist system and the United States, that's all, who else?—the official United States Government or the *Saturday Review of Literature,* almost anybody, I suppose, would be just as happy if I didn't exist because I've been complaining all the time . . .

AW: You think it's just as hard now as it was 20 years ago, making any sort of way financially . . .

PW: Well, listen Anne, I have about two dollars in my pocket right now and I've got 50 dollars that I'll give to Donald on the first of the month to pay the rent that we've agreed on paying, so I'll give him that, that'll be what—Friday or something like that—and I have another two, or a little more than two, three dollars and that's all the money in the world there is, there isn't any more. Sometime or another Harcourt will probably send me a check if there's any money coming in, if that book has sold anything in the last six months. I got a check from Ted Wilentz for about 30 dollars for royalties on *Like I Say* and it was actually for the sale of three copies and the rest was royalties for reprint rights for some magazine or anthology . . .

LW: You feel that not having money has affected your writing and your life . . . it's a conscious thing not to have money . . .

PW: No, it's just inconvenient not to have any then sometimes it's a drag not having any because there's been nothing to eat and I like to eat, and so for several days on end there's nothing to eat you feel sad and then also it's embarrassing to have to go about at that point and see people, to have to borrow money or say, "Invite me to dinner please because there isn't any food." And so at different times various friends have very kindly said, "Why don't you come over if you don't have any money and I'll give you some food." But other—you know—some days, you don't even feel like just doing that, but it's so time consuming, it wears down your nerves, you feel you don't have anything going . . .

LW: You ever think what it would be like to have all the money you want to do what you want to do?

PW: Well, what I know I'd do would simply be to read and write and play music and walk around as usual, that's all, the thing is, I wouldn't have to be worrying about where to find the bread. [LW: I was just curious.] And as it is, as soon as I can, I'm gonna try to, as soon as I get all of my junk here, I'm gonna have to sell quite a bit of it in order to raise money just to live. We went through all this one day—there's a long tape at KPFA about that, where Gary and Lew [Welch] and I had a long three-way thing with one of the guys there about how the poets make a living so . . .

AW: *Well, you'd be prepared to teach if that . . .*

PW: Oh, I wouldn't mind teaching part of the time but I certainly, not full time anyplace.

AW: *I don't know what the solution is.*

TC: I think the less money you make the less bullshit you have to take . . . but all that teaching and all that running around, it's good for guys like Bob [Creeley] 'cause he needs to discharge that energy, you know?

AW: *But there's some difference betwen having two dollars in your pocket and having a couple of hundred . . .*

TC: Yeah. I think the old patron system was great of the 17th and prior centuries . . .

PW: It was if the people had sense enough to use their time and to do what it was they were going to do anyway, yeah, but if they got hung up and, say, well now I'm going to make this thing, I mean I'm going to make this painting and it's gonna have a lot of blue in it because I know the Earl of Rochester likes blue and he gave me this two million pounds to play with . . .

TC: But everybody has some commitment of that kind going on, consciously or not anyway, you know what I mean. In everybody's time there's something to which, you know there's some contemporary goals, you know, things which will allow you to make money, moves you can make.

LW: . . . to just do what you do naturally and be paid for it . . .

TC: That case is similar to the *New Yorker,* that thing that you were mentioning, is similar to the *New Yorker* where you can just sign a certain type of contract with them. They pay you $15,000 a year and you give them first look at every poem you write and they don't have to use any of them or they can use three, and some of the people who've done it are—Rechy had a contract like that, Dickey had a contract like that. And what suddenly happens is that you start writing poems for [AW: for the Rockefellers!] for the *New Yorker* and you're conscious of that, similarly to where you have a patron and it becomes a moral. I mean, supposing you had a patron like that. It'd just be a moral consideration as to whether you were going to allow that to dictate to you. You know what I mean? If you didn't care you'd just write your own poems, and send them to them and not worry about the fact that next year they weren't going to renew your contract.

AW: *So you think that the patron will always want something from you?*

TC: . . . your own motives. I mean you realize that your patron might kick you in the ass if you do certain things then you still do them . . .

PW: But then the thing is that in those days if you lost one you could get another too, and I suppose if you were lucky you would have enough friends who were interested in you and they would introduce you to another patron. 'Cause that happened, different guys had different patrons at different times or there'd be a group of people around, who, if one got bored, the other one wasn't and would still be producing commissions.

TC: A lot of the places where there's been a patron system, there's also been a weird outlet at the other end where you could go and like you wouldn't have to starve if you were very poor, you know, like the famous Chinese poets who went up into the mountains, supposing that they could eke out some weird existence.

PW: Well, in China there is a family system to start out with and they didn't just go to the mountains for one thing, like the one who was called Tao Yuan-Ming who was called the poet-hermit or what not . . . what he actually did was, he wasn't living in the capital, he was living out on his ancestral farm out in the country surrounded by servants and farmers who worked the land and by his immense family and cousins and uncles and so on who took care of the children and helped with the cooking and what not, and they all lived in one huge compound. It was out in the country someplace and he raves about his humble hermitage and so on, he's actually living a very elegant life, a retired life in the country, but he wasn't working for the government and he was away from the capital where all his friends were, and then other friends, of course, were at provincial capitals being in the government but he had gone away and it wasn't simply a thing of leading a simple life. Han Shan and Shih Teh were legendary figures. They don't know who Han Shan was. The Han Shan poems may have been written by about ten guys or eight guys . . . certainly the ideal of splitting and living in the mountains and so forth was there and a lot of people did it for religious reasons and so on and lived at temples and so on and ate herbs and bamboo shoots and tiger whiskers and whatever but . . .

AW: I really like that . . .

TC: In Hungary where you know if you were a foreign writer and you published there you can't take your royalties out of the country but you go to this castle, like twenty miles from Budapest on the Danube where they have all these girls to serve you this really fantastic food and they have all these local dances and room service and you live off your royalties until they run out.

LW: In Rumania, apparently the king of Rumania is a poet and so the poets of Rumania in which there are hundreds, hundreds of magazines, are like the second highest class. It's like the civil service system . . .

AW: How's the poetry?

LW: . . . incredible magazines and they pay . . .

TC: In Hungary and Rumania and those countries, for some reason, books cost the equivalent of . . . somebody was telling me the collected poems of Blaise Cendrars has sold seven million copies in Hungary and the price of each volume is equivalent to one pack of cigarettes and people like the American writers Miller, Steinbeck, Kerouac, I think, and Saroyan have all sold over a million copies of lots and lots of books that, more than the more social writers. 'Cause the books cost like about twenty cents and everybody reads books.

LM: Do you think people would read books here if they only cost twenty cents?

PW: No, because we don't have a literate public. In Russia, for example, they'll set out a 10,000 copy edition of the poems of Voznesensky, it would be gone inside a week and the next week they can sell 10,000 more.

TC: I think that's because they've never developed this totally electric soft culture in between the high possible literature culture and the people. There's never been this other buffer swarm culture, you know, like the T.V. *Life Magazine* culture . . .

PW: But before it, listen, before the T.V. *Life Magazine* culture what there was was work and all the guys, all the people, in the other part of the world who would've been awake and buying books were out here breaking the sod and cutting down trees and the only people who had the means or the interest in books were a few people in the cities on the eastern seaboard, and all the rest of the electorate was out hewing wood and drawing water for about 200 years in this country and it's only in about the last 20 minutes that any sort of publishing system and distribution system for books has been going. It's still brand new, a brand new idea, books in drug-stores even; they still don't believe how they're doing that and . . .

TC: I don't think poets are into being involved in running the whole system, of moving product and, you can't do anything about it unless you are Rod McKuen or somebody who does a lot about it, I suppose.

AW: *Hit your head against the wall.*

TC: He moves a hundred times as much product as all of us here will ever move.

PW: Yes.

LM: . . . In one day.

MB: It's meaningless product though.

PW: Well, a lot of people like it.

LW: Rod McKuen's a good poet.

AW: *Have you ever been offered any teaching jobs?*

PW: No. It's even hard to arrange for readings. Everybody claims that they've got no money and it's only been through the help of Gary [Snyder] yelling at people and telling them that they have to invite me to read that I've been doing anything.

AW: *Don't you think it's almost by chance, though, how someone gets to be a celebrated poet?*

PW: No, Creeley has published a lot of high-grade material . . . certainly to invent a book like *The Golddiggers and Other Stories* is worth every penny . . . it's a great book.

LW: You ever give any readings in Japan?

PW: One time a man who was running the American Cultural Center down at Kobe asked me to come down there and read and so I did, but reading to an entirely Japanese audience who had only a smattering of English and certainly didn't understand the West Coast dialect . . . in Japan poets are not interesting to start out with because everybody there writes poetry and . . . there are maybe one or two people that they think of as great teachers of poetry and something like that that they would be interested in but otherwise it's just one of the things that ordinary people always do, they write poems . . .

LW: What do they do with them, publish them?

PW: Give them to their friends, hang them up in the sitting room, and, if they're good enough, their friends see to it that they're collected and published. What they believe in as interesting is what *Life Magazine* tells them about and so they know all about what's-his-name, that Yalie who wrote that book that was made into a . . . yeah, Erich Segal, they know exactly what he is and all about him and they know all about, probably about, what's that Southern writer [MB: Robert Penn Warren?] . . . no, no a newer guy . . . I was reading a review of his book—Walker Percy, they know all about Walker Percy because he's told about in *Life Magazine* and *Time Magazine* and what not and so they, the ones who read American literature, know that those people are there . . .

LW: What's your sense of Bolinas, in terms of all the poets staying in one place?

PW: Crowded.

LW: Crowded with poets?

PW: No, just people, just people of all kinds and it's a very attractive place for people to want to come to from the city on weekends and be around and it's a little inconvenient . . .

LW: Would you rather be elsewhere?

PW: Yeah, I'd like to live in a more isolated place or right in San Francisco where nobody could find me, it'd be much better . . .

LM: I think it takes a space of time being here, I was going crazy but I don't see people nearly as much as when I first got here . . .

AW: *Here we all are!*

PW: But then Lewis [MacAdams] was sort of expecting people today. He wasn't really planning on being able to sit in his drawing room quietly . . .

AW: I don't know if you want to talk about it, but I'd like to hear more about that peyote trip.

PW: Oh, well it was great fun. I didn't think anything was happening, see, all these people I was with up in Seattle had never done it before and at this party the hostess who was giving this party was a lady from Boston and she and her husband were both teaching at the University, I guess, teaching fellows, you know, they were graduate students, and somehow this lady had written to what was called the Tropical Fruit Company, I guess in Laredo or the Tropical Plant Company or some such thing and sent five dollars and they had mailed her this cardboard box about two feet by eighteen inches full of green peyote plants, not buttons but the green living cactuses. Well, I don't know who had given her the instructions about how to prepare this, but what we did was to take all the fur off first and then peel away the outside and cut away from the root and all the time you inhale this ungodly smell, this great smell, and then we each had four of them, they were about an inch and a half across, the cactuses, you have to chop them up in small pieces and then start eating and she said, "Well, I heard that you had to eat soda crackers with it. It's easier." It's just a terrible taste, it makes your throat contract and it makes your mouth pucker up and everything, it's quite a thrill and so, anyway, we somehow got all this down and then sat around waiting for what was going to happen next. Well, there was a religious ceremony of some kind going on with all sorts of guys in robes and things all standing around and marching back and forth and there was some kind of statue at one end . . . apparently I was remembering or bringing to life a photograph of some of those Buddhist caves in India, and anyway, but here were all these people in it and all orderly marching and chanting and there was music in it of some nature which was quite marvelous. Well, anyway, sometimes I was some of the people and sometimes I was some of the architecture and sometimes I was some of the music and sometimes I was part of the strange image that was at the end of the cave that was being offered or prayed to or something, and so that went on for awhile and then after a while I was sick and I was puking but it didn't change things very much. I kept on having various little trips and at one point I remember I lay down on the couch, and I could hear the traffic on Roosevelt Way outside, and at one point I had my arm over the side of the couch sort of flopping, and then I had this great take about how my arm stretched clear out through the house and across the front lawn and across the street to the other side and every once in a while a car would run over it and I would get this funny feeling (Laughs) which is quite lovely, and I don't know . . . I saw various other strange Hindu deities marching around, and then, at another point, when I was more organized and I was sitting up, I looked out of the sitting room and into the kitchen and I could see these great cracks developing in the walls and at that point I wondered whether I was gonna have some sort of a nightmare trip and I said, "Well suppose it does, then what?" And so then I imagined all this wall coming down and sort of insect claws and beetles and things marching out and at that point I was so tired and so bugged and so unstrung or something that it didn't matter, and so I was able to take that without wigging out or anything and it gradually went away, but anyway, there were various other instructive and interesting bits but gradually I came down to where I was feeling tired and interested still and by that time the sun was starting to come up and I thought well, I'll go outside and get a breath of fresh air, and then, I went out into the light and you know the garden was a miraculous garden. It was just something else, you know, it was just fantastic, and it got lighter and lighter and I was beginning, I realize now, to go "up." And then I walked around in the garden a little bit and then I thought, well, I'll go up the street to these people's house where I had been before and see them and find out how they are, and then I noticed that the people who were driving by in the cars were very strange-looking, they were really weird types who were driving these cars and then I got up to the top and got in and I was feeling better and better, and I said "How are you?" They said "Just fine. Come on in." And so we sat down and started this incredible rap session where whatever we imagined or whatever we would suggest to each other we would see in a flash what it was we were imagining, and so we had this great exchange, this great marvelous conversation about how there were mice in the room riding neon bicycles around . . . no, the guy I was talking to had taken some at the same time I did, so, I thought that was really strong and then I felt real good for another hour or so, really high really just absolutely whooppee, really great, real ecstatic and then gradually it just sort of wears off and you feel sort of tired again and you wish you could go to sleep and, of course, you don't, you stay quite awake . . .

LW: Had you ever taken acid before?

PW: Oh no, that was in 1955.

LW: Do you have any dope?

PW: Asolutely.
(Some unintelligible remarks)

LW: *You Didn't Even Try,* was that like a real, based on real events?

PW: No, it was all imaginary. No, it's very funny. I started one day, I heard this imaginary conversation, about one page of it, and I wrote it down and then another day I was wandering around in Mill Valley in the woods and it seemed like I could suddenly see that I had a novel in my head, all of a sudden, there was a three part thing lodged inside my little brain, and so then I went back . . . [MB: Three parts?] mm-hmm, it was a kinesthetic sensation, literally . . . no, just three blawps, they were in there, like the, what do they call it [TC: Three Stooges?] no, the cerebrum and the cerebellum and the medulla oblongata. Well anyway, so then I rigged up this, and I knew it would have something to do with that page of conversation so I looked at that and then the next day, I was living at Albert Saijo's place over in Mill Valley . . . [TC: . . . was working in all those factories, or did you make that up?] Oh no, that's a reminiscence of the post office and all those other places, but anyway I started then walking every morning in the woods. I started to take long walks in the woods around Mill Valley and pretty soon I would think about what was the next thing that would happen and I would write down a few lines in my pocket notebook and I would come back and sit down and continue from here, and pretty soon I had a whole lot of handwritten pages and then I decided well I'll type up this much and see what happens, and then I typed it up. It didn't make any sense and so I said well, I'll just rearrange those pages one of these days and I went on to some other stuff. And then I started typing finally one day and getting it all arranged and I was living with Albert Saijo and he hated the noise of the typewriter so after a couple of days Albert just said, "Well, I think you'd better go." So I said all right. So then I had to think very hard and very fast about where I could go next, so I phoned my friend Tommy Sales in town and I said, "Can I stay at your house?" And she says, "Yeah, there's a spare room in the back." So then I got everything moved into there and I said boy, there goes that novel. That's the 19th time that I've started a novel and written a certain amount and then something happened, or I, so I said there it goes again, it's just fucked up in my life again, and nothing's happened, but then after a day or two I just started writing the second part and I knew the second part would be a certain amount and I did the whole thing from then on, without stopping. I was doing it every day, and then there would be days when something would happen when I couldn't work at it at all or sometimes there were two or three days in a row when I couldn't see it, I couldn't do it, and I thought, oh god, not again. So I felt really, I thought let's get it over with . . . till I knew I had come to the end of it, and then copied it, you know, did the final typing of the first draft and then looked at it, rearranged it and cut it, messed with it and then recopied it and then I don't know, I forget. I guess the next thing that happened was yelling at everybody about how I'd finished this book, and being very happy and then at some point, I think Elsa wrote to me. Elsa Dorfman wrote to me and asked what was I doing and I wrote back saying I'd just finished this book and then she wrote back saying that Sara Blackburn was an editor at Pantheon or some such place and why didn't I send the manuscript to Elsa and she would take it to Sara and show it to her, and so, all right, I sent it out to her and she wrote back and said that she liked it very much and she would pack it around to as many places as she could in New York to see if she could sell it for me, and so, gosh, poor Elsa wore out I don't know how many pairs of shoes lugging that thing up and down the length and breadth of New York trying to get a publisher. And she also gave it to, what's that fancy publisher in Boston, Little Brown, and they wrote a nasty letter back talking about all the nasty language and the bad writing . . . all sorts of nasty writing and the bad words and they were sure that nobody in their right mind could possibly read all this and so anyway they didn't want it. Hah, and so this took, let's see, I did that in 1963 and I guess it was two years later that Koller and Brown had got organized with the Coyote thing well enough so that they said, "What have you got?" And after they had printed *Highgrade,* they looked at the novel and said, o.k. we'll do it, and so, then the next thing that happened was that they showed the manuscript or I showed the manuscript to several friends like Ed Van Aelstyn, for example, read it and boy he hated it. Maybe it was after it was published that he read it and he said, "Maybe it was all right for you to write it but you should never have published it. It's a bad book." And he told me why it was bad and it took him about 40 minutes of very serious talk to explain to me that the thing was a dreadful mistake from the word go . . . Yeah, I can't remember any of it. It was very real, it was very rational and everything [LM: Did it depress you?] Yeah, and then I showed it to, this must've been before we got around to, it must've been when Ed was still editor of the *Northwest Review* and was down looking for manuscripts, but anyway, I showed it to Mike and Joanna McClure. Michael looked at it and said, "Well there's too many words on the page." And Joanna looked at it and she said, "Well, I read into about half of the first part." And she said, "It's too much like real life. I don't think I can stand it." Duerden read it and he said he liked it and an old friend of mine, the guy who was here recently, he read it and said he thought it was real good, and another guy from Reed read it and he said it was all right, so then somebody else would look at it and say it's just rotten and so about half of the people that I showed it to said it was rotten and half of them said it was all right, and I never found out, it was very strange and then it got printed finally and then they've probably forgotten about it and now it's just fine. The only person that likes it I think is Ted Berrigan, I was surprised, Berrigan wrote a very nice letter and said that he was having his students read it and everything, but I think he probably reads novels like I do 'cause you know you read them for the fun of it and you either like it or not, and if you don't, well . . . that's all.

TC: One thing I was wondering is when you were writing your earliest works, what precedents did you have for that open spacing, and that form of notation of opening the poems up like that?

PW: Well, which poems are you talking about?

TC: Well, like in even the poems in *Like I Say* and *Interglacial Age,* the ones that are over the page . . .

PW: Oh, I see, I see what you mean. Ah, Cummings and Patchen, 'cause when I was in the army in 19 . . . I guess it was in 1944 that I got into Hollywood one day, at that time I was stationed out at Yuma, at the Yuma Army Air Field, I was able to get in, once in a while, I would get a three-day pass and go to L.A. and this one time somebody had told me about this bookshop in Hollywood where they had all sorts of contemporary literature, and so I went in there and they had that early, one of the first books that New Directions published, that one called *Sunday After the War* and a book, a very small book of Patchen's called, I forget what it was, it was all printed in red and black and it was a very pretty little book, and anyway, I bought those and I read them and then I read about Patchen in the Miller book and I went back and I got several books of Pachen's, *Journal of Albion Moonlight* and the volume of poems called *Cloth of the Tempest,* and I think that was it, oh maybe the *Memoirs of a Shy Pornographer* . . .

TC: You know that thing he started doing where he would do the drawings and then the words spaced around the page, I don't know when he started doing this, but he started doing it after you did or . . .

PW: Oh no, a long time ago, I saw those, as I say I saw those in the forties . . .

LM: How come you always marked the time of completion of the poem? . . . dated the poem?

PW: Mainly because many other people are all doing the same sort of thing. I mean I'll be here in Bolinas writing something about bee's nests hanging in eucalyptus trees and one thing and another and then it turns out that I will read in some magazine that somebody in Florida has got into the same time/mind trip and are somewhere into the same, so it's simply so that I can keep track of when it was I did it, whether I did the first time around or not.

LM: Do you think of another sense of time than the poems? . . . Well, I just always wondered. I mean, you say 7/14/57. I mean, like that's a different time than the poem.

PW: Oh no, that's the date it was written on, that's when it was manufactured.

TC: Do you think you'd like to try and . . . I mean writing the *Scenes of Life at the Capitol* is interesting because it's like trying to do the long poem. I mean you feel like you'd like to try and do it again?

PW: NO!

TC: Did you learn a lot by doing it?

PW: I don't know yet, but all I know is, as I was telling Anne earlier, I got into doing the thing and then I thought I don't want it to go over the edge and be *Paterson* all over again or *Maximus* or something like that, I could see that it would have to stop after it had reached a certain point and the thing is where was it going to go? But I cut, I cut and then I had all these pages finally, I had these pages all strung out across the floor and I could look at them and I could see, I could see where this page over here should really follow this page over here and that this page over here should really go down in the second row.

MB: Did you use all the pages that you had strung out there?

PW: No, I cut, I cut a lot.

TC: Did they have drawings?

PW: No, that's all words.

LW: Did you write any more novels?

PW: Yeah, when I was in Kyoto the first time in '66 and '67 I wrote a novel that is coming out in L.A. from the Black Sparrow people, supposedly. They wrote me again a reassuring letter and said that they would get the proof to me late in October. That's the most hopeful that they've been so far.

TC: What's it called?

PW: *Imaginary Speeches for a Brazen Head.* But it's very funny because first of all what happened was that I got this poem ["Waiting for Claude" in *On Bear's Head,* pp. 384–385] see, that's in

"The Winter," that has these women's names in it—Margaret Gridley, False Memories of Margaret Gridley, what's the matter with Margaret Gridley, etc. and then "whatever happened to Margaret Grimshaw?" Well, those people eventually, I really literally did wonder what happened to them and so I made up this novel to tell who Margaret Gridley and Marjorie Grimshaw—

TC: I thought they were American girls from New Hampshire who were going to become schoolteachers or American missionaries, one or the other . . . they're from the Kyoto tapes . . . Well, I'm glad that we finally got the information.

PW: But that was marvelous because when I was writing that I'd get up in the morning early and go downtown, well not downtown, but just down the street, to a beautiful coffee place that I keep raving about in "The Garden" and various other places, I've mentioned it also in *Scenes of Life* where they had the hot coffee and croissants. And it was, my house was so cold, I was living in such a cold place then, that the earlier I could get out of it and get up and out of bed and go down to this cafe the better, and so I would go down there and have coffee and croissants and write several pages in this notebook I had—it was a notebook I'd bought years ago at Reed College. It was a big one about ¾ inch thick, it had several hundred pages and I'd bought it years ago with the intention of writing a novel in it and then I had got scared of using it but anyway I wrote it in that book and carried it around with me. I wrote some out of those and some pages out of notes but mostly in that copybook, just what I remembered. Later it ran into two more notebooks, and finally I had to sit down and copy it at the typewriter.

TC: Maybe somebody ought to put up a plaque . . . you travel around England, man, you see these little plaques, Jane Austen wrote such and such here . . .

PW: That'd be great.

LM: There's a great one on St. Mark's Place where James Fenimore Cooper used to live . . .

AW: *How do you think people should keep their sanity in these "troubled times?"*

PW: Well, you know, just stay out of the way. Try to stay out of the way, try to stay out of the way of falling buildings and so on, that's all.

LM: What do you want for Christmas?

PW: Well, I'd like to have an organ for Christmas. One time, one time, I think that that's in this book someplace that that's what I want anyway. Yeah, I had a fairly good one when I was in Kyoto. I had a two-manual Yamaha trip with twelve foot pedals . . . well, this one was a larger machine, it really held a lot more noise. It was great, you could, having two manual pedals, you could . . . oh no, that's only when you're playing "Mighty Like a Rose" or something. If you're playing Bach you need as many buttons to push as you can get and that machine had quite a few of them—as many as I could handle, anyway. So, it was a great pleasure to play.

TC: . . . You couldn't transport it back?

PW: I gave it to the YMCA for a new building 'cause it would cost so much money to have it packed up there and sent to the boat in Yokohama and then to have it removed from the boat to here. It would have cost more money than the fucker was worth.

TC: Do you have anywhere to put it?

PW: Then I'll have to figure out some place else to be. Join the church, hah.

AW: You could come to New York and do a workshop.

LM: I heard somebody pissed in the organ and it fucked all the pipes up!

PW: . . . New York, it's sort of a scary outfit.

TC: There's a funny poem . . . you guys are playing a balalaika somewhere drunk on . . .

PW: Oh, that was, no, that was when McClure was living on Fillmore Street next to that big garage, in the building where Jay

De Feo and Wally Hedrich lived. We were horsing around sitting around a table in the kitchen and manufactured that piece, that was when we were getting ready to go to New York in 1959, that great tour that Ellie Dorfman set up. She was working at that time for Grove Press and on her lunch hours, or on Barney Rosset's time I hope, anyway, she organized this titantic trip for her friends. How many colleges . . .

LM: Is that when you went to Princeton and people put you down and hated you?

PW: Yeah, yeah, right. It was funny. See, what had happened is that Leroi [Jones] and Ray Bremser and Mike and Allen and I all appeared all at once or something like that somehow or maybe it was just Leroi . . .

AW: *Bremser was there.*

PW: Maybe it was just the four of us, seems like Allen was there but Allen didn't read or something like that, I forget how it ran but anyway we came out to find that here was all these pink spotlights and these cafe tables set on the stage with checkered red and white tablecloths and then down just below the stage on either side there were coffee machines set up and then there were young ladies in the costume of hippie chics, although at that time they were beatnik ladies wearing black leotard bottoms and weird things on top and looking like Vampira, you know, and zipping down the aisles and delivering this coffee, and there had apparently been some kind of entertainment just before we got there produced by the dramatic society who had invited us to be there and who were supposed to pay and, no, they were called the Bridge Lamp or something like that, the Bridge Lamp Players, but anyway, when, so here this audience was, it was just commencing to barrack right about then and Michael McClure looked around the edge of the curtains and saw those pink spotlights and says, "I am not going on until they get rid of those pink spotlights." Hah, so he was starting to freak and finally we got everything calmed down enough and we all went out on the stage and everybody starts wildly applauding. First they make this dumb introduction and then everybody wildly applauds for ten minutes screaming and raving, and I think Leroi read first and at that time he was writing very gentle things but

Kenneth Patchen. Palo Alto, California, 1957. Photograph by Arthur Knight.

then people still applauded a lot and stuff and then Bremser got up and started reading and he said fuck once or twice and everybody broke up and they were screaming, whistling and yelling and he kept yelling, "All right, shut up, or you won't be able to hear the dirty words Shut up! Goddammit! Grrr!" and then he'd read a few more and he'd say "shit" or something like that and everybody'd break up, and so, but finally we got through all four guys and we left the stage and at this point the management comes up and says, "Wait, hey, where you going?" and we said, "Well, we did our number and now we're through." "But we told the audience you were going to stay here till midnight reading poems. It was going to be like a beat coffee shop and everything, a beat coffee shop in San Francisco's North Beach." And we said, "Well, unfortunately nobody ever . . ." Elsa did the talking at that point and said, "Well, listen, where's the money and you didn't tell us anything about all this show and about how we were going to read till midnight. Everybody, all the people, who said they were going to read, have read. Where's the money? la-la-la, where's the dean?" so she went around and rigged some authority out of bed and picked him up by the ankles and shook him until money fell out or until it didn't fall out and she had to call him the next day or something. Anyway, it was an awful scene and the students, 'cause we didn't come back on stage, the audience was starting to run up and down the aisles and through the balconies and in and out of the windows and stomping and screaming and, oh, it was really marvelous, it was in that theater that was designed by Thomas Jefferson or something, it was a round theater with a dome on it and it's all made out of marble and pillars and stones and gorgeous . . .

LM: It was this little theater in the middle of the campus. It's really an old theater . . . there wasn't another poetry reading after that until I came to Princeton.

PW: Well, then the next thing that happened was that we were going to go to, this guy invited us to Muhlenberg College in Allentown, Pennsylvania and we got there and he met us and he says well, heh, heh, we're going to have the reading in the ballroom of the Muhlenberg Palace Hotel in glamorous downtown Allentown, because two weeks ago Leroi Jones and Ray Bremser were here and it was decided that their language was unsuitable, the language of modern poetry was unsuitable for the ears of the campus of a Methodist college, whatever it was, so we played this hotel, and, of course, it was just jam-packed with people and Allen read and Michael read his grand fuck ode and I was reading something raunchy—I forget what it was—and it was quite a lovely evening, but it was strange to be in this hotel ballroom with a very low ceiling and it looked like a convention of the American Legion or something like that. The man who was the teacher there later got canned, he, for producing all those nasty . . . [TC: . . little cotton earplugs for all the . . .] It was very sad. I don't know whether he ever got another job, it was very sad, he was a very nice fella.

TC: Nice fellas get jobs.

PW: Yeah, I hope so.

TC: Or else they get into computer programming.

PW: Right.

MB: We should turn the tape off.

AW: It's just two seconds more.

PW: . . . for a gentleman or a lady . . . [AW: Coquettes.] Oh, let me see, nice, let's cut.

4

FROM *GUILTY OF EVERYTHING*

Herbert Huncke

The Caribbean Sea at night is absolutely magnificent. One has to see it to really appreciate the beauty of it, not to mention the sky. At one point, a storm was brewing way off in the distance, and the heat was extremely intense. The sky was just literally loaded with these big rolling clouds and above them, long streaks of heat lightning that would illuminate these fantastic views. They were just simply so beautiful that I couldn't believe it. On starlit nights, almost anytime you look up you can see at least one comet racing across the heavens. The water is so full of phosphorous that it looks just exactly like little balls of sparklers dancing on the surface. Anything that moves through that leaves a streak of light. The wake behind the ship was fantastic. It was just an avenue of sparkling light. I'll never forget it.

We hit the Pacific with the moon almost full so that we sailed just directly down a path of moonlit water. I used to take the monkey—Jocko, of course, nice original name. He was such a cute little bastard. He stood about a foot and a half high, maybe not that high. He had a tail that was a good foot and a half in length, and it was his pride and joy. He could whip it around anything. If he could get anyplace where he could put this little curve at the end of it around something, he'd just swing back and forth and chitter up a storm. When he'd get angry, he'd sit and curse me out.

I came down into the fo'c's'le one day. All my shaving equipment was on a little shelf. The fo'c's'le was actually a four man fo'c's'le, but Phil and I had the two bunks. This was one side of the fo'c's'le, opposite the lockers. Then the bunks that were supposed to be up alongside the bulkheads we put on end, and that was Jocko's territory. I used to keep newspapers on the floor. There was a little porthole and a ridge there that he could run back and forth on or climb up and down on. I could span his waist with my thumb and my finger. It was so tiny, but his little chest was big and his arms were long. He had a snow-white face, snow-white on the back of his head, and his body was black.

Anyway, I came in one day, and there he was, smearing shaving cream all over the place. When I came in, I said, "Jesus Christ, what's happened here?" With that he gave a leap and a bound, whirled back in the corner. He knew damn well he was in trouble. I said, "Jocko, you are a bad monkey. I don't want to hear any of that tch tch tch." I thoroughly enjoyed him. I'd take him up onto the deck, and I'd tie the chain to something. He'd get up onto the rail, along the edge of the ship, and just run back and forth. I just knew one day he was going to go over, and I thought well, if he does he does. He never did, though.

The Pacific is all ground swells, and the surface really is almost smooth. it's almost like glass. When the sun hits the surface, at least down in that part of the world, the water literally gets a burnished bronze cast to it. Well, Jocko was sort of playing along the rail of the ship and I was gazing out over this fantastic scene. Maybe 50 yards from the ship, this gigantic fish just leaped into the air clear out of the water, made a perfect arc, plunged back into the sea, and left nothing but a spray of crystal drops. Boy, I'm telling you. It even startled the monkey. His little head cocked, watching it. It's a sight that I can see so vividly in my mind's eye. I so often think of it.

We sailed finally to Honolulu, which I was impressed with, but it's so Americanized and so commercialized. It left me feeling very sad, because the climate is so beautiful, and when those tropic breezes just sort of waft across the surface of the earth, it really does something to your whole physical being, and then to be surrounded by these tourist traps and these awful hotels along the beach and Dole's pineapple. I'll never forget looking down through the turquoise water to the white sand bottom. The sea gets such a vivid shade of blue. It's a really true ultramarine blue, and then gradually pales out to turquoise in spots. You can look down through it I don't know how deep. It really impressed me.

In the Mediterranean I've seen blue, but there's nothing quite like those islands in the Pacific, I'm sure. I've always wanted to see the Galapagos Islands. They've always held a certain fascination, the prehistoric monsters, the iguanas and various types of reptiles that still are in existence down there. I suppose everyone's had this dream at some time or another, but my dream was always to have enough money to buy a little island all my own someplace, preferably in the South Pacific, and invite my chosen few to come and live and forget the rest of the world, just let everything else go on by. No competition. You'd instinctively do your bit for the cause, so to speak, to keep it all in order. There wouldn't be any necessity for pressure of any kind.

After we came back, the first thing that happened is we met Bill Burroughs. There was a young fellow that worked up at this drugstore in the vicinity of Columbia. He and his brother had come to New York with the idea that eventually they'd be high-powered gangsters. Their names were Bob and Don. Just prior to the trip I took down through the Caribbean and to Honolulu, I had met Bob and had turned the apartment over to him while I was away. We were gone approximately 4 to 5 months and didn't make any money. We did have a royal time, and of course we didn't kick our habits. In fact, we came back with habits even stronger than the one we had before we started.

When Phil and I got back up to New York, we went directly to the apartment. Phil had picked up a little chick aboard the train on the way up from Newport News, and he didn't want to check in with his old lady until he'd bedded down this little girl. So he took her to my place, naturally, which I didn't like too well. He really scared the bejesus out of her, because she didn't know what she was getting into. He just suddenly appeared in front of her stark naked and ready for action, and she says "Oh, no," and he says, "Oh yes." Finally she gave in. She was obviously an experienced girl, but she didn't expect it to go down quite like that. Incidentally, it had been snowing very hard and the streets were just piled with slush and snow. When they were finished, he ordered her to get dressed. Then he walked her several blocks out of the way just to confuse her apparently, so that she wouldn't know how to get back to the apartment. I'm sure that she had no idea of where she'd been, really. He finally put her on the subway and said goodbye.

That evening, when Bob came home from work, he said, "Jesus, good to see you. Man, I've got a guy lined up, going to be down tonite. I want you to tell me what you think of him. He approached me the other day. He's been coming into the drugstore quite regularly, and he's been talking about capers of one sort and another. He just told me that he has a sawed-off shotgun and some morphine syrettes that he wants to get rid of." So Phil said, "Morphine syrettes?" We'd just been using morphine syrettes for I don't know how long, so it sounded good to us.

Sure enough, who appeared at the door that evening but Bill Burroughs. I took one look at him and said, "Jesus Christ, get him out of here, man. This guy is heat." He was standing there with a chesterfield overcoat on, his snap brim hat sitting just so on the top of his head, wearing glasses, and obviously pretty well groomed. Certainly his appearance was not indicative of anything suggesting nefarious activity. Bob says, "No, this guy's alright. I've been rapping to him, man, just take it easy, take it easy." Phil was interested in talking to him because he said, "Man, if he's got any morphine, we can really do a little business with him. Maybe we can get a little taste out of him." So he came in.

The kitchen was arranged so that there was a table dead in the center of it. It had a bathtub in the kitchen and then the kitchen sink right next to the bathtub. The bathtub was alongside the wall that faced into the living room. Instead of it being a solid wall, there was a window that you could look through into the next room. It was nothing for somebody to be sitting taking a bath and bullshitting with somebody in the next room. There were straight backed chairs around the kitchen. There was a large cabinet with dishes in it, and then there was a door that led into the bedroom. It was a typical railroad flat, except that it ran the full length of the building.

There were two apartments on the top floor. We had one of them, and there was a very frustrated, confused woman who was still fairly good looking. She'd come to our door, and there she'd be in her nightgown and her night robe. She'd come in and talk for a little while, things like that. She would have been glad if anybody had given her a little play. Her daughter, who was 15 years old, was just as bad. She'd come in the afternoon. The mother worked in some bar someplace, a barmaid, and the daughter was really just nothing but sheer trouble. A lot of the cats that were cutting in and out of the place were young kids, around 19, 20. They would come in and the next thing you'd know they'd be running next door with her. I thought, "Oh boy, this is going to lead to trouble." I'd sort of put the squash on the situation. I guess Bob had taken care of her several times while I was away.

Getting back to Burroughs, he sat down at one of the tables in the kitchen, and I sat at another one opposite him, kind of looking him over. Phil was also sitting at the table, and Bob was in the other room rolling up some joints. He was going to turn everybody on to some pot. Now Bill hadn't taken off his overcoat. I said, "Listen man, why don't you take off your coat?" He hesitated for awhile, then finally got up and removed his coat. Here he is in a very conservative grey suit and a tie and collar, the whole bit.

I still didn't feel comfortable with him. He obviously didn't know any of the underworld language. He appeared like a fish out of water to me, and I was sure that he was connected with the FBI and that Bob had really made a mistake in bringing him down. Finally Bob did get around to mentioning the sawed-off shotgun. I said, "Well, where did you get it?" He went on to explain that a young fellow that he had known for quite some time had picked it up someplace along with some morphine syrettes. In fact, his story was that the young fellow had broken into a drugstore, and he'd come across this sawed-off shotgun and the morphine syrettes. He had several gross of them.

Phil was just delighted. Bill didn't bring the shotgun with him, but he did bring along a pocketful of these morphine syrettes. He pulled out several of them and threw them on the table. Phil anchored into him right away. He and Phil got along splendidly. Phil knew how to talk to him, and I sat back and watched. So finally Phil said, "Come on Huncke, let's you and I shoot up. Man, this stuff's just laying here. You don't mind, do you Bill?" We were calling him Bill by this time. He says, "No, not at all. I've been thinking about this. You know, I'd like to try that myself. I've always had sort of an interest in that sort of thing." I gave Burroughs his first shot.

Phil and I walked into the bedroom and we cooked up enough for the three of us. Bill was very interested in watching the whole process. He'd come in and by this time his suit jacket was off and he was watching us. I shot up right away, and right after I shot up Phil did the same. Phil turned to him. "Now look," he said, "there's enough there in the cooker for you to shoot up." So Bill said, "Well, what do you think? How do you go about this?" He was very hygienic about this whole thing. He thought it would be a good idea to first rub a little alcohol on the arm. Then he thought that it would be a good idea to clean off the spike first before he wanted to run the risk of injecting morphine into his system. Of course in those days hepatitis hadn't become quite as popular as it did later. We managed to dig up alcohol, and then we dipped the spike in alcohol. We drew up what we figured would be a fix that he could handle.

Morphine, incidentally, can be pretty frightening the first time you shoot it up mainline, because it gives a terrific pins and needles sensation. You can literally feel the drug travelling through the system, and it usually hits finally right in the back of the neck. You get this flush feeling, sort of a heat wave, and if you're not prepared for it, it's pretty frightening. Whenever I have been in the presence of people that are using drugs for the first time, I have always made it a point of trying to describe what the sensations might be, so that they're sort of prepared for it. It's so completely different from anything else that one has ever felt or reacted to, that if you haven't a little idea of what to expect, it's apt to throw you for a loop. So, not knowing Bill or how stoic he might be, I felt it was wise to describe a little of what I felt that morphine might do.

We tied him up and we gave him a very effective tourniquet. He rubbed a little alcohol, and then he turned his head the other way. I got the needle in and drew up a little blood and I said, "Loosen the tourniquet." He sort of loosened the tourniquet, peering down at his arm, and he began to feel the sensation as I shot the morphine into him. All of a sudden he said, "Well, that's quite a sensation." He kind of looked around and said, "Well, that's very interesting." He gave the impression of being sort of scientifically minded about everything. He hadn't given me any indication of where his interests lay, but he was so methodical about everything. I did think that most of his approach would be from a purely scientific standpoint, or something similar to that, and as I discovered later, it was. In other words, he became a drug addict principally as a result of research more than anything else.

I learned a little bit about Bill later, which sort of justified my original feelings. He had been raised in the Middle West. He was a member of the Burroughs business machine family. I think it was his great-grandfather, or great-great-grandfather—some member of the family in the past had invented the business machine, the comptometer or whatever it was. The family in general had money. Bill apparently had been sent to the very best schools. He had studied psychology in Vienna. As his high school graduation present, he was sent to Europe where he sort of hobnobbed with the so-called in people at that time in the European scene. He married a very obvious lesbian in order to help her obtain papers for becoming an American citizen and brought her back to this country with him. As I began to know more about him, I discovered that as a very young man he had been in love with a young student, or young friend, who died and left him fairly brokenhearted, to be somewhat romantic about it. He never spoke in those terms. He never discussed that with me. I picked that information up from Allen and from other people that were part of the scene around him.

That night, after he had shot up, we made arrangements to see how many morphine syrettes Bill actually had, and we decided that there could be something done about the sawed-off shotgun. Frankly, I don't know whatever became of that particular item,

Allen Ginsberg, 1980.
Photograph by David
La Chapelle.

because I think that it was handled mostly between Phil and Bill. He felt a certain rapport with Phil that he never felt with me.

Bill evidently started to write *Junkie* shortly after having met Phil and myself. After that particular night we began seeing a lot of each other. He, of course, formed very different opinions about me. He wasn't very flattering, I must admit, in his first book. Bill described having gone down to this strange place on the Lower East Side, this weird apartment. I must say it was pretty weird. In the living room, where we did most of our smoking and entertaining, we had painted the walls black with yellow panels. We had yellow and black drapes which covered the window, and then the ceiling had been painted a Chinese red with a huge medallion in the center of it, consisting of all of the Oriental colors, plum, and off-shades of yellow, orange, greens, reds, every color in the spectrum so to speak.

It had been done by Bob. One day when we were smoking in the summertime and drinking beer, just sort of enjoying ourselves, we had decided that we should really turn this place into a den, and make of it what we thought would be a good environment for getting high. Let me say that Bob never used junk. His interest in drugs consisted of marijuana and hashish. Also, he used these poppers, amyl nitrate. He liked those and he occasionally liked benzedrine, because it gave him a lift. After having partied all night, he would go immediately to work and not feel the wear and tear of the long hours without sleep. Then he finally would break down and sleep for maybe a day or a day and a half. All of this was happening while I was getting to know Bill and had been introduced to Bill's friends.

Bill was a little bit reluctant about inviting Phil and myself up to where he was living at the time that we met. I suppose it was just natural caution. In fact, it happened that he had a place on Waverly in the Village when I first met him. It was just about that time that he was living in the Village and attending classes at Columbia, I think in journalism, although I'm not sure. He was part of a very select group that consisted of a fellow, Hal Chase, and Allen Ginsberg, young and starry-eyed at the time, who wasn't quite sure what he was going to become. From a practical standpoint he had decided that it would be best to become a history teacher, since he had specialized in history. Meanwhile, he was attending a poetry course under Lionel Trilling, I think. In fact, Trilling was very "anti" his first poem, a thing called "The Doldrums."

At the same time I met Allen's brother, who was studying law and who is now a lawyer. He changed his name, and now lives somewhere out on Long Island with a large family. He married a very lovely girl who was the daughter of a Methodist or a Baptist preacher. How they met I don't know, but it was one of those young, calm attractions, one for the other. There was nothing impetuous about it, nothing exciting. They were just two young people that found they liked each other, and I guess their liking became a sort of love and respect and they decided to marry. Frankly, I think she did a great deal for him.

It surprised me to meet this rather reserved conservative young man who was Allen's brother. He certainly didn't fit into the picture that Allen had surrounded himself by. Allen's interests were far more flamboyant. He was going through a stage where he didn't know whether he was heterosexual, homosexual, autoerotic or what. He had naturally sought out the people that were the outstanding people at Columbia at that particular time. That group have all become fairly well known in their respective fields. Most of them were literary or interested in psychiatry or in journalism or things of that sort.

Bill was very interested in hypnotism, and had tried to hypnotize Allen on several occasions. Whether he was successful or not, I don't know. Bill was interested in many things. He was one of the first weightlifters I ever met, and it was very funny because he wasn't at all a weightlifting type. To see him with these huge barbells in his room really struck me as being incongruous. It just didn't fit his personality. At any rate, he introduced me to all of these people that sort of congregated at Joan Adam's apartment.

Joan later became Bill's woman. He said that he married her. If they got married, I don't know when. She had apparently lived with some young man going to Columbia when she was attending classes. She had a daughter by him. When I first met her, the daughter was approximately a year old, still a toddling infant. Bill had moved from Waverly Place up to her apartment.

The first time I met Jack Kerouac was at Bill's room on Waverly Place. He was living in one of those brownstone fronts converted into studio apartments. I ran into him one afternoon, Sunday afternoon if I recall correctly, and he invited me up to this room on Waverly Place and I met Jack Kerouac. Somewhere Bill had picked up something. I can't recall what the drug was, but he wanted to know if I knew anything about it. I had never heard of it. I didn't think it was the kind of thing that I'd want to fool with, simply because I didn't know anything about it. He decided that it could be shot intramuscularly. We did shoot some into the muscle, and nothing happened at all. I think he tried to talk Kerouac into shooting up, but Jack said no, he would pass it up.

At that time Jack would smoke a little pot, or reefer or ganja or grass or weed or tea, whatever you want to call it, but he was a little bit leery of the needle. When I first met Jack, he was a typical young clean-cut American type. We had a saying in those days about people like Jack. He looked like an Arrow collar ad type. They always had these clean cut young American progressive businessmen with their hair cut just so and with sort of a twinkle in their eye, and right there up and at them. That was Jack. That was the first time that I met him. Time went by, and all this time I was living on the Lower East Side. How I was living financially I can't really say, except that occasionally Bob and I would go out breaking into cars and stealing things.

Jack Kerouac. Tangier, 1957. Photograph by Allen Ginsberg.

At some point along the line someone brought a little fellow named Jack into the apartment. Jackie, it turned out, was the son of the secretary-treasurer of the Eastern seaboard Mafia. That goes back now to the 20s. His father had been a don, and when he died he turned a lot of his business transactions over to his wife. She was a real character, an incredible woman. She looked like something out of the wildest gypsy story you could possibly feature. She was an old crone if there ever was one, with hennaed hair that stood out in sort of a halo around her face, which was very chubby and full. Her cheeks were like apples. They were just puffed up, and her eyes took in everyting. Every finger had a ring or two on it, diamonds especially. She wore two or three different kinds of necklaces around her. She walked with a cane. She was the mother of Jackie, Frankie, two other sons, and two daughters.

Frankie, being the oldest son, assumed the responsibility that his father would have automatically assumed if he had been alive, as far as the family was concerned. He was a lithographer, one of the best. He really was considered a good man in his field. He works for a well-known outfit here in New York. I don't think he has ever gone out on any kind of a caper himself, but he does know how to dispose of merchandise. He has his own family, which must have at least 50 or 60 members, uncles, aunts, cousins, nieces, sons, the whole bit, plus his friends, who also have big families.

Later on Jackie, Bob and I worked together. We cracked a dress shop out in Jamaica. We just grabbed rackful after rackful of dresses, dumped them all into a little panel truck, took them right straight up to the house and hung them up. It was like sale day at Macy's. The price tags were still on the dresses. Everything went for half price. Two days time, we didn't have anything left. Of course, Mom had been gifted with several outfits for herself, and the daughters were allowed to come and pick out what they wanted with one or two friends. But the rest had all been sold. I don't know how much money we made on that little deal, but a nice piece of change. I didn't have to go out for quite awhile. I never really enjoyed working with Jackie, because he always felt that he should be the boss. I always felt that there should be no boss, that partners should be partners.

In the meantime Phil had returned to Kay, who had an apartment at about 157th Street and Riverside Drive, just where Riverside Drive ends. A very reasonable place, and a beautiful little apartment. Phil had been insisting that she try to find a place downtown. He was tired of making that long trip up, and when he'd wake up in the morning, he'd be sick and he didn't have any stuff. It was kind of hard on him. He'd have to make it all the way downtown, sometimes all the way over to Brooklyn, since he was using doctors at that time. Very few pushers on the street. In fact, it was almost impossible to cop horse then on the streets. I can't recall running into any of it for quite a while. It was in the 50s when it did come back.

I wasn't seeing a great deal of Phil at the time, but I did discover that he and Burroughs had become very good friends. In Burrough's book *Junkie,* he tells of going out with Phil on some of Phil's routines. They'd work what was called the hole, or the subways. Bill acted as sort of shill for Phil, who was a qualified pickpocket. Of course, this was all very exciting to Bill, and Bill was a perfect shill. You couldn't have found anybody better to work with from that standpoint, since no one would ever suspect him in the world, and then they'd think twice before they'd accuse him. So he was going out with Phil on capers, and Phil was taking him over to Brooklyn to meet doctors. Bill was gradually building up a habit.

I sort of dropped Bill and Phil. I didn't see much of them. I was caught up in my own problems, and they were working on a thing that didn't include me. Several times I did go out with them. The three of us went out together and made doctors out in Brooklyn and got together on our scripts. Usually Bill would have the money to finance these things, and money was a scarcity with me. Even when I'd made a good touch it would go very quickly. We were paying rent, and we had our electric lights and gas. We had gotten by by hooking up the lights to an outside line for awhile, but that didn't last too long. They finally caught up with us, and we were very nearly arrested for that.

While all this was taking place, Bill decided to move up into Joan's apartment not far from Columbia, where he was taking a course. Now, Joan had rented a large rambling apartment. I think there were actually three bedrooms and a gigantic bathroom with a tub in it. It was an old fashioned apartment that had been built about 1915, when that area was just beginning to be developed. It was right in back of Barnard there on 115th. She took this apartment at, I think, a very reasonable amount of money, by today's standards practically nothing. I think it was something like 75 dollars a month for this gigantic place. She kept the kitchen and the dining room and the living room for herself, and the three bedrooms she rented out to students from the university.

When she met Burroughs she immediately was attracted to him, and she saved her prize room for him. It was really a beautiful room, gigantic, in which he had his books and a desk and a bed for himself and the whole works. Then just a little bit beyond that was the bathroom and beyond that was Hal Chase's room. He was in one of the history classes and now teaches history, I think. There was some other young fellow that was just sort of in and out, not really a close member of the clique.

The clique consisted of Joan, Bill, Allen, who had a place of his own but spent a great deal of time there, myself, and later, Jack Kerouac. Then there were several Oscar Wilde types. I don't know what you'd call them. They were certainly effete, if I use the word correctly. They were very witty with a terrific bite, almost vitriolic in their sarcasm. They could carry on these extremely witty conversations. They were people that I didn't care much for, partly because I was intimidated by them. I couldn't always understand them, and it used to make me feel sort of humiliated because I obviously did not know what they were talking about, and I felt embarrassed.

Joan particularly fascinated me. I had never met a girl quite like Joan. As a young teenager, I had met several girls that I was attracted to, and one that I had sex with. I was primarily a homosexual at that time. In fact, I was going through many changes about my homosexuality. I didn't know whether I was purely homosexual, or bisexual. In fact, I didn't know if I could have sex with a woman for a long time. Well, I say for a long time. I was about 16 or 17 before I actually had sex with a chick, and then that was very quick and over with and done. After that, occasionally I'd ball with a girl, so I could have sex with women. That relieved a great deal of the personal problem that I had at that time but that was the Chicago period.

As any young person does, I had dreams about the future and what would happen in my life. I didn't know whether I wanted to be an actor, or a dancer, or a writer, and I had always excused my escapades into the more or less questionable environments by saying to myself, "Well, this is sort of like gathering material for the book." It was very funny. I would speak of it at that time fairly openly, until one night I heard someone make that statement. "Oh, I'm gathering material for the book." This person was just so obnoxious, his whole presentation of himself and his personality, that from that point on I made up my mind that I would never say I'm gathering material for the book, no matter what. To this day I really don't think about ever saying, "Well, this is something that I'll write about."

Anyway, I wanted to finish up about Bob and the end of the Lower East Side apartment, because it was very funny in a way, and tragic in another. Bob had dreams of becoming a gangster. He was out of Ohio. He had spent some time in Cleveland, but I think he was really born in some little town somewhere in Ohio. He had a brother, Don. After many years had passed, Don and I went to sea together.

So, Bob had this wild dream of becoming a mobster of a sort, and I must say he had the potential, except that underneath all of his swagger and his bravado he was really a very gentle guy. In fact, he would much prefer lying up in bed with some chick and making love to doing anything else. But when he wasn't doing that he was scheming ways to make money.

Now Jack, the son of the Mafia guy, had been part of a group of fellows that were working around Washington and Baltimore. They'd drive down on a mapped-out caper, something that had been planned, and they'd break into the place and make for the safe. One of the fellows in the crowd was one of the best safe men that New York had at that particular time. How true that is I don't know, but he was very highly recommended. He worked only when a job had been cased very thoroughly and he knew almost to the dollar how much would be in the safe. They called him a first class box man.

Well, they decided to take Bob into the crowd. They also picked up some outsider that I didn't know much about. He was a young kid who liked to drive cars, and he could drive, no question about that. They had organized this particular take right to the letter, and at the time that they met this young kid they needed a driver. They called him a wheel man. They either had to make the take that weekend or forget it altogether.

This was a theater. I think they were actually working with some guy on the inside who was going to let them into the office, and who knew to the dollar what the take was. It was to be on a late Sunday night, so that there'd be the receipts from all day Saturday and all day Sunday. It was almost guaranteed that there'd be something like thirty thousand dollars. As it turned out, there was ninety-two thousand dollars in the safe. Bob was very excited. This was the first time that he'd really been in on anything this big.

Sure enough, they went down. They made the take. They split the money. But, the kid that was driving the car had gotten nervous, and he'd been smoking cigarettes one right after another while he was outside. He'd run out of matches, and when he went to use a new pad of matches, he threw the old pad outside onto the sidewalk. Naturally ninety thousand dollars called for attention from the government. The law enforcement organizations got very busy. Two days after this happened, everybody was back in New York, sort of lying low. Everyone was feeling pretty good. Bob had given me a thousand dollars which I stuck into the bank. He was spending money pretty recklessly, and I told him to watch it a little bit.

Vickie had come to live with us at that time. It happened that she had run into a streak of bad luck, and she called me one night and said, "I just can't take it anymore, I've got to have a place where I can hole up for awhile. Can I come down?" I said, "Well, sure, come on." We just gave her the bedroom to herself, and sometimes I'd sleep with her, sometimes Bob. At any rate she took care of the place, kept things in order, and she was a pretty hip chick. She knew how to herd these cats around so that they behaved themselves. So naturally Vickie was benefitting by all this.

About three o'clock in the morning, we got a telephone call, and it was Jackie's brother saying, "You better clear out. They found a match pad which has been traced." These guys really tracked the thing down. It was just a matter of time until everybody was going to be grabbed. So we closed that place up. By daylight we were ready to sell all the furniture. We got a second hand furniture man up there. The apartment was empty the following morning by ten o'clock.

Vickie and I went uptown and checked into a hotel. Bob, unfortunately, had a lot of places. He wanted to keep his working record clear, and they traced through that. That's how they finally caught up to him. As soon as they got his name, they started snooping around. The story is that the young kid that had been the wheel man or the driver had fucked up somewhere along the line. He'd done something wrong.

Now Jackie got a big break. Mama knew everybody. A few years after this routine, he got busted in Columbus, Ohio, and got 10 to 20. Mama didn't stop. He was out of that prison and back in New York in four year's time. That old woman hobbled out to the airport and boarded the plane and negotiated with people until they found some loophole to get him out. Jackie was her baby, and she wasn't going to stand for him being put away for 20 years. How it was worked, what was done, who was seen, I don't know.

Getting back to the caper I started to tell you about, when they all got picked up, the money that had been made on the deal went for lawyers and things like that. Bob got a very light sentence. They couldn't pin anything directly on him. As I said, I don't know what they did with Jackie. At the most he did two years or maybe a ten year max.

That was the end of Bob really as far as our relationship was concerned, although later I did see him. We were always very good friends. There had never been any homosexual relationship there at all.

Going back a little, after my earlier trip on the tanker I was blackballed on the American Transports. I was so stupid that I thought that meant that I couldn't go back to sea at all. In talking with Bob's brother Don one day, he said, "Well man, how could you be so stupid? They haven't touched your papers. There are other ways of going to sea than American Transport." This was during the war. I said, "Well, I'm ready for a trip. I'd sure like to go to sea." He had been sailing with the Isthmian steamship people, and they liked him very much. He took me down there. We got aboard a liberty ship, and we had one of the best trips I'd ever had in my life. That was really an exciting trip. We sailed into the war zone. We were off the coast of Normandy about three days after the invasion. They were still coming over in black waves dropping bombs all over the place.

Our chief steward was half Portugese, Filipino, and God knows what else thrown in. I worked right under the head cook. Don was the baker and we had a pot and pan kid in the galley. I was the second cook, supposedly. The chief could take a knife about a foot and a half long with a blade that could slice a hair, and he could kill a fly with the tip of that knife. He was something else. He was a marvelous guy. Cookie, we used to call him, of course. He liked me, too. He was a stone thief. When he hit the other side—my gosh. They were unloading our cargo onto these amphibian trucks. Well naturally, when they'd come out a lot of the cats from shore would come out, and they had their pockets full of morphine. What they wanted was something to eat. I was in the galley and I used to just stagger to the door and deal as fast as I could. I had a beautiful time. When I came back, I had Italian berettas. I had commando knives, and air force jackets, and God knows what else.

We sailed to Newport, Wales, and stayed there for three weeks. I went up to London, spent time in London, and came back. I went to Cardiff, had a little trip up the Rhone Valley and got to know the Welsh people. Of course, it was wartime, but I used to smuggle sugar off the ship. One day I went off the ship and I had these huge salamis. I had one shoved up one sleeve and another one up the other sleeve. I had a taxi driver in town. I guess the customs agents were pretty hip. They were afraid that we'd start to do black marketeering, but I would never sell a penny of any of that stuff. I took apples and bananas. I showed a banana to a child. He had never seen a banana. He didn't know that they existed. And when I produced an orange! We had all the best supplies that you could possibly imagine. The stuff we dumped overboard, as garbage, would have fed I don't know how many people. It was really criminal.

Well, that was a long trip and I made very good money on it. When I returned, I had to go back to Times Square. Bill frequently would appear at the Angler Bar in the evening. We'd meet down there, and one evening he brought Joan with him, and Kerouac and his wife at the time, little girl named Edie. She was also out of Grosse Pointe. She finally divorced Jack. Very hip looking little girl, very hip chick. Apparently Kerouac wasn't too successful with her sexually for some reason or another. I think that was the big drawback, because they were going through very funny changes at that time, which were obvious to people who were part of the crowd. She was friendly with Joan. She would stay up at this apartment on 115th Street.

Angler's became a regular meeting place and almost every night, sometimes two or four nights in a row. Bill would show up and he'd want to cop some pot. At that time, I'll be very honest, I didn't like him really. I'm afraid that my feeling toward him was that I had him pinned for a mark. Now Kerouac I was somewhat indifferent to. Allen was really the most entertaining person of the group, Allen and Joan. I found that I was attracted more to the two of them than to anybody else in the crowd. I felt sort of self-conscious with the rest, I guess.

At about that time another very funny thing occurred. I was sitting in Chase's cafeteria one afternoon, and a young girl walked over to my table and said, "May I sit down?" She was carrying several books in her arm and was obviously a student. She said, "There's someone who wants to meet you." I said, "Yes, who?" She said, "Well, a Professor Kinsey." So I said, "Yes, Professor Kinsey, I've never heard of him." She said, "Well, he's a professor at Indiana University and he's doing research on sex. He's requesting people to tell about their sex lives, to be as honest about it as possible." My immediate reaction was that there was some very strange character in the offing who was too shy to approach people himself, who probably had some very weird sex kick, and he was using this girl to pander for him. But I sounded her down.

She obviously knew what the score was insofar as sex, but I

didn't know. I didn't want to shock her, but at the same time I wanted to find out just exactly what the score was, so I questioned her rather closely about this man. My first reaction was why he hadn't approached me himself, and she said, "Well, he felt that it would be better if someone else spoke to you. He has seen you around, and he thought you might be very interesting to talk to. I'll tell you what I'll do. I'll give you his name and his phone number. He's stopping at a hotel." At that time he was at a very nice East Side hotel. She said, "You call him and discuss the situation with him." I had nothing else to do and I said, "Well, I might as well find out what this is all about."

I called and he said, "Oh, yes, I'd like to speak with you very much." I said, "Well, exactly what is it that you're interested in?" He said, "All I want you to do is to tell me about your sex life, what experiences you've had, what your interest is, whether you've masturbated, how often, have you had any homosexual experiences, heterosexual. Just a complete record as far back as you can remember, and some of the interesting experiences you may have had." I said, "That's all you want?" He said, "That's all I want." I said, "Well, I think it's only fair that I tell you. I don't want to sound crude, but I do need money." He said, "Well, I'd certainly be willing to give you some money. Would ten dollars be all right?" I said, "It certainly would."

He wanted me to come up to his place, and I said, "No, I'd rather not do that. I'd rather meet you somewhere first." I still didn't trust him. There was just something about the whole thing that sounded very offbeat to me. So I arranged to have him meet me. "Well," he said, "I'll meet you at a bar. I don't drink, but I'll buy a drink." I said, "All right, that's fair enough." So we arranged to meet, not at the Angler but at another place that was also popular. He said, "I'll know you when I see you, so you just sit down and order yourself a drink, and I'll be there in a little while."

I didn't have enough money to buy a drink, and I sort of kicked around in front of the place until suddenly a cab pulled up and I saw this man get out. Kinsey had a very interesting appearance, strictly professorial. His hair was cut very short. It was slightly grey. He had a round face, very pleasant appearing. He was dressed in a nice suit, obviously a conservative man.

He walked up to me and said, "I'm Kinsey. You're Herbert Huncke. Well, let's go in. You'd like to have a drink." I said, "Yes, I'd like to talk to you for a few moments before we go to your hotel." He said, "All right, we'll go in." He again gave me much the same story that the girl had and assured me that the only thing he was interested in was the discussion, except he also wanted to measure the size of the penis. He had a card he showed me which had a phallus drawn on it. He said he'd like to know the length of it when erect and when soft. Naturally, I was wondering when he was going to get to the point. It was really very strange, and I still didn't believe him, but I thought, Well, hell, I might just as well go along with him and see what it's all about.

As it turned out, it was a very delightful experience. As I got started I just sort of unburdened myself of many things that I had been keeping to myself. I have always masturbated up until just the last few years. I sort of lost interest in sex around about 50. Of course everybody told me I was off my rocker. I must say I was sort of thankful by that time to get it out of my system, so to speak. I earned my living by it at one time. I have met all kinds of people, really some very strange fetishes that I have had experience with.

I told him most of the things. For example, in the *Journal,* I described an experience, a very interesting experience for me. It tells of being approached by an older man when I was a young boy about eight or nine years old. A young fellow, about 20, who, after telling me dirty stories and arousing me with pornographic pictures, suggested that we go up into a building together. We did, and he suddenly startled me by dropping his pants. There he was with an erection on. This thing looked gigantic to me, because it just happened that it was dead in front of my face. I sort of drew back, but at the same time I was sort of interested. I must say that in all honesty, I had felt no fear.

He wanted to feel me. I was very embarassed by comparison. Here was this little tiny hunk of flesh, this gigantic thing standing in front of me. It just didn't seem right somehow. Anyway, he did try to convince me that it would be a good idea if I would allow him to put it up my rectum, which I certainly drew the line at. I knew that that would be very painful, and I assured him that I wasn't about to cooperate. He didn't press the issue. He proceeded to masturbate very furiously and then he ejaculated. That was my first experience with anyone other than children.

It was the thing that I thought of when I began to masturbate. It would excite me. Instead of following a normal course, I suppose, and being pleased by visions of a little girl, I was very attracted to this big phallus, a cock. It was quite an experience. I had never told anyone about it until I told Kinsey. It was that sort of thing that I unburdened myself of. As I went along, he was so adept at his questioning and his whole approach that there was no embarrassment really, and I found myself sort of relaxing. He turned out to be a very interesting man, a man that I learned to respect and that I saw quite a bit of. The one thing I couldn't supply him with was a size of my penis. He finally gave me a card and asked me to fill it out and send it to him later on, which I never did.

We met several times. He only remained in New York a short period of time. I think there was some difficulty about the grants at the time to enable him to continue on. He had to return to the university later. Then he came back with his companion, very nice young man, someone who had studied with him and that he had broken in himself to follow in his footsteps. I think he is still with the Kinsey reports. I was one of the first in New York to be interviewed, and certainly one of the first from Times Square.

Kinsey had seen me and he was fairly sure that I'd have information to give if he could get to me. He had walked up and down 42nd Street, and he realized that there was action of some sort going on down there. Of course, he didn't know too much about the underworld aspect of it, but it's pretty obvious. You walk by doorways and you see young men with tight pants and their whole profile on display. Then there were many flagrant queens that used to fly up and down the street, not to mention some of the more sinister types that could be seen and still can to this day. The area isn't nearly as interesting now as it was then. There weren't as many pornographic bookstores. Things were not quite as nasty then. It was more in the open. Broadway was lit up bright and sparkling all night long. There was a different feeling about things.

I wanted to mention this. Kinsey gave me money for the interview, whether it was a full ten dollars or not I don't know. I wouldn't perhaps have accepted money from him if I hadn't needed it very badly at the time. He said, "Now if there's anyone else that you know that you think might be interested in being interviewed, by all means send them up. In fact, I'll tell you what. For every person you send me from 42nd Street, I'll give you two dollars. I know you can use the money." I said, "Yes I can." It was nice to know that when I was uptight I could get two dollars. All I'd have to do is just waylay somebody that I knew, and I'd say, "Hey man, do you want to make a couple of bucks?" "Well, what do I have to do?" "Well, all you have to do is just sit down and tell this man all there is to tell about your sex life. There's no hanky-panky involved. The man is doing research work on sex." Of course, there was no problem. I sent Vickie up to see him, and I think he actually interviewed Burroughs at one time. I introduced the two of them at the Angler Bar.

Bill is a very knowledgeable person. He's been all over the world, and as a young man he had studied psychology in Vienna and could talk the man's language. And Joan was very interesting and pleasant to be with. It was a good crowd. Then of course I was the wicked character, rushing in and out. I'd see somebody. I'd say, "Excuse me, I'll be back in a little while." I'd go out and rap for a few minutes with someone, or I'd say "So and so's looking for you," and that sort of thing. Then I'd introduce various people and it sort of went on like that.

This was when Kinsey came back the second time. At that time he was working with men, and then of course later on with women. I pretty much made his Times Square study. There were others, too, that he met through me that sort of took over. It got to be pretty competitive for awhile. I always liked Mr. Kinsey. One night when I was very sick, I bumped into him. I said, "Look, I am really uptight for some money. Can you spare five or ten dollars?" He did it, reluctantly. "Now look," he said, "I don't want to make a habit of this. I'm in no position to do that, but yes, this one time I'll be glad to help you. Just forget it." When you meet people that understand or are somewhat responsive, it always leaves a good feeling. So that was how Kinsey came into the scene and was part of it for a little while.

I had about three dreams as a kid. An actor, a dancer, a writer. If I've held on to anything of so-called value in my concepts anywhere along the line, I have always respected creative people, music, painting, writing. Science I didn't know anything about it. But anyone who was doing something progressive, this was something that I secretly dreamed about and thought about. These were thoughts that I carried deep inside of me no matter what was happening.

For a long time I tried to justify my actions and my behavior and the things that I did. Of course, it finally reached the place where I couldn't do that. I have done things that don't hew to the line by any means. I don't know whether I feel any shame about them or not. I don't think I really do. I can see where I might be a person who, if one was going to pass any kind of judgment or opinion, one might certainly object to my behavior. I don't believe that that is right. I think that's a very bad way to think about people, in terms of judgment or opinion. I try not to have them about people. Of course, there is such a thing as instinctive liking, instinctive disliking. That's the way I would refer to it. My feeling is automatic. It's something chemical, I suppose.

I finally decided that I couldn't write myself. The way I was living there just wasn't any time, although I would make little attempts to write in a notebook. A lot of that stuff was just simply lost. I don't know whether it matters any, because it wasn't until I was really about 30 that I could evaluate correctly. Then I could evaluate sensitivity, responsiveness, perception, all those things.

Prior to that I'd been pretty callow, especially when I was in my teens. I say with no pride at all that my only interest in people was how I could use them. If I wanted to tear it all apart and say whose fault it was, I suppose to a large extent it's the fault of my parents. To a large extent it's my own lack of discipline. There's nobody at fault. I think that applies to almost everyone.

I finally reached the conclusion that if I couldn't write, everytime I'd meet somebody that could write, I'd encourage them. I found that no matter what kind of life I was living, invariably there would be two or three people of that nature that would either seek me out, or I'd somehow get to know them. It sounds so silly, but it really was like that.

I wanted someone else to do it, since I couldn't. I would try to recall some of the things that had hung me up and prevented me from really doing some of the things I'd wanted to do. I could see where people were unhappy because of trivialities, much of their time wasted with trivialities in the final summing up. It really didn't matter one way or another morally, from the standpoint of whether it was right or wrong. Nobody deliberately sets out to be wrong. There may be some that do, but basically people are shooting to do whatever they think is the best thing they can do. They play it by ear.

So, when I met all these people that were literally ebullient with the desire to write and to see the world, it was sort of exciting for me. I was very pleased that they'd even allow me to be a part of their circle. This was all underneath of course. I don't know how many of them were aware of it, or whether they ever thought about it. I became very close with all of them. My life, in terms of making changes, probably did a little bit, although I certainly didn't stop misbehaving. I continued to live on the streets and to steal.

Meanwhile, Bill had gotten himself, along with his room uptown, a little funny apartment for about 30 or 40 dollars a month on Henry Street, about two blocks down from where my place had been. He threw a couple of beds and a mattress into it. What his purpose was, I don't know. He let me live there, but of course he made a very nasty crack.

Bill always irritates me. He calls me Herman in his book *Junkie*. First of all, he gave a rather hard description of me as being scrawny-necked and sort of emaciated looking which I probably was at the time. This was his reaction to entering the kitchen at Henry Street. He said he looked around and somebody introduced him to this sort of strange looking person whose name was Herman. Later, he said in passing, "Herman lived in a little place I had on Henry Street. Of course, it never occurred to him to pay the rent."

Since then he may have learned, because I understand there have been financial reverses in his life, although he's living very comfortably now by his own work and effort. I still believe there's a trust fund that he can draw on if necessary. But at that time he certainly had his family in back of him, so he had no conception of what it meant to be strictly on your own and scuffling to get by. He could very well say, "Well, it never occurred to him to pay the rent himself." Damn sure didn't. I was hoping, as a matter of fact, that he'd never bring the subject up. I was certainly grateful for the place, because, God, I'd spent many a night out in the cold wandering the streets.

That place never became quite the spot that the other place did, although a bust took place there. Some kid that I had helped out fingered me. He couldn't help it. I have learned not to be critical of people, because, hell, they don't know what they're doing a good percentage of the time. I'm sure that the kid was terrified of going to jail. I think what happened is that one night he had been stopped by the cops, and they had said, "Well, look, if you'll finger some dope outfit or something like that." They frequently do that. "We don't really want you, but we would like to get a good arrest on our record. Maybe we can give you a little break if you'll cooperate."

I had them approach me once and offer me money to set Ginsberg up. They offered me freedom, and I guess I could have

*Herbert Huncke. New York City,
April 1979. Photograph by
Gordon R. Robotham.*

had a little supply of dope occasionally. A few years back there were two detectives of the narcotics squad—well, of course then so many of them have been corrupt. It's hard to pick out who I mean. These two were a couple of the first to come to the attention of the public. They had a list of people. I guess they were interested in money. I didn't know that then, but they probably would have set up a nice little business for themselves. "Give us a few hundred dollars and we'll forget the whole thing." If you're going to nail somebody, nail the distributor. Now, I can't even say that about the average pusher, because the average pusher is just some poor guy who's trying to keep his own habit going. He buys half-loads at a price, and half of that he shoots up himself, so he's in a bind. It's really pretty awful, the whole thing. All it does is jack up the price of drugs on the street.

This kid probably thought, "Well, you know, shit, why not Huncke? He's laying up there in a pad. There are works up there.

There's bound to be some junk around or at least a little bit of it." Sure enough, he met me on 42nd Street that night. I was always trying to tell him to go home. He was really a kid that didn't belong on the scene. He didn't have the stamina for it. I'd helped him out several times and taken him down to the place. I'd always tried to look out for people if I could, and then I've always had an eye on kids anyway, or young men. They attracted me pretty much at that time. I didn't try to force myself on them but a lot of them were pretty responsive, and he turned out to be that way. I'd taken him down to the pad. I suppose he justified it on the strength of that. Unnatural sex practices.

The kid told me that he was going to go home. In fact, he had wired home and had given my place as an address. He was expecting a telegram and he really would appreciate it if he could come down there and stay that night. So sure enough, at 11 o'clock there's a knock on the door. I said, "Yes?" "Western Union." I went to the door, and two bulls walked in. They pretended like they were going to take him along, but it was pretty obvious that they were going to give him a boot in the ass and tell him to split when we hit the street. I didn't say anything.

One guy had the nerve to say to me, "You've certainly deteriorated. You're living here on the Lower East Side, and it's a pretty barren place you have here." Jesus, here I'd been on my ass the whole time anyway. He had known me when I was working with Eddy back in the days of the prescriptions and the doctors. I had been living pretty high, wide and handsome then.

They busted me. As a result of that bust, they do a lineup on Bill, because the place was in Bill's name. So Bill got busted, and that was his first bust. His family immediately got him out of that and took him back to St. Louis. That left Joan with her mainstay gone, and the place began to go to shambles up there. Ginsberg was going to sea. Kerouac was sort of making a play for Vickie. I think at about that time Vickie was actually turning tricks. She had gotten lined up with some so-called madam on the East Side, and she'd get calls and go out. She tried to keep on the upper scale, 50 dollars a night and stuff like that. I think there for awhile she was actually doing pretty well.

Eventually I came out after having served my four months. Following that, I went up and I stayed at Joan's place. While I was staying there a Polish fellow from Buffalo appeared. He had sort of been the pride and joy of a black queen that had lived in the Times

Square area, some friend of Spencer's. They had given up their apartment in the Times Square area and had moved to Fox Street in the Bronx. I still know very little about it, but Fox Street is pretty notorious. I think there was actually a heroin factory up on Fox Street.

This black queen didn't use drugs. He was strictly a juice man and could drink an incredible amount of whisky. He'd have open house from Friday night on. There'd usually be a couple of chicks there, and there'd be maybe a couple of good looking hustlers from Time Square, and then this Polish guy that I just mentioned, who was a car thief, together with his partner. I got sort of chummy with my Polish friend. They were driving a stolen car from Buffalo.

Some chick visiting this black queen's apartment had left her valise there, and somebody took it. It was decided that it must have been me. I didn't, but I was fingered for the deal. So who appeared at the apartment with this chick and the police one night but this black queen, looking very righteous. They knocked on the door and just came in. Joan was absolutely horrified. This was the first experience with the law that she'd ever had. Of course, they couldn't touch her. They were primarily interested in me. It ended up that they finally took me and the Polish guy. The queen pointed out the car downstairs in front of the house. She really was very spiteful. Sure enough, all three of us, he and his partner and myself, ended up in the Bronx jail with this case on our hands. Well, I beat it. We all beat it. They were held, of course, for the car theft, but they couldn't do anything to me. They had to kick me out of the case. This was just about the end for Joan.

When I came back out, who appeared on the scene but Bill, in a station wagon. Incidentally, he was a member of the Harvard Club here in New York, and occasionally he'd take everybody up there for dinner. He'd come marching in, very dignified, with these weird looking people, and everybody would sit and have a good meal. This was around Christmas, and he was going to Texas. A friend of his had interested him in truck farming, the son of some multimillionaire, a playboy who had nothing to do but just fly around Texas in these high-powered sports cars. Finally, he rammed it into a tree and killed himself. I don't know how many broken legs he had and so on.

They have nothing to do. These people live on these elaborate farms or plantations. They've big comfortable houses, and they have people working citrus fruit, tomatoes, things of that sort. It's a very good business. His father had set him up down there and of course he didn't have anything to do but just sit back and collect money. This sounded sort of good to Bill, but Joan didn't like that particular element. While they were looking around, they found this incredibly beautiful little cabin back from Waverly, Texas. It's East Texas, Brazos River territory. Bill decided that it would be a good place to experiment with growing pot, and maybe try his hand at Oriental poppies to see if he could produce a little opium. Of course that never materialized, but we did produce a good growth of pot.

To get back to when I came out of jail, I remained in New York. I went back to 42nd Street. It was like home. I sort of fucked around for a little while. I would see Ginsberg occasionally, who had returned from one of his trips and was still going to school up at Columbia. It was during this time that he introduced me to his mother, who he wrote *Kaddish* for. She was insane. They couldn't permit her to stay outside. It was best to take her into the institution, but at the time I met her she was somewhat rational, a very sad woman. There was something very uncomfortable about meeting her for me, but Allen took it very well, as he does most things.

At any rate, he received a letter from Joan and Bill to have me come down to Texas. I had absolutely no idea what part of Texas I was going to or anything. They had sent money to Allen and the instructions had been to get Huncke on the bus headed for Houston, where Bill would meet him and pick him up. Now I had a habit at the time. I of course had immediately started fooling around. The first little bit of money I got I ran right to the connection. I figured that Bill would probably like a little taste of something. He had sort of hinted that it would be nice if I'd bring something along.

When Bill settled in Texas, he had cased every little town for miles around for paragoric. He had succeeded in getting a paragoric habit. He'd chill it overnight, skim the surface off, burn the alcohol out of it, and end up with a somewhat clean texture of opium mixture and shoot it mainline. It would give a nice lift, but he really didn't like that. So we were very anxious to get hold of something closer to the real thing, preferably morphine.

When I had left it had been mid-winter, and Ginsberg put me on the bus and started me off for Houston. I don't even remember getting on the bus, actually. All I recall is waking up somewhere over in Jersey, en route for Houston. I still had a little for shooting-up purposes, and I tried to string it out, but it was long gone by the time we hit the Gulf of Mexico, Gulfport, Mobile, that territory down there. I was ready to find something else. I didn't really have bad withdrawal at that time. I did go through some changes, naturally, but they weren't too bad. When I got to Houston and met Burroughs, he had paragoric. It sort of helped me through. Bill Garver, in New York, would send ground-up pantopon through the mail, and he sent it pretty regularly. Burroughs would send the money order to him, and he would save a little for himself and send a fairly good supply of pantopon down to us in Texas.

Meanwhile I had started using benzedrine inhalers along with Joan. The very first day I was in Houston, as we were driving out from the bus station we passed a drugstore, and I said, "Bill, I think that drugstore could be made." He kind of laughed and said, "Well, sometime when you're in Houston you might try." It wasn't long afterwards that I did make a trip into Houston. Supposedly, I was to have brought pot seeds along. Vickie had saved a half a Mason jar of pot seeds. Why I was never told about it I don't know, but in all of the confusion in getting me started en route to Texas nobody had said anything about this jar of seeds. Bill was terribly disappointed that I didn't have them. So, since we were so close to the Mexican border, I said, "Well look, why don't you let me have some money and let me go on down to Mexico, and in all probability I can score. At least I can score some pot, and if I can score pot that hasn't been cleaned, we can get seeds that way." So Bill thought that it might be all right. He gave me 200 dollars and got me into Houston.

When I got into Houston, instead of making arrangements to go to Mexico, I decided to try Houston first and see what luck I'd have. Sure enough, there was a little shoeshine stand just about a half a block from a hotel that I checked into. The hotel had apparently been the NMU headquarters for seamen in Houston. The idea that Houston was a seaport had never entered my thinking at all. Even to this day it seems sort of hard for me to think of Houston as being a place to ship out from, but they actually have union halls there and the whole bit.

Apparently during the war, this particular hotel had catered to seamen coming in and out of Houston. It was really a typical old Southern hotel, sort of tropical in atmosphere. The rooms were furnished with wicker furniture. There was one of these two-bladed fans that kept slowly revolving in the center of the ceiling. The hotel was really an interesting spot, because it looked out over

Houston's Chinatown, which consisted of about three buildings with pagoda-like trimmings, a little area where the Chinese had congregated and had their headquarters. There are Chinese in Houston that have laundries, and they have clubs or tongs that they belong to, and that was their headquarters.

So here was this sort of strange hotel with the Southern atmosphere, the slowly revolving blade in the center of the room, wicker furniture, and a very lax air about who came through the lobby and who didn't. There was nothing really shabby about it, but at the same time it wasn't really genteel either. It was clean. The maids were very accommodating. There were nice black girls that were still affected by their Southern background. They did everything to make one comfortable that they possibly could, and I'm sure that they would have been even more accommodating had anyone pressured them.

Right around the corner from that hotel was the black belt. There were two or three beauty parlors and places of that sort, and a shoeshine stand with these typical Southern blacks that really had a little routine going with the shine rag and the whole bit. I fell up to the shoe shine stand and started rapping to one of the fellows and he said, "You sure don't sound like you come from around here." I said, "Well, I don't. I come from New York." "Oh, you come from the big city, the big apple?" "Yes, I do." He said, "Well man, I"ve always wanted to go to New York."

We got to talking. I said, "Listen, you don't know where I could maybe turn on to a little smoke, do you?" I don't think I said smoke, I probably said grass or tea or something. He was a little reluctant about owning up that he knew where I could get some grass, but finally he broke down. I said, "Well, what I really want are some seeds. I'm visiting some friends here in Texas. We've got a big spot and we'd like to plant some grass. If I could get just a jar, it's worth 20 dollars to me." Twenty dollars at that time was big money, and it sounded very good to him. I could see his eyes light up. He said, "Well man, I just might be ble to do you some good. Listen, I can't knock off here until a little later in the day, but if you want to we'll meet. I have a taxicab and we'll drive out to a couple of spots I know. I'll turn you on to a decent joint, a stick, and you can decide whether you want some of this or not. When they clean up, I can tell them to save the seeds. Sure, I can get you 20 dollars worth of seeds."

I considered myself very fortunate, because first of all I was white. I haven't been down that way in years, but the people in Houston think of blacks in one way and themselves in another. There's a big division, which is typical, I guess, all through the South. I thought I was very lucky to sort of fall into these people to cop. I did meet him, and we drove out to a couple of honky-tonk places. He didn't let me go in with him, but he let me sit in the cab. He went in and I guess he rapped with his boys, and he finally came up with some grass to smoke and also some seeds.

I still hadn't contacted the drugstore. Joan made me promise that I would see what I could do about getting some inhalers. So I had decided that when it came time to go to cop some inhalers, I'd hit on this one drugstore. Lo and behold it turned out this drugstore was the main spot for connecting. I used to buy benzedrine inhalers by the gross. He gave me a regular wholesale price for them. He offered me anything in the way of the barbiturates that I wanted, nembutals, amytals, anything I could think of. What I did was go in and ask for a couple of benzedrine inhalers. In a conversation with the guy, I said, "I don't suppose that if I wanted a dozen of these, you'd let me have them, would you?" He said, "Well, maybe something could be arranged."

That was how the whole thing built up. I became a steady customer of his from that point on. I'd make that trip in from the cabin at least every two or three weeks for a fresh supply of benzedrine. Sometimes I'd pick up a few downs along with it. Also, we were in a dry county in Texas, and Bill wanted his drinks in the evening. So I'd pick up liquor in town, too, and take it back out to the place with me.

I don't know how I knew the place could be made. It was just an instinctive thing. I knew that Bill was going to drugstores. I'd heard that he was driving around these small towns all around New Waverly. He was a little reluctant to make his business too well known right there, but he would drive over to I don't know how many little out of the way towns and buy paragoric. All you had to do was sign for it. He was becoming a little paranoid about it. Not only would he buy paragoric, but he'd have to buy Joan's supply of benzedrine. He was sure that he was attracting too much attention, and as a matter of fact he was.

Bill was very interested in guns, and he'd purchased a .22 target pistol. It was really a beautiful gun, and he'd stand out back of this little cabin and aim at the barn. There would be sound through the area. One day when we went over to a little place not far from where we lived in the woods to buy some supplies, the people at the place said, "Oh, you must be the fellows that live over there near such and such a place in the pine woods. I thought there were a couple of gangsters over there, there was so much gunfire." They were a little curious about what we were doing over there. There's no question about that.

Stephens was the name of the people that owned one side of the bayou. There was actually a feud going between the people on one side of the bayou and people on the other side. It had been going on for years. One day I had a chance to ride a horse all through the territory. There were little paths that led back through the pine woods and down along the edge of the bayou, and a place to cross. It was really incredible.

They had a whole world of their own in there. Old man Stephens, of course, was the big shot on our side of the bayou. He used to come over on horseback and climb off his horse, and he'd look around and he'd say, "Well, how is everything today?" He was really a typical hillbilly type. His mother-in-law was dying of cancer, and he really made us shudder one day. "Well," he said, "the old woman's about ready to go. Her breast is just literally eaten away." He sort of gestured and kind of scooped his hand around right in front of his chest. He says, "There ain't nothing left. Poor old girl." She died, too. He invited us to the funeral, but we didn't go. They were really strange.

He had big hounds. There was always a big gob of saliva dribbling from the corners of their jaws, and they were monsters, literal monsters. A little cat had sort of wandered in out of the pine woods. I put some milk down, and from that point on it was our cat. When these hounds would come bounding through the woods and over toward the place, that cat would know it instinctively. I'd see him just literally splitting like a streak of lightning way back under the house. They really were anxious to get that cat. One clamp of the jaw and it would have been the end.

There were armadillos all over the place, the trees draped in Spanish moss. The whole bit was fantastic. Little chameleons all during the summer, when they'd mate, you'd see them with their little throats bubbled up. They get sort of rose colored. There were snakes. Fortunately, I didn't see any poisonous snakes. There were supposed to be pine rattlers.

Getting back to Houston and this drugstore. They were very accommodating. Later on, I asked him if he knew a doctor that I could go and see to get prescriptions for morphine. He thought for a few minutes, and he said, "Well, I do know two doctors. You might try them." Incidentally, I never did. I got to thinking about it and thought, well, maybe it's just as well that I don't. We were really not hooked on anything. It was just as well not to get hooked, because it would have been too much of a hassle.

I was completely in the dark as to what Bill's eventual intentions were. When we finally did leave it came sort of like a shot out of the blue. We were there from January to October of 1947. I think when Bill first went to Texas he had some idea that he would sort of get in with the wealthy crowd, but Joan didn't want that. Joan was not interested in keeping her nails painted red, with all of the sitting around and socializing. That wasn't her stick at all. She wanted to get back in near to nature, so to speak.

The place was completely out of the way. Our nearest neighbor was at least a mile and a half over through the pine woods. Although there were people living all through the area, there were none that were close to us at all. We had this whole section to ourselves. I think he bought about 93 acres. It went down from the top of a little hill right down to the bayou itself. I'm telling you, it was fantastic. In the summer it was just a mass of all kinds of flowers, tropical flowers, and everything was so lush. A lot of cedar trees, hibiscus bushes, these big coral-colored blossoms on them, really beautiful.

But Bill was ready to pack it in. He didn't want to face a winter down there. I think they were sort of fed up with the whole situation. He also wanted to see what we could do with the pot, see if we could make any money on it. Also, I think he was sort of disgusted with things. That was my impression. He just didn't like being so completely removed from everything.

His son was born while we were there. Apparently Joan had become pregnant during the time that I was in jail, just before Bill had been pinched. I gather that they were making it together. I have never been able to really figure that whole scene out, because to my knowledge there was no physical contact to speak of. I know there wasn't while we were in Texas, and yet she was pregnant. It had to be Bill's child. So, one morning about two o'clock, she calmly knocked on Bill's door. He had his own room. I had the room across the way from him, and there was a little section with a chemical toilet to one side, and then an area that had been partitioned off for storage space and hanging clothes and things like that. Then she used the front room as her room. There were a couple of chests of drawers and a big table that I'd put together as a dining table.

At any rate, she knocked on his door, and she said, "Bill, I think it's time." So he said, "All right, just a few minutes." He got his clothes on. Naturally I got up to see what was going on, and she said, "Well, I'm going to have my baby." They hadn't made any arrangements at all. There was a hospital just a short way from New Waverly. Here was Joan ready to have her baby any minute, and it's darn near three o'clock in the morning. I guess Bill had to find somebody to direct him to the hospital, and sure enough he came back the following morning and said, "Joan's had her baby. It's a boy." The following day she was back.

What always astounded me about Bill was his complete indifference to other people's comfort, especially to Joan. I could never understand that relationship at all. I think he respected her. As far as love in the accepted sense of the term is concerned—of course love is such a vague thing anyway—but in the accepted sense of the word, I'm sure he had no deep affection for her. She was sort of interesting to him, and that's all. He didn't like to be annoyed with her too much. She demanded that he give her a little attention each night. She'd go in and just before we'd all go to sleep, she'd spend maybe an hour with him in his room, and they would talk. She'd leave and go into her room. It was a very strange household, all the way around, but off from everything. It was very weird.

Joan went back to New York on the train. She had nowhere to go. She had to wait in the Grand Central Station until Bill pulled into New York. He was short of money at the time. I guess the family had suddenly raised a lot of hell with him. Joan had a big old-fashioned trunk. You could pack everything but a stove in it. There were several things that she wanted to save, and she had packed everything. Bill hadn't bothered to pack much of anything. His guns that we wanted he stashed away behind some clothes that were still hanging there.

We got back to New York. Neal Cassady, Bill and myself drove right straight from New Waverly, Texas, almost without stopping. When we reached New York Bill said, "Where do you want to go?" I said, "Well, you better drop me off at Vickie's." I knocked on the door. Vickie of course was very excited about seeing me and wanted to know all the details of the experience. Bill had to drive over to the Grand Central Station and pick up Joan.

That was almost the last time I saw Joan. I was told that

something had happened to her leg, and that she had to use a cane for a little while. They found a little house out near the ocean front around Brighton Beach. They disappeared from the New York scene altogether, except for their contact with Allen and Kerouac and people like that. I was very definitely cut out at that point from any association with almost all of them. I didn't see Ginsberg at that time. I didn't see Kerouac. I did see Neal Cassady once and asked him what he intended to do.

He sort of hung around with me for a couple of days. Vickie had become involved with a lesbian down in the village, who was the sister of a guy I had knocked around with a little bit. He had been a seaman, and he had introduced me to his sister Stephanie, who was a junkie, and of course automatically we all became very close because of that. During the time that I was in Texas, Vickie started using drugs. Prior to that she had been death on heroin. Anything that involved the needle she wanted no part of. I was very surprised when I returned to discover that she had a habit going, and she and Stephanie were making a scene of a sort.

Stephanie had a comparatively large apartment not far from the police station. Vickie had moved in with Stephanie. I was going to stay there for awhile, but they didn't want me around. One night there was this incredible scene in which Vickie ordered me out of the place very dramatically. Said that I didn't need to think that I was going to move in there and sponge off of them. I can't remember all the details, but I was on the street.

Stephanie was a pianist and she was working these little bars out in Brooklyn as an entertainer. I never did bother to go out and hear her play or get involved with any of that scene at all, but Neal did. I introduced him to Vickie and Stephanie, and it happened that Stephanie had to go to work. Neal had driven in from wherever Bill and Joan were staying with the jeep, and had run into me on 42nd Street. He had the use of the jeep for a few days, and we hung around together for just that short period of time. So he drove Stephanie to work. I guess they saw each other once or twice after that. I presume that he tried to make her. Maybe he did, I don't know.

I don't know what was happening with Vickie at that point. All of a sudden there was an anti-Huncke attitude on the part of practically everybody. I was out in the cold all the way around. I don't know just exactly what happened. I think the anti-Huncke attitude sort of came from Bill and Joan. I think that I got on Joan's nerves while we were down in Texas.

I don't know what Joan really thought about me to begin with. I was never quite sure. I was very much smitten by her in a strange sort of way. During that time in Texas, once or twice I came back from Houston very zonked on goofballs. One night Bill and I had an incredible argument. There were just a lot of things that had been building up inside of me, and somehow or another the barriers were down and I proceeded to tell him off. I can't recall all the things that I said to him, but I said many things that were very insulting. I recall Joan telling me that I was making statements that were utterly ridiculous. All of that is very vague.

There's a very strange story about Neal and Allen. When they came to visit, we were sort of pressed for sleeping quarters. I knew that there was some kind of relationship between the two of them, and it occurred to me that they'd probably prefer the privacy of a room. So, I volunteered my room. For some reason, we were short of beds, and I tried to build a bed for their room. We had a couple of sideboards from the bed and an old army cot, and what I tried to do was stretch that canvas from the army cot in such a way that it could be used as a bed. It was a total failure all the way around, and there were a lot of meanings read into my efforts that were not true. It appeared as though I was trying to make things comfortable for these two lovers. The whole thing was so damned ridiculous that it's always irritated me. It's still a thorn in my side.

Bill and I were never really very close. I think it was Joan's idea that I join them in the first place. She thought that I might be able to help, and I tried. God knows I tried to keep the place clean. I helped put up a fence. Bill didn't really know what he wanted to do. The first thing that annoyed him was that I hadn't brought the fucking seeds. There was just an accumulation of things, and I always have felt that that is probably why there was a sort of an anti-Huncke attitude at that time.

When Allen arrived on the scene with Neal, he was still a typical student, unsure of what he was going to do. He didn't know whether he was going to teach or write poetry or what. He had made an effort to write poetry, and he had succeeded in writing "The Doldrums." He and Neal were not as close as he wanted them to be. There was a whole lot of emotional confusion.

Another thing. I made a trip into Houston with Neal. I think this was the final kickoff. When I would go into Houston, I'd check into this hotel and I'd usually get all my business taken care of, whatever I had to do, getting supplies, mostly from the drugstore. There was a very good delicatessen, and I'd pick up smoked oysters and various things of that sort, so that we had little snacks with the drinks at night. I'd get all of that taken care of. Bill was very lenient with money, and I'd have a good time. I saw no reason why I shouldn't.

One weekend I had come in on the bus. I'd checked in the hotel. This was a long weekend, maybe the 4th of July. I was planning to stay in over Saturday and Sunday, then come back Monday night. Bill was to meet me at the bus stop in New Waverly. I met a couple of cats. There was a place that I could go and get a little record player and pick up a few records, so I did. I set myself up very comfortably for the weekend. It was Saturday afternoon.

About five o'clock in the evening, who appeared on the scene but Bill. He had not mentioned coming in at all. Well, Bill proceeded to get very drunk. Meanwhile, there was a young cat that I'd met that I had eyes for, and I planned to have him stay with me. He also had a room in the hotel. When Bill had gotten so drunk he could hardly stand up, I said, "Listen, why don't we put Bill down in your room and let him stay down there and sleep it off? You stay here with me." This was perfectly agreeable to him, and we got Bill up enough to get him downstairs and onto the bed. It was the first time that I ever recognized that Bill could appear beautiful. This was with all of his defenses down, his glasses removed. He was lying on the bed. He has very fine features, a sharp nose, thin mouth, the eyelids almost lavender in color, and his hair had sort of fallen down in a shock over the forehead. He really looked extremely beautiful. I had been hearing about dear Bill from practically everybody, and I had never seen it, but this time I did. It sort of surprised me.

Everything seemed to be all right. I went back up to my room, and the next morning there's a knock on the door about 9 o'clock. It was Bill. I answered the door. He said, "I'm leaving." I said, "All right. I don't feel like leaving yet. I'll come back as we planned." So Bill drove back to the cabin, and I guess he and Joan talked that situation over and Joan didn't like the idea of my taking Bill and putting him in a strange room. She thought that I wasn't showing loyalty. That was another thing that went wrong.

Then there was another episode very similar to that in which

Herbert Huncke. St Mark's Church in the Bowery, New York City, June 13, 1973. Photograph by Evan L. Arthur.

Neal Cassady, Allen and myself were involved. Another weekend, and I was supposed to come back with Neal, but I was having a very good time and I didn't feel like going back. I can't remember why it was so important for me to go back with them, but when I did get back there, I was greeted by hostility. Something that I had done that didn't sit well with them. I don't know just what it was. I know I thought that somehow or another they were unjustified in their attitude, so I didn't pay any more attention to it.

This was almost the end of the whole routine anyway. Of course, I didn't know that. There was never any discussion with me about their plans at all. What happened finally was that one weekend out of a clear blue sky, Bill announced that everybody was going back to New York. That's the way it came about. I undoubtedly had done many things that didn't sit well with them. I don't feel as though I was terribly guilty of anything really gross or detrimental to the peace of the whole place. The main thing was that I was the third person. Three don't get along well together. I know that very decidedly.

5

"HIS ABSENCE WAS ALL THERE WAS"

AN INTERVIEW WITH JAN KEROUAC

Gerald Nicosia

It was one of the great complaints of Jack Kerouac's life that he never received public recognition for a lifetime of literary labors. The publication of over a dozen books within half as many years may have astonished the many thousands who fell in love with *On the Road*, but the feat brought him not even one nomination for any major or minor American literary prize. At the time of those books' publication—the late Fifties and early Sixties—just the mention of nominating Kerouac for, say, a Pulitzer Prize would have brought a hearty and probably also snide laugh from most of the major critics and English professors in this country.

Part of the reason for my writing a biography of Kerouac was to help establish, for the first time, his rightful place among the greatest innovators in American fiction and poetry. When I was asked to speak at the 1979 convention of the National Society of Arts & Letters, I determined to see that Jack's fate would not befall his daughter, Jan Kerouac, who promises to be a major literary innovator herself. Jan has written a great deal of poetry and is finishing an autobiographical novel, *Everthreads* [since published as *Baby Driver*, 1981] that has already drawn praise from several editors (a selection from which has been published in the *City Lights Journal*). When I introduced her to the audience, she stood

firmly on her own accomplishments as an American creative art-
ist—but in some sense, I like to think, it was also as Jack Kerouac's
closest living representative that she took a long-belated bow before
the artistic establishment.

The following interview was conducted in Chicago on June 4,
1979.

Gerald Nicosia

GERALD NICOSIA: *Do you remember when you first heard who
your father was?*

JAN KEROUAC: Ever since I can remember my mother talked
about him. When my mother left her second husband, she told me,
"Well, now it looks like your name is going to be Kerouac, like it
ought to be," and so there was a big to-do about learning how to
spell my real name. I was nine when I first met him, and I
identified with him—he seemed to be sort of a larger version of
myself. I was never interested in the legal hassles that my mother
was undergoing with him, and I always viewed them as being
unnecessary, because I didn't really care if I got support checks. It
had something to do with a paternity test to see if I was really his
daughter—a blood test. His lawyer was Eugene Brooks, Allen
Ginsberg's brother. I don't think my mother had a lawyer. But we
met him out in Brooklyn somewhere with his lawyer, and we went
walking along the street, and I remember looking at this character
who was my father and feeling very interested in him. The first
thing he did was suggest we go to a bar for lunch, instead of to a
restaurant, and I thought it was kind of cute because it shocked his
lawyer. His lawyer said this little daughter shouldn't have to go to a
bar, but I'd been in millions of bars already living in the Lower East
Side. So we went into a bar—it was the day the astronauts first
went up in space, in 1961. I remember the TV set up in the corner
was blaring with white-and-black images of astronauts as we sat
there, and my mother and father reminisced about their early life
together, and I looked back and forth between them, and felt for
the first time a certain wholeness. I always had suspicions that I
was a real human being with two parents, and now it was being
confirmed.

GN: *Did you know that your father was denying that you were
his child?*

*Jan Kerouac. San Francisco,
California, August 29, 1983.
Photograph by Arthur Knight.*

JK: I knew, since my mother told me, that the whole problem was that he had told *his* mother that I wasn't his daughter way in the beginning, to protect *his* mother, who was kind of hysterical. She had been worried that someone was trying to bother her precious son, and he consoled her and told her that he didn't really have a daughter. He couldn't go back on this lie, and so he sort of talked himself into a corner. But I never really felt like my being his daughter was of primary importance somehow. I understood that he was doing something very important—that he sacrificed fatherhood for something grander. I knew he was out there bumbling around in some kind of very important universe.

GN: Did you know that your father was King of the Beats?

JK: I knew that all the people that my mother knew were in a certain category. They were *hipsters*. That word was used all around me from a certain crowd of people on the Lower East Side who were different from so-called straight people. I felt proud to have my parents belong to that crowd, like we were special.

GN: *When you met your father, did he live up to your expectations?*

JK: I can't remember what my expectations were precisely. The main thing I remember is that I thought he was very handsome, and I felt a certain strange pride—almost like the type of pride that a parent would have for a child. I felt sort of as if *I* had created him. I saw him staggering around the street and acting like a real noodlebrain—just as I figured any father of mine would act. He had a way of talking that I recognized as similar to my own.

GN: *How did he react to you?*

JK: He acted like a shy young boy on his first date. We'd both heard a lot about each other, and finally we were meeting. I wanted to be his friend, his buddy. I looked at his way of relating to my mother with a kind of awe. He said to my mother, "You always used to burn the bacon," and things like that—very mundane little memories, and she would laugh and say a few things about something that he used to do. After we finished sitting around at the bar, we all went to a clinic, where Jack and I had blood tests. It may seem funny to call him *Jack,* but I really like that name. I had this feeling that there was some substance in our blood, just Jack's and my blood, that no one else had in the world, and that they needed it for some special experiment. I had no shadow of a doubt that he wasn't my father—it was just obvious to me, and I know it was obvious to him too. But in his haze he just chose not to acknowledge it, and I understood. Then we went back to my neighborhood. That was the highlight of the whole thing because he came to my apartment, and the first thing he wanted was to go to the liquor store, so I had to take him there—very proudly, because this was my father, and nobody else had ever seen my father before, and nobody knew I had one. Of course they probably thought it was just some old anonymous guy that I was walking with, but I didn't care because I knew it was my father. I took him to the liquor store on 10th Street, and he got a bottle of Harvey's Bristol Cream Sherry. On the way back we didn't talk to each other much. I didn't want to

Gerald Nicosia, Paddy O'Sullivan, A.D. Winan. City Lights Bookstore, San Francisco, California, July 14, 1983. Photograph by Arthur Knight.

disturb him too much—I felt he was kind of precarious or something. Back at our place, he actually paid more attention to my half-sisters than he did to me, which I was a little bit resentful of. But I didn't really blame it on him, because I knew it gave him a way of avoiding the more serious question of me. To my sisters he was just another funny guy that came over to entertain them, but *to me* he was my *very own* funny guy. So I let them stay there and laugh at him as he drank his sherry and made little jokes. What he was doing was tearing off black plastic pieces of the bottle and putting them down on the table. He'd point to a little piece and say, "Heesh a Russian! Heesh no good!" They erupted in peals of daughter, and I just watched him and waited for him to say something to me, which he didn't do very often. When he left, I looked at the door in a daze, as if I knew he was about to come back any minute. And he did. He came back and said, "Whoops! I forgot my survival hat!" We gave him his hat, and then he said, "Well, see ya in Janyary."

GN: *Would you say that your father had a strong influence in the way that you grew up from then on?*

JK: Naturally I had more of an image of him than before. About a year later I talked to him on the phone. Somebody gave me his number. I called him and talked to him for hours. He was drunk and so he was talking very freely, and telling me about the family crest—referring to it as *your, our*—acknowledging that it was mine also.

GN: *When did you first start reading his books?*

JK: I had been in this juvenile detention home in the Bronx. One morning I woke up and I had welts all over my body. It turned out I had hepatitis and had to be taken to Lincoln Hospital. While I was there, my doctor noticed my name and said, "You ought to read *On the Road*," and he gave me a copy. That was the first time I read anything by him. I've never been an avid Kerouac reader because I just didn't feel like I had to. I come upon his works from a different direction than most people—from underneath, maybe. It seemed very natural to me to be reading *On the Road*. But I was constantly aware of the fact that this doctor had forced it on me, because I was his daughter and I *should* read it. Later on I read other things on my own. *Maggie Cassidy* was one I really identified with, because I was living in Santa Fe, New Mexico, with all these chicanos and this very Catholic situation—which was like Jack's adolescence and his Catholic upbringing. I read *The Subterraneans* in London, when I was just beginning to write my book. *Lonesome Traveler* is about my favorite. I've read snatches of *Doctor Sax* and *Visions of Cody*. Eventually I *will* read them all. But I don't have an overwhelming curiosity. I feel like he's in my blood somewhere. I'm coming out of the fountain rather than stumbling on it dying of thirst. I feel like all of his feelings and his tendencies are already inside me.

GN: *You only saw Jack one more time in your life? When you were fifteen?*

JK: I was on probation from the Bronx Youth House, and I was pregnant. They would take routine samples of urine to see if the girls were pregnant, and if they were, they'd send them right away to the Hudson Girls Reformatory, and they'd stay there till they were 21! So my mother had me bring a bottle of her own urine in to the probation officer—we switched the bottles. That way they let me off probation. We told them we were going to Washington, we were turning over a new leaf. But I didn't go to Washington, I went to Mexico with my future husband. First we went up to Lowell, Massachusetts, to see Jack for the last time, because that's where he was living in 1967. I *had* to see him one more time—I didn't know it was going to be the last time, though. We managed to track him down by getting in touch with all the Kerouacs that were in the phone book, and we finally got taken to the right house by a bunch of other relatives, who were very happy to see me. At that point he was married to Stella, and Gabrielle [Jack's mother] was there. Gabrielle had already had a stroke, and she was in a wheelchair, and kind of in a daze. We told him we were going to Mexico. He was drunk, sitting in front of the TV, in a rocking chair, watching *The Beverly Hillbillies* and drinking from a quart of whiskey. He said, "Oh yeah! Go to Mexico! You can use my name."

GN: At that point you had already had an awfully hard life. Did you feel that Jack was at all responsible for it?

JK: No, never, that never occurred to me. I realized from the very beginning that he was kind of a baby, that needed to be protected. I didn't want to bring the harsh reality of my needs to him, but I definitely would've loved to have known him better.

GN: It was fairly soon after you returned from Mexico that you heard of his death?

JK: I was living in a small commune north of San Francisco. One day I was out in the garden, and the girl who lived there came running out in a frenzy and said to me, "Jan, your father just died! I heard it on the radio!" And I stood there and just looked at her—just blank. She had these sort of tearful eyes, and she was searching me, waiting for me to burst out crying. Probably as a kind of defiance I just stared at her blankly. I said, "Oh. That's strange." And inside I was thinking, Hmmm . . . I wanted to know him better. Now he's gone and *died* without even asking my permission. It seemed like kind of a dirty trick to go and die without my knowing about it. Several days later things started hitting different little subconscious points, and I started having dreams about him. Gradually it hit home. I'll never completely realize it because it takes forever to realize things like that.

GN: Now you have a very definite sense of yourself as an artist. Is that related to your father at all, or is it you?

JK: Partially my father and partially me. I know I have my own style of writing, which is very different from Jack's. I'm not as subjective as he is. He was very emotional, and everything he saw was directly related to his soul. Whereas I always tend to think things out. I'm not that worried about shining out from under his shadow. People may read my stuff and think, This is Jack Kerouac's daughter, let's see if she's as good as he is. But it's not necessary to make a comparison like that, because I wasn't trying to emulate his type of writing. Three years ago, when I started writing my novel, I just thought, Gee, I've actually done so many things in my life that it warrants writing about it.

GN: One editor has suggested that your writing seems like a search for your father. Do you agree with that?

JK: Now that I think of it, all these travels that I've been on, there might be some truth in that. It might just be something organic, something out of my control, that I haven't even intellectualized. I very often had this wish that I was some kind of masculine bum, so that no one would know who I was and no one would care. This desire to be male or at least neuter definitely has something to do with my father and a lack of his presence. His absence was just all-encompassing because that's all there was.

GN: How do you feel about your father's sudden rise to notoriety after having been largely forgotten for many years?

JK: Things go in generations, in fits and starts, and gradually a little element of society, or a huge element, gets enriched by something that happened a long time ago—like Shakespeare, like all kinds of different authors, keep coming back in cycles. The whole world, the literary world, is just breathing. There are in-breaths and out-breaths. I'm glad that they're remembering him again.

GN: This time his fame will be more lasting. In the Fifties he was famous just as a cult figure, a leader of beatniks. But now they're going to start filming his books, and people are going to be writing critically about his books. If he's given a lasting place in American literature, how is that going to affect you?

JK: It will affect me just by the fact that I have his name. It'll also do something to my subconscious. I'll probably become closer and closer to him, because everything will become more manifest. I *am* learning more and more about him—learning all these things I always suspected anyway, because I've had a natural intuition about what he was like.

GN: Do you regret any part of your past?

JK: Your past is the foundation on which your life is built. If you regret your past, it's senseless. I suppose I could say I regret not having known Jack better. But in the same breath I realize that there was a reason for everything that happened. If he had hung around and been a father to me, he wouldn't have written all his books—he wouldn't have gotten all that inspiration. I'm perfectly happy to be the missing element that enabled him to be who he was. My father was one of these very intense people, who have to hide a lot of their feelings. One of those feelings, one of those secrets, was me! I know that. I could tell just by looking at him.

6

LETTER TO ALLEN GINSBERG

Jack Kerouac

May 10, '52
c/o Williams (Burroughs)
Orizaba 210, Apt. 5
Mexico City, Mexico

Dear Allen [Ginsberg],

It took Bill and I 10 days to find this splendid type-writer and ribbon and only recently we resumed work on our respective books.

I have no idea how it could have been possible for Hilda, Joan's siren friend from Albany (you know, the brunette) to write, a month ago, a letter to Kells' wife telling her I was coming to Mexico unless somebody in New York who knows my movements is hipping her and possibly Joan, not that it matters but why? Try to figure this leak for me, it ain't right.

Neal left me at Sonora, Arizona, on the Mexican border. He had his car with the seats all out (station wagon) and had pillows and babies and Carolyn all gypsied and happy in the back; I left the happy domestic couple and started on my new adventure, at dawn. Crossed the wirefence into Sonora (it was NOGALES Arizona, excuse me into Nogales Sonora I went). To save money I bought 2nd class bus tickets south . . . it became a tremendous Odyssey of bouncing over dirt roads through jungles and changing buses to cross rivers on

Larry Rivers, Jack Kerouac, David Amram, Allen Ginsberg, and Gregory Corso (in the stocking cap). New York City, 1959. Photograph courtesy Walter Gutman.

makeshift rafts with sometimes the bus itself fording the river up the wheeltops, great. I hooked up soon enough, around Guyamas, with a Mexican hipcat named Enrique by asking him, as we stood in front of some nepal cactus if he ever tried peotl; yes, he had; he showed me you could eat the fruit of the nepal for the palate; mescal is the peotl cactus. He started teaching me Spanish. With him he had a hand-made radio repair ohms and amperes gadget for appearances, also it was one of his crafts (he's 25) but actually we ended up using it for, pour cacher la merde, if you dig, which we picked up in an Oriental village or town called Culiacan, the opium center of the New World . . . I ate tortillas and carne in African stick huts in the jungle with pigs rubbing against my legs; I drank pure pulque from a pail, fresh from the field, from the plant, unfermented, pure milk of pulque makes you get the giggles, is the greatest drink in the world. I ate strange new fruit, erenos, mangos, all kinds. In the back of the bus, drinking mescal, I sang bop for the Mexican singers who were curious to hear what it sounded like; I sang "Scrapple from the Apple" and Miles Davis' "Isreal" (excuse, it was written by Johnny Carisi whom I once met in Remo) (wearing checked topcoat with fur collar). They sang me all the songs, did "Ah va va va vav vov vov" that Mexican laugh-cry; in Culiacan we got off bus, me, Enrique, and his 17 year old footman tall 6 foot Indian Girardo; like a safari we started off down hot dobe streets of midnight, straight for the stick hut Indian outskirts of town; near the sea, in the tropic of cancer, hot night, but pleasant, and soft, no more Friscos, no more fogs. We came to a gigantic space between the dobe town and some huts and crossed in the moonlight; one dim light ahead, in a stick hut; E. knocked; door was opened by white garbed Indian in big sombreo but with downturned hunkey like Indian face and scornful eyes. Some talk, we went in. On the bed sat a big gal, Indian's wife; and then his buddy, an Indian goateed (not by style but didn't shave) hipster-junkey, in fact opium eater, barefoot and tattered and dreaming on the bed-edge, and thin, Hunkey [Huncke] like; and on the floor a drunken snoring soldier who'd just eaten some O after lush. I sat on bed, Enrique, he squatted on floor, Big Girardo stood in corner like a statue; the host, scornful, made several angry remarks; E. translated one of them, "Is this Americano following me from America?" He had once gone to America, to L.A., for maybe 12 hours, and someone rushed . . . well he the hero of the gone heroes tribe of Mexican Fellaheen Afternoons and Mexico (I saw the Lord Star from a bus) gave me a medallion to look at which was either torn from his neck or from another torn, see, but I think it was torn from him but he recovered it and he gestured showing how this American (maybe cop) tore it from his neck in LA, that's what he did, was crucified in Los Angeles and returned to his Night Huts. Thus anger . . . understand, Allen, that everything is going on in Indian dialect Spanish and that I am digging everything, all of it, almost perfectly, with my French Canadian mind in the middle of the Dakar village.

I thought I was beyond Darwin's chain,
A phosphorescent Jesus Christ in space, not a Champion of the Fellaheen night With my French Canadian mind.

Then Scornful, who was very husky and goodlooking and dark, handed me a pellet and instructed my boy Enrique (who was squatting on the floor pleading for friendship and coolness but had to go through certain tests, just like two tribes meeting) so I looked at the pellet, and said Opium, and Scornful laughed and was glad; pul'd out the weed, rolled several cigars, sprinkled O in them, and passed around. I got high on the second drag; I was sitting right next to the Indian Opium Saint who, whenever he succeeded in breaking into the conversation, made apparently vacuous or maybe mystic remarks that they in their practicality and hepness avoided—everybody, young Girardo, blasting. I got high and began to understand everything they said, and told them so, and chatted in Spanish with them. Scornful brought out a statue he'd made in Gesso . . . you turn it over and it's an enormous cock; they all put it on their flies seriously to show me, laffing only a little, and on the other side a, I think, woman of some kind, or human figure. They told me (it took a half hour, with writing in my notebook) that in Spanish the other word for Gesso was Yis, or Gis. I showed them things like Zotzilaha, the Bat God, Yohualticitl, Lady of the Night, Nanahuatl, Lord of Lepers, Citalpol, the Great

Star; and they nodded (from my notebook). Then they apparently talked about politics, and at one point, by candlelight, the host said "The earth was ours," La terra esta la notre or however . . . I heard it clear as a bell and looked at him and we understood (about Indians I mean) (and after all my greatgreatgrandmother in Gaspe, 1700, you know, was an Indian, married my ancestory French baron) (but so they say in the family)—then it was time to retire, the three travelers went into Hunkey's hut and there they gave me the choice of the bed or the ground, the bed was a straw pallet on crisscross sticks with a piece of cardboard for insulation under which the Saint Junkey kept his fixings and shit. He was offering his bed to all three of us, it was too small, so we stretched out on the ground with my seabag as a common pillow, I tossed with Girardo for the outside position, I lay down, Hunkey went out to get some shit, and we blew out the candle. But first Enrique promised to tell me all the mysteries of that night in the morning, which he later forgot. I wanted to know if there was a secret underground Indian hipster organization of revolutionary thinkers (all of them scornful of American hipsters like John Hoffman and LaMantia who came down among them not for shit or kicks but with big pretenses of scholarship and superiority, this is what Scornful indicated) and not with pure Allen Ginsberg-like friendship on the corner on Times Square is what these Indians of course want, see, no bullshit and hinct, they need Hunkies) (in Frisco, the last week, I visited LaMantia with Neal, he is living in the former stone small castle of Hymie Bongoola (you know the name) overlooking Berkleley Calif. he was reading The Book of the Dead, was reclined in a sumptuous couch with book and Hymie's old cancerous 14 year old angora cat, and fireplace and rich furnishings and turned us on, three friends from Calif. U dropped in, a psychology major who is apparently his Burroughs, a tall handsome owner of the house (who is somewhat the Jack K.) (lounging on floor and sleeping eventually altho maybe his queer lover) and a young eager intelligent kid who was like you; this was his circle, and of course he was being Lucien, they talked about psychology in terms of "I saw that damned black background to the pink again in yesterday's peotl," "Oh well (Burroughs) it won't hurt you for awhile," (both snickering) Then: "Try this new drug, it may kill you, the greatest kick of all, man." (snicker, turning away, real serpentine and hateful he is, LaMantia, very unfriendly, very queer, I touched his hand briefly while exchanging joint and they were cold and snakelike) He showed me his poems about the Indian tribes on the San Luis Potosi plateau, I forget tribe name, they deal with his visions on Peotl, and they, the lines are,
        arranged
            like
                this, for effect, but more complicated.

But I was disappointed in Neal that night for not at least digging the new things instead holding the floor all night talking about his goddamn railroad, who gives a shit, "Chug chug, there's the engineer, easy as you go," acting like an Okie, or worse as I told him later, we were like two Italian mountain peasants allowed by local nobles of the castle to chat with them for a night and had failed on account of Guidro talking about his cart and horse all the time.) This made Neal mad, and the next night, for the first time in our lives, we had a fight—he refused to drive me to LaMantia, outright. He made up for it the next day (at Carolyn's urging because she loved us both) by buying a Chinese dinner, my favorite. But when I left Neal at Nogales I felt an undercurrent of sad hostility and also that he had hustled me there awful fast instead of the picnic we were going to have by the side of the road in Arizona or Imperial Valley even. So it goes, I dunno. But Neal was great and generous and good and my only complaint is cheap, i.e., he never talked with me any more, just "Yeah, yeah," almost sullen, but he was busy, but he is dead, but he is our brother, so okay, forget it. He needs another explosion, I can tell you that much; for now he is all hungup on complete all-the-way-down-the-line materialistic money and stealing-groceries anxieties and Nothing Else, positively. Carolyn has to stay in the house for months at a time while he works every day, 7 days on railroad and other jobs, to pay for things they never use, like cars not a drop to drink in house usually, no shiazet any more, nothing and Neal always gone). This was my observation; Carolyn is a great woman. I think it will work out when they move to San Jose, in the country, and then C. can at least grow a garden and get her kicks in sun, there being no sun where they live now, or nothing, although I never was so happy in my life than in that splendid attic with 11th edition Encyclopedia Brittanica . . . but my complaints are the least of it, and I want to tell you in person later, and you understand, I dont want to appear to be the ungrateful brother-in-law guest yakking in behind their backs which I aint, I was happy and secure for the first time in years and the first thing Neal said was "Do anything you like, man." But to Culiacan: the candle out, I lay awake for an hour listening to the night sounds in the African village; footsteps crunched close to our door, all three of us stiffened; then they moved on; and sounds, rhythms, beasts, insects. Hunkey came back and slept, or dreamed. In the morning we all leapt up simultaneously and rubbed our eyes. I took a crap in a 1000-year old Indian stone crapper in the outdoors. Enrique went off and got me about 2 ounces of shit for equiv. $3, which is expensive down there but I had dough they knew. Then I got high again and sat listening, squatted, to noon sounds of village, which is a cooing, crooning, African, world Fellaheen sound, of women, children, men (in the yard was Scornful with a spear splitting twigs on the ground with great strokes of perfect aim, chatting

and laughing with another spear wielder, mad); Hunkey just sat on bed with eyes open, moveless, a dead mad mystic Francis I tell you, down. Enrique rolled enormous Indian joints, laughed at my American sticks I rolled. In fact they roll em just the size of Lucky Strikes so they can smoke on street unnoticed, round, firm. Then I got shakes (from no eating and bouncing for days) and they wondered at me; I sweated. Scornful went out and brought me hot food; I ate happy; they gave me hot peppers to revive my system; I drank a pop with it; they kept rushing out for soup, etc. I heard them high on tea discussing whose food it was . . . "Maria" . . . they gossiped about her; I saw enormous complexities of Indian noontime gossip and love affairs, etc. Hunkey's wife came in for a brief giggling look at me; I bowed. Then I was surrounded by cops and soldiers. Guess what, all they wanted (tho my heart sank) was some tea; I gave a lot of it away. "I'm going to be arrested in Mexico finally," was my thought but nothing happened, and we left, safari, waving, and cut; in the heat of the day Enrique made us stop in the old church for a minute to rest and pray; then we moved on, left Girardo in Culiacan with tea and 20 pesos, got bus for Mazatlan, were entertained by young intellectual busline employe (two Mission Oranges) (at sidewalk crazy cafe) who said he read Flammarian . . . I told him I read existentialists, he nodded, smiled. Enroute to Mazatlan Enrique got a woman who offered us her house and food for 10 pesos in M. that night, Enrique accepted cause he wanted to lay her, but I didn't feel like being a watcher of Spanish lovers, but I agreed; in Mazatlan we took our gear to her two aunts' house in the Dakar slums (you know Mazatlan is just like an African city, hot and flat right on the surf, no tourists whatever, the wonder spot of the Mexicos really but nobody hardly knows, a dusty crazy wild city of beautiful Acapulco surfs) and then Enrique and I went swimming, blasted bombers on sand, turned and looked at city and great meadows and five miles away we saw, in the clear sunset, three muchachas, girls, making the center of an enormous bat-wing Rubens view of fields and cows and horses and gardens and worlds, beautiful. "Look at the muchachas make the center of the world"—three little Biblical gals in robes and (I don't know why I'm writing this I've got to do my typing) Let me finish, instead of staying the night with the gal I insisted we move on to Guadalajara, anxious now, as I got close, to see Bill the Champ. So he kissed her gobye and she got mad and yelled at me but we cut, and in the morning Guadalajara, where we wandered in the great market eating fruit. The beach at Mazatlan when we look'd at the girls five miles away and the red, brown, and black horses in the distance, and the bulls and cows, the enormous verdures, flat, the great sun setting in the Pacific over the Three Islands, was one of the great mystic rippling moments of my life—I saw right then that Enrique was great and that the Indian, the Mexican, is great, straight, simple and perfect. Towards late afternoon, bussing now from Guadalajara (incidentally went through Ajijijic little stone village of Helen but rolling) I slept; there is no more beautiful a land and state than that of Jalisco, Sinaloa is also lovely. We arrived in Mexico City near dawn. Not wake up Bill we instead walked in slums and slept in a criminal's hovel for 5 pesos, all made of stone and piss, and blasted, and slept on miserable pad . . . he said to look out for the gunman. I avoided his learning Bill's address, for obvious reasons, told him I'd meet him that night in front of Post office, went to Bill's, with seabag, the dust of great Mexico on my shoes. It was Saturday in Mexico City, the women were making tortillas, the radio was playing Perez Prado, ate a 5 centavor powder candy that I first dug 2 years ago with Bill's little Willy; odors of hot tortilla, the voices of the children, the Indian youths watching, the well dressed city children of spanish schools, great clouds of the plateau over piney thin trees of morning and future.

    Bill was like a mad genius in littered rooms when I walked in. He was writing. He looked wild, but his eyes innocent and blue and beautiful. We are the greatest of friends at last. At first I felt like a beat fool brought to a far flop in a land of centipedes, worms and rats, mad with Burroughs in a pad, but not so. And he persuaded me to stick to him instead of Enrique, somehow got me not to meet the kid that night, and I aint seen my saint Enrique since . . . that is, a guy who could teach me where, what to buy, where to live, on nothing-a-month; but instead I turned my mind again to the great St Louis of American Aristocracy and has been so ever since. Wasn't that right decision? The kid, I mean, I feel sorry for standing him up—but Bill cant afford any contacts save Dave you know, his position is delicate. His "Queer" is greater than "Junk"—I think now it was a good idea to put them together, with Queer we can expect big Wescotts Girouxs and Vidals to read it avidly, not only Junkie-interested types, see. Title? "Junk or Queer" or something . . . hey? JUNK OR QUEER OR JUNK, OR QUEER JUNK AND QUEER. But title must have indications of both. Bill is great. Greater than he ever was. Misses Joan terribly. Joan made him great, lives on in him like mad, vibrating. We went to the Ballet Mexicano together, Bill danced out to catch bus, we went on a weekend to Tenencingo in the mountains, did some shooting (it was an accident, you know, no doubt about it anywheres). . . . In the mountain canyon there was depth. Bill was up on the hill striding along tragically; we had separated at the river in order to go separate ways—always take the *right road* Bill had said night before about cobblestone road and asphalt regular road to Tenencingo—so but now, he was taking left road, climb along ridge to mouth of cut, and back along, to road, avoiding river—I wanted to in the inexpressible softness of Biblical Day and Fellaheen Afternoon wash my feet at the place where the maidens left their cloth parts,

Allen Ginsberg giving or taking piano instruction to or from Bob Cain. Committee of Small Magazine Editors and Publishers (COSMEP) conference, California, Pennsylvania, June 1980. Photograph by Arthur Knight.

and sat on a rock (shook spiders from it first but they were only the little spiders that watch the river of honies, creek of God, God and honey, in the flow of the gold, the rocks are soft, the grass just reaches to the lip, I washed and laved my poor feet, waded across my Genesee, and headed for the road (holes in my shoes now, I'm at my last ten bucks in this foreign land) interrupted just once by canyon where depth and tragedy made me circle further, met Bill in a Tenencingo soda fountain waiting. We came back that night, after turkish baths, etc. Bill's Marker has left him; I had two women so far, one American with huge tits, and a splendid mex whore in house. Met several great Americans . . . but they all got arrested yesterday for weed, tell you their names later (Kells among them, as if Kells was a teahead) (or pusher) Bill and I clean, cool; we have Dave. Bill and I want huge letter from you about Wyn situation, for both of us (my ms. coming soon, 530 pages); more news about Genet, first-degree murder? news about everything, and again I want to know where are the first 23 pages of *On the Road* goddamit! (Will insert into ms. for me?)

WRITE *J*.

7

LETTER TO
JOHN CLELLON HOLMES

Jack Kerouac

June 17 or 15 or 21   52

Dear John [Clellon Holmes],

Bravo old tool! The Hip Generation is exactly what I will do now, after several days thinking it over, and re-reading your inspired letter several times, and talking with Burroughs about it, I see that you're absolutely right. Bill says I could make some money, I should make some money. He says "That Doctor Sax you're doing is alright but you should—it ain't timely—you should concentrate all your immediate attention on Hip Generation, make Doctor Sax your hobby." Poor dark Doctor Sax.

Doctor Sax has had a strange history. No one has noticed here that I wrote it; in letters, in sending occasionally excerpts from Doctor Sax, no one mentions it. It's like an invisible inexistant book that nobody knows about .. ideal for Doctor Sax which is a study of darkness and secrets and shades. I am finishing it this week, this minute, in bursts of concentrated marblefist writing . . . I am mounting up the great flood of 1936 right this moment—yesterday I wrote The Song of the Myth of the Rainy Night, to illustrate a minor point in the novel . . . Sax is full of secret . . . But I won't quote any, there's too much. Rather talk to you about your Walden Blue. You are writing great mad prose, the best in the states right now. Vidal's imitative Faulkner sentences have tacked-on clauses that you can see

Jack Kerouac. Photo by Allen Ginsberg.

through—yours are solid clauses, you meant what you started and finished to say . . . you're writing very well, you have hit your stride and maturity—yet strangely enough it isn't anywhere near what I'm doing now, yet exactly what I was on my way to do with Ray Smith Red Moultrie On the Road and deviated to the now-present ways I have which are general lassooing of the meaning in heaven and in the air kind of hallucinated, clairvoyant type trance Yeats prose which I call modern prose now. . . . . But I like your prose and am glad to see you've succeeded. Yes, you must publish Walden Blue; you might delete just one thing, "bop was in the air," I have those exact words in On the Road somewhere—publish it and also for God's sake write your jazz book (but Good Christ if Rae Everitt liked my Road jazz scenes so much why didn't she publish them? now I'm outdated by you)—Your Jazz Book, Walden Blue the first chapter—is apparently deeply ingrained in you and we couldn't get it out—but you quite rightly in a vision saw there was no no sense in my quibbling over the jazz-plot when the whole generation plot would do just as well and vaster . . . so you give me the Hip Generation idea, which I already had partially in mind as a super T & C with homegrounds in Kansas and bop brothers etc., and accept from me the jazz book idea.

I am starving to death. I have no more money, not a red cent. I weigh 158 lbs. instead of 170. Bill thinks I'm mad at him because I was writing when he got up and retired to the bathroom with my tea and pencil pads, so he's gone, has only money, nothing to eat in house, it's cold . . . I sit here yearning to get back to food and drink and regular people . . . I'll personally return this copy of Walden Blue to you this summer .. no money to mail it back, of course. I've had to resort to writing to Neal for money for traveling back to a job—I simply am destitute. I hate to bother poor Neal, especially since he's right, all I have to do is go to Frisco and earn and save $2000 on the railroad before Xmas—but I've got other things to do—other places to work.—.. with my family . . . SUNDAY MORNING Just got a letter from Neal and Carolyn in Frisco, they tell me about how they bought a big hot quart of wonton soup in Frisco chinatown and Jamie the 2½ year old jumped right on it in front seat and splashed onions and wonton and soup all over car—that Neal is about to buy himself a new all-steel station wagon, is making $500 a month on railroad— they live happy rich life, with 3 kids, wonderful baby boy Jack Allen Cassady (named after me and Allen)—they have life. I have nothing but death. They have house on Russian Hill, marvelous attic where I wrote On the Road and listened to the greatest bop disc jockey in America, Pat Henry, with his midnight to 6 program of carefully selected, carefully commented latest bop by big and small groups . . . Brendt Halberg, Jack Noren, Baritone Lars Gullin, Shorty Rodgers, Shelly Manne, Dave Brubeck . . . he likes to feature Californian and Scandinavian elements . . . (I dont like Brubeck.) But what difference does it make whether I like Brubeck or not when all I've got is death. Where shall I go now? News comes to me that my sea union is on strike, that a seaman I knew in Frisco (Charley Mew, 4 foot 10 tall, he's in the Tape part of Road as Charley) is driving a cab in Baltimore!—another seaman Al Sublette, is hungup in New York duration of strike; Now John you must ABSOLUTELY look up Al, he's the greatest colored cat you'll ever meet, he's from St. Louis . . . Here's how to do it, *and you'll be doing me a particular favor John* because this cat will help me ship out from any American port . . . but particularly I want to catch him in NY to go to Birdland and Harlem with him, he's a musician—Here's what you do: if you're taking a walk on the waterfront drop in at the Marine Cooks and Stewards Hall at 148 Liberty st. right off the waterfront street, North River . . . look for Al, ask for Al Sublette, he'll be paged, if he ain't there leave a message with your name, phone number and that your Kerouac's buddy. Better and easier than this for you is if you simply call up, EVERY MORNING TILL YOU GET AL, call up the hall and have him paged: the phone number is RE 2-8655, got that I repeat, RE 2-8655—have Al paged, when you get him on the phone tell him who you are and rush to meet him, kicks man . . . you ain't known about the new hipness in America till you've dug the younger Negroes who call New York the Apple . . . Al is 21 years old, has one bad eye, wears hornrim glasses and is a real cat, wears gray fedora, lapell-less jacket, checked, sharp. He's got $1000 right now, just came from around the world on the S.S. President Monroe, American President Lines, American President Lines pier in Jersey City, you can also try to get on the ship by ship-to-dock phone, here's the number: (it's in the book, woops). S.S. President MONROE he's in Steward dept. This is what I'd be doing right now in New York if I had the money to be there, looking up Al and trying to ship out .. God I feel awful today, that letter from Neal and Carolyn, the doom that surrounds me now . . . I don't know why. What have I got? I'm 30 years old, broke, my wife hates me and is trying to have me jailed, I have a daughter I'll never see, my old mother after all this time and work and worry and hopes is STILL working her ass off in a shoe shop; I have not a cent in my pocket for a decent whore. Goddam sonofabitch sometimes I think the only thing that's ready to accept me is death, nothing in life seems to want me or even remembers me. John, you know how I feel about this lousy life .. lyric epic novels aside, and all things, and my talent if any exists, I still know that there's nothing but doom and despair on all sides waiting for everybody and especially for me who am so alone . . . I'm the loneliest writer in America and I'll tell you why . . . it's because I have written exactly three full-length novels since March 1951 or less almost less than a year ago and not one is wanted now . . . NOW NOW their bloody cheatful Now of blindness and materialism .. if I ever stuck one foot in my grave and heaved half a last sigh all those fucking dirty bastard publishers including punk jew Solomon and the whole stinking commercial bourgeois lot of them would pounce on my books to publish them "Posthumously"— what a pretty word, it looks so nice on a bookjacket.. All they know now about my work is that they read it, without effort because I went to pains to make it smooth and beautiful and mad and because there was no effort and the plot didn't stick them in the nose but sort of existed and rambled in subterranean passages . . . a vastness of prose and wildness of the life idea and grandeur theme on ALL LEVELS not just one measly "novel" level—and not even knowing that they're too ignorant to understand what's in front of them, they turn, with pious sneering faces, and make this judgment: "Kerouac can do better." Any other bum they publish right away and he rushes off to his 7 months in Paris . . . I, a French man, haunted all my life by a spectral dream of Paris, can never go there, I never have enough money—probably the greatest living in America writer today—and the most despised bum, you realize don't you that Giroux not only feels that I'm irresponsible and "uncooperative" but also that if I could write a great book still I wouldn't do it out of sheer irresponsible spite and no-goodness. This is what my contemporaries think of me.

Paste it on yr hatbrim and study it—it happens every time to the most earnest and thoroughgoing bloke in any art at any time in history. . . . I feel like Wilhelm Reich . . . all, barring not a singleone prick, ALL ALL the doctors and scientists deny him and say he's a fool and spread rumors that he's in a madhouse . . . which he isn't . . . meanwhile, slowly and insidiously, they're stealing every one of his ideas one by one, giving him no credit whatever for anything, and soon he will die in disgrace, poverty and loneliness. It will happen to me.

Jack

8

LETTER TO
NEAL CASSADY

Jack Kerouac

early April 1955

Neal Cassady
Brakeman
c/o Southern Pacific Railroad
Yard Office
San Jose, Calif.

Dear Buddy,

Please don't go thinking "Here's old shitty pants Kerouac again coming on with the buddy-buddy talk now that he's been away from me long enough to have gotten over his latest imaginary peeve" etc. or any such type thoughts you may have, all of them I do humbly or at least regretfully admit are logical and tenable for you to have. But I want no more bullshit between us any more; and believe me and dont mistrust your own senses when I say, it was all my fault and you were not to blame, because you're always the same and very constant in your own way that I understand now. Like, the hassel over the money and the weed-power, etc., pure neurosis on my part; forgive me, I apologize; silliest of all then having the nerve to ask you to drive me into town so we can "talk"; I don't blame you for being horrified. I have a hangover because I went out last night and was bored by everybody (George Wickstrom, etc.) and drank a lot to

Jack Kerouac. By Carolyn Cassady, 1977.

drown the boredom; there were some new chicks around that look good; I'm arranging a jam session to make an album for Jerry Newman's record company, with Allen Eager on tenor, for which, with written notes, I get fifty bucks, with which I'll buy a phonograph and $20 worth of records. That was why I went to town. So, hang- over, now as I write to you I'm drinking brown beer and regular beer mixed together in little wineglasses and every now and then I get up and refill, because without beer, with hangover, my whole system shakes, I'm just the biggest drunk that ever hit town. Meanwhile I have the local Jumpin George on my radio, right at this moment wailing Charley Parker who drank iodine the other day after a fight with his wife and on the television I have a picture-clear view of the Giants-Cubs game with Willie Mays, Dusty Rhodes, everybody, so you see what kicks we would have if you were here, for instance; and of course I also have all the shit in the world too. Like you I spend all my time in really lost lonelinesses blasting and masturbating and there's no hope, and yet, there's plenty of hope. That's why I'm writing this letter, buddy, and mailing it to you at your railroad so Carolyn wont see it, tho there's nothing in the letter to hide from her, it's just that I want to write to YOU now without having someone read over your shoulder even tho it be your sweet protective Caroline.

Thinking about the Allen hassel which is really a wild comedy, but I don't actually laugh, I mean it's like a Three Stooges vision, of people hassling, people tied by iron bands to the vices of their delusions selfconsciously crying out in the night; certainly I'm not exempt from any of this comedic material. The point of my letter is, I want you and I to be big buddies again, not that we're not big buddies anyhow; in thinking about Reincarnation and Cayceism I'm not too sure that maybe you arent my brother Gerard reborn, because he died in the summer of 1926 and you were born . . when? in 1927. Sometimes I explain it to myself that way, what is almost the holy feeling I have for holy Neal, maybe he's my brother at that; it was you first said we were Blood brothers, remember?—I approve of your Cayceism interest, I have the same interest in Edgar Cayce, I think he's great and I think you're the greatest. Think how wild it is, for you to be Proust, which you are. (Monte Irvin just hit a homerun to tie the score! scorin Willie Mays in front of him, and Willie's happy! happy for Monte's come-back! it's like I feel about you, Buddy!) Please believe me, Neal. . . we got a long life ahead of us, I'm on good terms with your wife because I actually do love her as a person and your children are like as if they were mine. . . and I'm not queer. . . and I'm happy for you when you make it, like Willie Mays for his brother Monte Irvin just now. I understand all your vices because I have them myself; I dont agree at all that you're crazy, as the Rorschach says, because they had one about me too, just the same, in the Navy, and Allen and all those city-types who are so terribly afraid of insanity, which is after all just an arbitrary dualistic conception laid upon the un-dual eternal principle of Mind Being . . pah! you, the greatest writer in America, crazy? So was Whitman, so was Thoreau, so was Poe. Burroughs is Poe. He's crazy too. So what. But the "First Third" by N. Leon Cassady is to my mind the greatest extant begun-work in America. It exceeds, that is, now I'm talking about Joan Anderson and the style of loose narrative Joan Anderson which Third will reach, anything I've written myself, because when I wrote *On the Road* in 1951 with my sweet little wife God bless her I miss her I'd not yet learned looseness of talking-speed and was imitating a kind of anxious Dashiell Hammett of Wm Lee,— by the time I had made the great discovery of Sketching, writing fast without thought of words, in that same Fall I'd lost my contact with speech-styles and began writing in what I write now, a kind of special stylized Proust-like but American private monotone, Modern Proust, indeed. But in Joan Anderson you combine the looseness of invention with natural perfect rhythm and perfect natural speech, where it gets real hot in the jailhouse when you're talking about the Salvation Army cunts. Man, for you to stop writing, for you to say, as Allen wrote, "I quit" is ridiculous. . . . in reality of high afternoon, which you and I only understand, you are in bed, an invalid, writing the remembrance. . . . right? Every detail of the conductor catching and seeing you; of the 70-year old lay; of the little boxes going up and down Santa Clara Avenue in the afternoon; even every redbrick in the Bayshore Roundhouse; and every detail about Chittenden and sidings and that immortal sight of Watsonville Jct as seen so many times spectrally from the crummy (or the engine) in late afternoon when you've finished your run and have stopped at the big farmhouse tree waiting for the herder's come-on. . . . this is Neal Cassady, a great world genius, this is someone we rank with Proust. Never mind what Carolyn says about sex-writing being "dirt" instead of art . . . of course she knows it's art, it's new art . . . but I dont want to start new fights, I wont even mention Carolyn or ever mention your writing to her at all in fact, I'll just say, if you want to write about Sex, and in fact what else is the complete First Third and the Second and Final Third, but really a gigantic and exhausting analysis as only you can wind out of the perfection of your holy brain, of a tremendously complicated sex-life. . . . a confession about sex . . . It's not a Cayce sin, not when it's got the holy connotations that your approach has . . . Ah Neal, listen to your buddy, your older brother, and do what he says: write on, dont stop, in secret even, dont tell C. maybe, scribble, type it up, or I'll type it for you, in fact scribble it and send it to me and I'll regularly type it and send it back to you at the railroad—To do this typing job for you is one of the honorable reasons why I am on earth. I know that both of us are on the right track, that it's a track of greatness. . . . consider, too, that our friendship and brotherhood has really been a Literary association, djever think that? They'll say, years later, Cassady and Kerouac got together to discuss their work, they wont realize that we were mysterious brothers of the blood across the ages . . . Boy, I wont bother you with Nothin means Nothin no more; that nothin means nothin, is the saddest thing I know, and you know How sad I am all the time. . . . But rather than cling to that ridiculously obvious truth, I'd rather, at the age of fifty, be going out to get the groceries with you, sitting in the front seat of the car, with the kids in back (Kids'll be grown up!??) looking at you waiting for whatever you got to say next . . . my name Shadow—I be your shadow—because for the rest of my life, I'm dedicating my self to enormous artistic labours, for better or worse, I dont give a fuck whether it brings me riches or nothin. . . . it's the work itself, I want, want to see the ordered sentences typed up neat on perfect pages under a soft lamp, wild prose describing the world as it raced through my brain and cock once. . . . and as far as I'm concerned, the rest of my life is going to be spent part of the time with my mother and sister in the house in the South they're now planning with a room and private bath all of my own and rolltop desk etc . (and my secret crops in the forest), part of the time in Mexico City in the slums or in the country or in some house I may be able to buy, and part of the time staying with you or in your yard (buying my share of groceries from now on). . . . . there isn't much else, and anyway all of it is there. So dont quit, ... dont be frightened by Rorschaches and INKBLOT demons on all sides. . . . . I tell you, I'll write you big letters now, for your reading pleasure, sending you excerpts etc. and crap to keep us warm and close till I see you again sometime, and if you can possibly make it, write back to me, even scrawls, and if you want your First Third typed up (because busy on 7 day railroad) send me the scrawls and I do it for you. You know what I'm gonna do, I'm gonna buy a $100 panel truck and put a mattress in it, this winter, and go carbumming west, see you then. . . . . you know, I'll park my truck in New Mexico desert for weeks at a time, with supply of beans, cabbage and wine, and Buddha books for my everpresent by-my-side Proust, did, and really enjoy freedom and life.

In closing, I want you to remember the night we met in a crummy in Watsonville and you said "We dont talk any more" with tears in your eyes . . . Forgive me, O Neal, for everything that I done wrong. Holy Angels bless you.

Jack

The private works of jean-louis are going to be all pornography. Remember when I said I couldn't be saved and picked up that big old bottle off the floor in Al's room? Hey?

You see, I love everything, even wine. I love Ruth Brown's "What a Dream I Had Last Night"————I love weed. I love pretty girls. Somehow I must have been made for a girl. There's a girl, with legs smooth and full, comin my way. Ere I go. . . . Big football fights—starts at parties but really in a field like Bridge Street haunted house across from Mike's where Ma and I go to watch scrimmage be photographed by Fred Dressler (high school line coach) and another guy with small movie camera and suddenly (Charley Justice of North Carolina U. 1950) and others in the backfield, Justice is stopped dead at the line of scrimmage, the ball bounces around, and guys start fighting over it at the wall-sidewalk sideline—and Ma and I who've been watching from a bush "Watch out, Ma!" take hands and retreat—the fight spreads, overtakes us, goes all over the field and into the street and up on iron structures and buildings and permeates elevators and halls—Everybody's slugging everybody, Ma turns into a lil boy who wants to see and I hold him high on a frightening girder as he fidgets with his lil pants in fear and men pound running and fighting (not like they're doing right now out there in the warm sunny streets of Richmond Hill) slugging with fists on all sides——Up in the elevator 4 opposing fighters start right in in the rickety little lift and the girl was sassy anyway so we pile out in a halfway down lobby, I spar—"He's got the style to fight that guy!" laugh the 2 partners—a kind of maniacal ballet dance begins, in the fight, with bodies flopping—Meanwhile it had been Lowell and I'd gone down

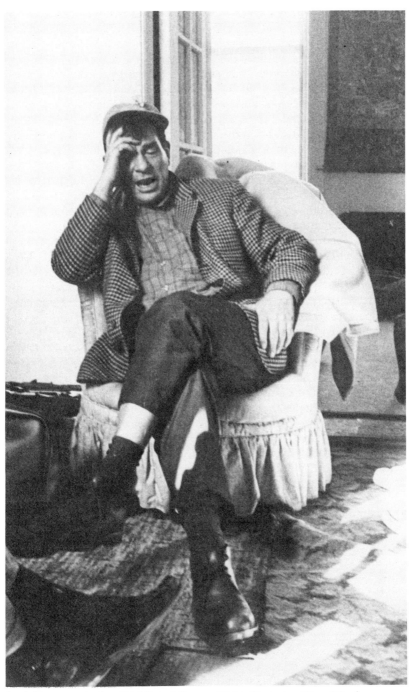

Jack Kerouac visiting 704 East 5 Street, 1964. Photo by Allen Ginsberg.

the street to G.J.'s cottage and he was alseep, night, about 11 o'clock—tan as a Greek berry I see him (all the lights & the radio on!) face down on a white sheet bed, poor G.J. as ever tired from work and now living alone so that I mourn for his poor black robed mother tho she's just across town (this is about Crawford street)—and it's sad spectral night as if oilcup flares of ditches at edge of town—GJ *is* like Allen Ginsberg, he's a Lowell newspaperman and tho still a big champion Lucien Carr drunk has responsibilities, is married, holds his job down—I stand in the soft night road begun earlier at parties where I'd been exposed and humiliated by some girl like the L.I.R.R. girl, Irish, roundfaced, I think sarcasting—BOOM! G.J. had furniture, a whole life ranchero concrete California style cottage "pitifully his"—all in little sad Lowell. Now I remember it's not far from the cottage of the B—— sisters' I'd had in dreams and in itself not far from the woman with The Virgin Mary Altar (uniting streetwise Moody & Lakeview)——THIS IS A GLIMPSE INTO BOOK OF MEMORY.

the B—— sisters, wow, if you'd seen them. long tits and blue eyes—I mean by long, they stood out from their tight jersies way out . . . nothin short about em. Beautiful long black hair, white skin, blue eyes, red lips, secret bodies——I saw visions of their cunts, I kept imagining what it would be like to lift the skirt off P——, or better, tear her shorts offa her, and make it with the warm, bright spot there, jam right in and hold her and look dig her eyes and see her coming with lips. Wow, we fuckin all day long and all night too cause I own her all day and all night, wow.—I got her in a hotel room, in Miami, I'm richer than Rita Hayworth . . . I'm fuckin the ass off her and when I get tired I get hi, and when I want to swim I go out and swim, and come back and she's laying here the lounge chair with a black slip and I see a flesh of creamy thigh there and want ta slup it all up. Right.

soft, hey, to run your lips over the soft jersey of the tight sweater over the long under tits that have no bra and the nipple stands out thru the jersey, and you rub that too with your lips, hands, fingertips, cocktip

later.

as al says.

Regards to ole hinkle dinkle the communist here of the wild west.

9

TO EUROPE
AND RETURN

Letters, 1957–58

Jack Kerouac and John Clellon Holmes

June 23, 1957

Dear John,

How are ya old partner? Excuse me for not writing to you from Europe but I didn't have a typewriter and it was really hectic traveling, I had a flying trip and endeavor now to outline the story for you . . . . After Allen and Pete and I left you (by the way, were you BUGGED by our madness, or bugged because I was acting madder than I feel? anyway thank God for the quiet humorous night with Alan Harrington) we went back New York, Allen loaned me $200 and I got on a Yugoslavian freighter all by myself because Allen and Peter had to stay behind to arrange with lawyers to spring Peter's mad Dostoevskyan brother out of the madhouse, which they successfully did so meanwhile I sail alone out of Brooklyn, with a double stateroom all to myself, with a big going-away party with Lucien and wife and kiddies, two days out to sea a huge storm when I think we're going to founder and I get a strange Catholic-like vision of the personal attention of God, i.e., "If I am to drown tonight, dear me, it will be into the snowy arms of God," all the Buddhism vanished in a crap of green fear, yet I saw a white glow over the raging black sea, that is, a definite vision of an eternal assurance that God's snowy

Alan Harrington, Jack Kerouac, John Clellon Holmes. Old Saybrook, Connecticut, November 1965. Courtesy John Clellon Holmes.

arms will fold us in for sure, a Personal God you might say, dont know, tho now I'm safe in that old bedroom I have to (logically) agree with the Lankavatara scripture which says "there's nothing in the world but the Mind itself" (notice they capitalize "Mind" so you might as easily substitute "God," or, as I do, "the Golden Eternity of God's Mind"—Anyway, finally the storm abates and the Ygos let out the little ship cats so at moonlit eight there they sit facing each other on the peaceful hatch, and the moon rises over the sea, and soon it's shining over Africa, and one afternoon we see the litle white city of Tangiers and by blue dusk I'm seeing my first vision of Africa, a put-put boat run by seedy arabs but with one fat guy in a business suit wearing a red fez standing arms aback clasped, come up to our bow to ask for job as "watch-a-man" . . . Well no need for such detail, anyway I'm writing a book about the trip, will call it *A Dharma Bum in Europe,* but I stayed in Tangiers about six weeks, on the roof in a room with patio facing the sea, over Bill Burroughs' own dingy pad on the main floor with a garden full of cats and Arab boys sneaking in at night over the wall—Burroughs having become an absolutely mad raving genius, having written THE WORD (originally we were going to call it WORD HOARD which turns out to be an old avant-garde magazine title), it is a book that supersedes Genet and de Sade and Alistair Crowley and even Allen and all the sex writers completely, it scared me to see it, no need to describe it here but to say it's apocalyptic truly and no one, NO ONE wants anything to do with it not even Bernard Frechtman (translator of Genet) to whom I took it in my rucksack in Paris . . . only Allen Anson and Ginsberg believe in it (and me) and worked with Bill on it after I left . . . i just missed seeing dear old Anson, tho damn it, who is now back in Venice, at % American Express, Boca de Piazza, Venice, Italy, if you want to write to him, and Ginsberg will be there also this summer but Burroughs hates Venice absolutely (says you can hear the shrieks, the pathetic shrieks of fags from St. Mark's Plaza on a windy day) (and says he has a vision of Venice as rich old American bitches and Truman Capote blowing Gondoleers out in the middle of the Grand Canal)—such style stuff, too, in his mad book, the funniest thing you'll ever read . . . Burroughs writes like this now (examples) (from what I have):— "Motel Motel Motel loneliness moans across the continent like foghorns over still oily tidal water rivers"—and—"boys jack off in the dark musty bedroom on summer afternoons and eat the berries that grow from the old man's bones and body, mouths smeared purple like whores who don't care"—and—"is them my peeled balls them boys is playing with?"—and—"did you ever suck up the sweet dark water from a cray-dad hole?"—and—"a mad prophet scream pure sound through him out his mouth, out across a great brown river whole trees float down, huge green snakes in the branches and pensive lemurs watch the shore with sad eyes"—"behind dobe walls smell of dried excrement, black dust blow over lean bodies, ragged pants dropped to dirty bare feet"—"sweet empty canary twitter"—"the boy looks like a nun so pure and alive for the moment to take the death vow it hurts a soft blue blast of sadness"—finally——"Oh what a rash and unsanitary deed is this!"—So in restaurants with me, always the best in town, he spits his bones out, curses, howls, raves, like Mr. Hyde he is now, scared Allen too—But Bill and I had long pensive walks together among the mountains and Berbers and Arabs—by myself I walked the sea, watched the ancient fishermen, you'll read all about it in *Dharma Bum*——Meanwhile, then I went to France, hitchhiked, or mainly hiked, thru Arles, Avignon, etc. Aix en Provence, went to Paris, stayed a week without easing the bite of it (Paris TOO great, you must go there someday) then to London where I saw tired (tho young looking) disappointed Britishy poor Seymour who listens to Alban Berg but ocassionally played me Getz and Kai and Jay Jay—Seymour disappointed in me because I had become such a big drinker—then I walked in the fog in Chelsea, and thought WHO WILL STRANGLE THE BOBBY IN THE FOG . . . O a thousand things I cant detail, such as the immigrations wouldnt let me into England (you know, John, I cant remember for sure whether I didn't get drunk sometime somewhere and write you this already) (did I?)—but when I showed immigrations the article about me in Nation, where I'm mentioned with Henry Miller, they remembered Henry Miller himself, same story, and let me thru laughing . . . Henry Miller's "From Dieppe to Newhaven," I believe its called. Well,

Jack Kerouac at Burroughs' Villa in Tangier, 1959. Photo by Allen Ginsberg.

enuf, let me just chat . . . first, my ex wife Joan has finally got a new sucker and is getting married and's got my signature to a Juarez divorce so I think now I'm completely free and meanwhile (as you see from postmark) I'm in Calfiornia, with my mother, but as this new development, my mother wants to go back to New York and anyway work a few days a week, she's lonely and idle, so damn, here we go again, back to New York, about this Fall, certainly before Xmas, and finally I'll go see you again in Saybrook Old around the holidays . . . Meanwhile I'm very pleased to see my very best "wild" prose appearing at last, in *Evergreen Review* No. 2, just coming out now, a nice piece about the railroad which we substituted for *The Subterraneans* when editor Don Allen wanted to pull a Giroux on me all over again and presented me with an eight pound baby 60 percent cut with all the long sentences cut up into little faggish sentiments wherein I heard not the mad voice of JK but the dry tones of Don Allen, it was disgusting, even my agent noticed it and saved the day by sending photostats of said castration to me in Tangiers . . . so I have laid down my ultimatum with publishers and I publishes as is or not at all—*On the Road* is just about as originally written on that block long (around the block?) sheet of Cannastra's drawing paper (secret: Viking thinks it's a 5 year extensive re-write job I gave them, it's the pure shining original by God) and that's the way to write, I say, who wants everything hidden under a bushel . . . Also, a mad story, "Neal and the Three Stooges," just appears this week in a little special avant-garde magazine called *New Editions,* and that's a pleasure to see in print, just about as written except for the printer's bewilderment . . . where he changed "THE GOD BONE CONNECTED TO THE BONE BONE" to a weak, watery "God's bone's connected to the bonebone"—Horwkwi!—and substitutes my famous dashes (which give reader a visual forewarning of end of sentence) with Celine-like dots . . . but that's no matter, I use dots in letters—Meanwhile, Gregory Corso was in Paris, got me drunk and made me spend all my money in one night, so thats why I left Paris so quick, but I walked 50 miles around Paris, mostly with my rucksack on back, because the Queen of England was there and no hotel rooms anywhere except for onenight shots . . . I stuck my nose up against Van Gogh and Rembrandt oils in the Louvre . . . I haunted churches, St. Tomas d'Aquin, Sacre Coeur on the Montmartre Butte, Notre Dame but this little poem scribbled angrily in a cafe over coffee and croissants indicates my bugginess at the time:

All the Martinis, Dubonnets, Raphaels,
    Flowers irises tulips of Van Gogh
    French songs voices coffees
    and sausage sandwiches
Are for death
      All the old churches of Europe
      scare me like the Children's Crusade
All the coffins of black and white
    contain gutters of symbol saturated
    with horse shit water blood & wine
And the voice burble gurgle richness
    of French girls crap—
Coca Cola me that, Arizona ash tray
The bottom of the cup begins in Heaven
The world is true but too heavy to bear
Gay floors gay chair-bottoms
    dead cats
    old rivers
    dumps
    home
It never mattered that Villon slipped
    into cathedrals stealing tresors
And golden Italy created light
    because I tell you my name
    Dead butts
    Abandoned Greeks
    lost children running to automobiles
Queers of the capitals of the world
    tombs
    longnose white saint statues
    Nobody has the right to his name

Names represent Nostre Nada Rien
And I see that the mirror reflects
     just as well as I
The short fly-life of cats

SO ANYWAY, I came back on the Niew Amsterdam and flew thru New York (a subpoena out for me at the time) pickt up my mother in Orlando and got movers, and she and I got on a bus and rode cross-country day and night drunk, my mother singing and hugging sailors all the way, what a mad cat she is, got off at New Orleans where we ate oysters standing at a counter, and at Juarez where a little bird leapt out of a cage and told her fortune, where she bought a Virgin of Guadaloupe medal and offered cigarettes to silent Indians in the park, and on, on, across the red mountains of Texas, to California, where inside one day we found this comfortable pad at 1943 Berkeley Way and now my typewriter's here and I can go on writing anyway, writing new book, and feel lonesome to hear from you, let me hear latest from you John—meanwhile scene in Frisco hounded down by cops so much, and banning and impounding of *Howl,* I would advise you as friend NEVER COME TO CALIFORNIA . . . silly place for old people—see you in New York on the holidays—God knows where I'm headed but I'm still trying and writing too and how can anybody blame a man who blows, how can anybody criticize Stan Getz on LOVER COME BACK unless they be negative shits? Who would have told Bud Powell as he sweated at the keyboard with bandaged hand in 1948 "Man you're repeating yourself" (which is what they tell me about my prose) Well fuck em all, I know better, you know better, besides who cares and who wants to be negative & dead?

Jack

February 26, 1958

Dear Jack,

Again I find myself in the position of not knowing where the hell you are, and having lost or mislaid all addresses but for some that must be certainly out of date, and so having to rely on Viking to forward this, despite the fact that Grove Press might have a better idea where you actually are. We are, as you can see, back in Connecticut snows, now after a week gone to slush, after over two months in Europe. We went over on the *America,* which was taken up with a Christmas singing contest between healthy German farm-boys going home, who cried "Ein Zwei zuffaf!" at the drop of a hat, and a beery collection of Irish exiles who held up the ship's bar from eight-thirty in the morning until thrown out around dawn, crooning *Mother Macree* to themselves in high, fleeting tenor voices, while the Ger-

John and Shirley Holmes at Gillette's Castle in East Haddam, Connecticut,
early 1960s. Courtesy John Clellon Holmes.

mans brawled, and pounded the tables, and oogled the girls. Our
three days in London, before going to France, were a haze of martini-
hangovers, and finding myself pounding on the doors of pubs at ten
in the morning, in terrible need of ale, and not understanding about
the complicated hours, and so slinking back through Green Park past
Buckingham Palace to find them changing the guards, as the band
played "Around the World," and I imagined Mike Todd counting his
money on the bridge across the duck pond in St. James's Park.

We rushed, still hung, down the Dover Road, and somehow
made a plane (car and all) which whisked us to bleak, drear, northern
France in twenty minutes, and I felt like a commando or something
suddenly set down in the dripping woods, with the abandoned sum-
mer villas there along the channel. We flew towards Paris through
empty tottering villages, green with moss and mould, and absolutely
uninhabited as far as I could see, with their still-ruined cathedrals in
which you could see your breath, even though the windows were
boarded up, and Christ himself shivered like a wax bean on the cold
staves of his tree. Paris for Christmas Eve, where all the loud speak-
ers were playing Mahalia Jackson's "Silent Night," where just at the
end of phrases the bluesy, jazzy slur comes in; and the city was, as
guaranteed, the City of Light, complete with fifty foot Christmas
Tree, all silver with blue bells, all illuminated in the square outside
Notre Dame, and we tried to get in for Mass, but the chilly old nuns,

holding leather pouches into which I dropped twenty francs, assured us there was no room, and so we went across the bridge toward St. Michel, and waited for midnight in a little cafe, and suddenly the whole city erupted in glorious celebration of That Old Nativity, and the restaurants and cafes were filled with girls, all Sagon-haircutted, and chic, with their bony-faced, intelligent-looking French dates, and we found ourselves drinking wine and eating huge *coq au vin,* and a Peruvian quartet was playing their harpy Peruvian jazz, and the night flowered. And so it went, we got into Notre Dame Christmas Day, and gaped at windows and statues, and ambled through the Tuileries, where all the "naked women" were delicate and green with age, and looked for a drink somewhere in the Bois, and finally found ourselves having pastis in St. Cloud, and ate somewhere in the market district where the whores leaned against cold walls, and stared at you and blew smoke in your eyes, and we did much, much more too, before we took off one morning in a pea-souper, out through St. Cloud towards the west, and Chartres, which once the pilgrims could see on the horizon for three days before they actually got there, but which we didn't see at all until we were a quarter of a block from it, because of the fog. I lit a solitary candle, and thought it the most beautiful building I have ever seen, and we sped on to Fontainbleau for lunch, in the great drear forest where Fragonard painted the court ladies at their grand frivolities, and where now the palace stands as a dull monument and the French army is busy cutting trees. On and on down the Rhone valley, the wines getting better and better, and cheaper and cheaper, and every lunch (picnic-wise by the side of the road) was made up of choice roquefort, and saucisson, and wonderful creamy, tasty French butter, and huge slabs of pate and of course the bread; Auxerre, Lyon, Vienne where the Romans built an amphitheater on the site of an old Gaulic church, and where the Christians built a chapel on the site of the Roman pagan temple, and where every century has left its own church; on and on, down into Provence, Avignon where all the walls said PAIX EN ALGERIE, and out to Petrarch's little mountain town of Fontain Vaucluse where the primitive caves still lord it, dark and patient, over Roman churches, and new little auberges; and from there, by back roads, down through the Durance Valley, where every town is out of Pound's early poetry, and sits, red and invulnerable and graphic in the clear air, right on top of a hill; and ruined forts, and tumbling monasteries watch the river; Aix en Province where, in ski parka and dark glasses, I felt like a wild horseman from the winter Caucasus, suddenly finding himself in a Georgian town by the Black Sea; and on, right over the big solid mountains until there was the Mediterranean, Marseilles a great smudge of smoke off there to the right, and Bandol, like a little heap of bright colored paper right in front. We ambled down the Cote D'Azur, estimating the amount of money represented by the shipping in the harbor at St. Tropez, where all the bookstores sold the Marquis de Sade in English, and the pastries were huge and delicate and would blow away at the merest breath; and Cannes and Nice, and above Nice, up the Var valley, where the river is dry and the bed sandy, to a little town, Gattieres, full of gypsies with their dark knowledges, and the grubby dogs, and their fat women stirring (actually) great caldrons of lungs, where we had New Year's—Madame herself cooking our chickens over a huge fire of faggots, and everyone drinking brandy with funny paper hats on, and all this in this little Casbah of a town in the dark night with the doleful church tolling steadily and solemnly away, and the radio playing Les Elgart. Down through Monte Carlo, where they wouldn't let us in to the tables because we didn't have ties on, but where avid, pale-faced little men were waiting for the ten o'clock opening of the great doors, and gathered around the tables like so many wan Dostoyevskis, and we contented ourselves with losing a couple of thousand francs in the slot machines, and then went over into Monaco (just down the block from the Casino) for Ricard and water right on the harbor-front, right next to Onassis' yacht, and someone watched us from the deck, and so I took a hundred franc piece and threw it in the water to show we didn't care. And then we went on into Italy to have our picnic lunch on the great wild cliffs near Ventimiglia, and came back over the Grande Corniche where the Alps are on your right hand and the sea on your left. And the next day we went up the Var Valley right into the screaming, manless center of those terrible mountains, along one-car roads, past cordoroyed road-menders with handle-bar moustaches who lead a lonely life, to Valberg, six thousand feet up, for skiing and meditating on the great frieze of mountains farther north where only the hawks go. And after a couple of days there we started down the other side, running out of gas eighteen kilometers from the bottom, and so having to soar, like a great silent bird, all the way down to just come to a halt in front of the first pump in an Esso station. North, north to Grenoble along the Route Napoleon, and the next day into Switzerland in a raging blizzard, and lunch along the lake out of Geneva where little children gabbled out the windows at us, giggling and passing confidences, and then over the Alps in one wild, slippery, sliding, sinister push through the blinding snow, into the wild Jura and an inn where they went out and caught our trout in the leaf and log swollen Ain twenty minutes before we ate them, and set us up to vin aperitif at nine the next morning, and we pushed on to Dijon for the mustard, and then up through the scarred and fatalistic Mame country, where the gently rolling fields give no sign of all the agony, all the waste, all the loss; and farther up, into Reims where the cathedral is being slowly rebuilt, and farther up, into Ameins where the walls said, in great white splashes, "Guerre = Misère," and back to Touquet-Paris-Plage again, dreary and windy and cold as all summer resorts are in the teeth of winter, and early one morning out we flew again, and back to England. England we loved, and prowled, finally getting used to the money and the afternoon break in drinking hours; and we read inscriptions in the crypt below St. Paul's and the marble slabs in the floor of Westminster Abbey, and skulked around Soho where the Teddy Boys wear fish hooks on their sleeves, and everyone needs a haircut, and has paint splashes on their trousers, and then went down along the embankments, into the depths of Fleet St. and the India docks, and up along Park Lane where the whores stand around waiting for their regular matinee-customers at 12:30 each day, and into Hyde Park where desk-clerks were playing soccer in their tight overcoats, and those great shaggy rangy English dogs were sniffing tree trunks. And stayed in London three weeks, and then, on a sudden, dashed off to Hardy's Dorset, and a seven century-town, called Carfe Castle, the castle ruined now by act of the Long or Short or Rump Parliament, occupied only by startled sheep, clatter-hoofing over the overgrown stones, and we walked over the wild and featureless downs, where the ponies loom out of the fog at you and go veering off, right down to the chalk cliffs over the boil of the channel, where we threw our lunch to the intrepid gulls, and froze our balls in the stiff wind, and where the sun came out in bleak patches of old gold light out over the grey sea. We played darts in the evening with 70 year old pink-faced "boys" in overalls, and talked about the old days when they burned wagonettes in the square and sat in rocking chairs all night on Whitsun near the beer kegs, and used to have wrestling and dart matches on the castle-green. Back to London, another week there, much, much, much, and then home again on Cunard, the crew disgruntled and sullen and the service and food rotten, and not, as you pointed out, anything like an American ship. To sit on the pier in New York in the middle of a coldsnap for four hours while they got the baggage off a piece at a time up one miserable, clanking conveyor belt.

Back to a blizzard, the house empty and closed up and cold, and the snow four feet deep in the backyard; back to copy-editing *The Horn,* which now they say may be out in late spring sometime, and all to the good for that; back to a raft of sad fan-mail on the *Esquire* piece: forlorn musicians in Miami, whose wives were "butchered" by incompetent doctors, whose five-year-old son's left eyes were gouged out by "brutal hoods," who have lost their jobs because all they want to do is swing; and who have lost their faith in God, and what, what, what can they do? I write back to say that I am just a man like them, and have lost my eyes too, but they can make it, and they should go out into Miami's streets and breathe the good air, and go home and cleave to their scarred wives, and love their winsome, wistful children, and don't think that God has forgotten them, because they are in His Eye, and the hoods are in His Eye, and the quack doctors and the greedy club owners are all in His Eye; and God loves us all the same, and loves the tranquil heart most of all, and God cannot forget. And other letters: you know them all, you have had them all too, I am sure. So I sit here in front of the fire all day answering those letters, trying for gravity and humility, and every now and again I go on reading things on something called The Beat Generation, by poor old Herb Gold, who's a nice enough guy, but he has to work hard to pay his alimony and he hates the "beat generation" because they don't work, and he writes so fast that he doesn't think too deeply into what he's writing about, content to catch the lingo and the surface, and to misquote with some maliciousness, and, after all, he's beater than anyone. That strange little old man, Sam Boal, shocks me with his strange little old pieces on "beat parties," veteran of da-daism, and ever-so-slightly wearying now. But then, as antidote, I read your really beautiful thing in *Esquire,* old buddy, a really solid, final state-ment of the historical curve of this whole thing, and no one of us need write about it again. How I love your belief that we are entering a time of "the last things" again, and, of course, I say amen to that. And it was so strange because just last wek, after reading the Gold, Boal things, I thought: "God, god, are all these people really having what they call 'beat parties,' and acting this way, and how immeasurably square I would seem if I was ever caught at one, wanting louder music and flushed faces, and enthusiasm, not this cold storage trapping and escaping in words. Jesus, Jack and I thought this up out of smoke those afternoons long ago, and it suited the tang and chill and excitement that was in the air then, and all of a sudden it's gotten completely out of hand . . . Man, when I see a girl bare from the waist, I don't, goddammit, reach for no foolish tone arm . . ." And here you go and say something so like it in *Esquire.* "It was a vision we had . . ." Yes, yes to that.

I haven't gotten *The Subterraneans* yet, but I'm eager, and will have it this week, I think. And I am starting in on a new book, to be written rapidly and very loosely, and to be well under way by the time poor old Edgar Pool makes his appearance among the knife-sharp-eners of the daily press. This one, all about God and the apocalypse and the last days; this one, all spiritual and with some strange things in it too, I think. Until then I'm trying to keep us alive and warm by foraging for article-things, with a good chance to do something on jazz for *Esquire's* August issue, if I can find the way into it, a panoramic sweep of the whole jazz scene right now, at this moment in time, to lead off an issue they are doing on what they call "The Golden Age of Jazz." It's still up in the air, but by next week I might have some word, and I'm fooling with it anyway.

And I read D. H. Lawrence, that inspired traveler, who was almost the first man to realize that the spirit erupts out of the intuitions, and who put all that down on paper, very fast too, I imagine. And St. Teresa, and Emily Dickinson, and Mauriac, and lots of other people, picking and going on, picking and going on.

And I wonder what is with you these days, and where you are, and what are your plans. You are probably in Europe and we missed connections yet again.

Later.

And if we have missed connections, indeed, as I suspect, I see you in Paris somewhere, at the Deaux Magots where we sat on Christmas afternoon among the no-Sartre's, and the strange, cute little thin raggedy girls in black stockings of runs, and large-heeled, old-fashioned pumps, and great poofs of Renoir hair hanging over their solemn, pale foreheads, with their strange men who did not look or talk or notice them, as the saucers piled up; and there was no one there that drear, sort of soft winter's afternoon, but some old argumentative men, bundled in overcoats out of 20's German films, with their bundles of newspapers; they, and a dainty, perplexed American queer reading the Paris equivilant of *Cue,* who wanted to borrow a dictionary from us, and strike up a conversation, but we were cooling everything, and finally he left; and drinking pastis continually, under the great mirrors and the mustard-colored pillars with great wood carvings on them, and the waiters who had seen everything before. Or in London, which you know and too have skulked, down along the docks particularly, and in the public (not the saloon) bars of those dreary, smoky pubs, forever lost in river fogs even when Parliament meets, where inquisitive, scrawny kittens come out from behind the bar, and skirt around the stool-legs, and perch on the beer-sloppy top of tables, and the little grates are red and warm with coal, the thin curls of thin and delicate and Chinese smoke sucked silently up the tiny flues; and the barmistress, who lives in Camden town, or up on the Edgeware Road, and across the river somewhere in the great twenty-mile glut of London, draws your bitter, and you wrap your coat closer around your empty belly, because it's cold in the public bar where the fire is smaller, and all the good blowsy, beery talk comes from the saloon bar behind the opaque partition, and you hear the laughter, and the cat gets up and skirts around the stool legs again, and plays with your trouser hem, and you finish up the bitter, and get up and it's almost three in the river-afternoon, and the alleys are booming with the trucks, and the pubs are going to close so you go back to the embankment and start home. Or, perhaps, in the rush and hurry and thrill of New York now, you wheel along Sixth Avenue from one thing to another—the immemorial Sixth Avenue of secretive bop musicians, where the bins of records used to be so eagerly turned over by wild-eyed fanatics reading matrix numbers, and where, outside the union hall, the cats and the squares separate, and those who do not tote horncases you know automatically are piano-men. Or perhaps in San Francisco, which I do not know at all. Where are you?

I am full of the old days, and full of the new days too, and eager for the work: all, all of it to the good. I want to go to Spain, and Mexico: I want to see the "hurling sort of run" which Lawrence describes in Indians; and brood upon his sublime phrase, the consequences of which reel my brain, "the old doom of matter," and by this (I know, I know it for a fact!) he means no Harrington-gnaw because of death, no agony of mortality alone, but the "old old doom of matter" which, despite our charging spirits, drags us back to time's necessities, sleep and sex and food and boredom and the itch again, and then again. "The old doom of matter" . . . I want to think, and have the time for it, and go the way I know that phrase will go for me, ah well . . .

Tomorrow I go back to New York, and as always I cavil somewhat at the thought; this time to help the copy-editing of *The Horn*, being taken out to lunch by the high-pitched, thrilled little girl whom I talked to on the phone, who baits me with mysterious "mutual friends," and titters softly and quite genteely, and will frown and shake her head over my commas, and three-dots, I know. "We'll have to argue, I'm sure of that," she says, and I don't intend to argue, but simply say, I thought all this one out, I thought all this one out very carefully and in the loneliness of wintry-country afternoons while Shirley worked. I know just what I meant, and let's standardize the punctuation but not argue as if it had any meaning. So for another bleak New York day, and then back up on here on Saturday, driving this time with friends, and the weekend, and next week to make some money from *Esquire* to afford the future in which to do the next book.

So I raved a little, and I'll send this off, old pal. Enough to say I'm back, and let's get together sometime, somewhere. What of Allen? Horribly mixed connections everywhere again; ironies too ironical to mess with now. American Express and its monumental goofs, and too little time, and hangovers, and everything not two blocks away. I cursed but roundly.

So. I'm off.

John

10 AN INTERVIEW WITH JOHN CLELLON HOLMES

John Tytell

For over twenty years, John Clellon Holmes and Jack Kerouac shared a special friendship. It began as a literary relationship: Kerouac showing Holmes the journal entries and notebook drafts of a novel that he was arduously composing into his first published book, *The Town and The City;* Holmes eager to learn about the new world which Kerouac inhabited, and its strangely illuminated orbits—Allen Ginsberg, Neal Cassady, Herbert Huncke, Bill Cannastra and others. Holmes yearned to capture some of the freedom from more traditional allegiances that these figures had won in their respective ways, but for Kerouac he was a bedrock of value, a man whose judgment was dependable because he retained a sure sense of rightness despite an exceptionately volatile environment. Kerouac confided in Holmes because Holmes, too, was ready to abandon the old answers that would no longer work, but even more because Holmes was a serious spirit, a man genuinely struggling in his art and in his life to discover valid responses in an anxious time without simply escaping in a flagellant nihilism. To Kerouac, Holmes was a marker, a buoy, a man on the border between straight and hip, past and present, a man with the sensitivity to make discriminations, and the openness not to fear what may have seemed bizarre to the many.

As Holmes' novels and other writings demonstrate, he is a writer who sensed and understood the social and intellectual changes catalyzing the Beats. *Go,* his first novel, captured the curious mixture of despair and new direction that enervated the lives of writers like Ginsberg (David Stofsky in the novel) and Kerouac (Gene Pasternak). Later, in *The Horn,* Holmes tried new fictional explorations into the world of jazz and hip values. These rare books—both because of their literary merits, and because they are now unfortunately out of print and as difficult to obtain as certain of Kerouac's books like *Tristessa* or *Maggie Cassidy*—inform us of what was then virtually unknown but vitally significant, the nascent stirring underground of the fifties. In "The Great Rememberer" section of *Nothing More To Declare,* and in a more recent eulogistic piece which appeared in *Playboy* called "Gone In October," Holmes has done more than any other writer to define the power and person of Jack Kerouac.

During this interview—conducted in two late-night sessions around a fireplace Holmes built himself—Holmes articulates that process of definition a bit further, substituting for the elegant flourishes of stylistic evocation which writing permits with a precision of statement and perception. He sees Kerouac from a variety of vantage points: ranging from Kerouac's reading habits to his technical intentions; from Kerouac's moral sense to his introverted nature and disappointed idealism. Holmes traces the ideological ramifications of the Beat movement, offering the image of a broken circuit for the sharp break in value systems that occurred during World War II, showing the Beats' attraction to a pre-Laingian therapy of "madness," ecstasy, jazz, even criminality, were means of generating new energies in a deadening time.

I drove to Old Saybrook from New York City—normally a 2½ hour drive which was complicated by a fierce late March blizzard into a 7½ hour crawl over icy roads—and arrived at ten on a Friday night. By midnight, we began recording and did the first part of the tape. Of all the interviews I have done, this was the most organic, flowing as a discussion among willing participants along a natural course. For the rest of the weekend, I ensconced myself in Holmes' study to read his journals and his collection of over one hundred letters from Jack Kerouac, from Mexico, from Denver, from the west coast, from Tangiers—letters which were more revealing of

Anatole Broyard's girlfriend, Jay Landesman, John Clellon Holmes, Shirley Holmes, Stanley Radulovich, Fran Landesman, Gloria Kaiser, unidentified bongo player, Anatole Broyard. Broadway, New York City, July 1952. Photograph by Harry Fine.

the literary intentions of the writer than any I had read. Late Saturday night, after a hearty stew and wine dinner, we returned to the fireplace and continued the tape. Before leaving on Sunday, Mellon took photographs, and John Holmes gave us a tour of Old Saybrook and vicinity. But the most enduring memory of the visit, for me, was the generous spirit, the warmth and hospitality of John and Shirley Holmes.

John Tytell
May 28, 1974

INTERVIEWER: *You were one of Jack Kerouac's closest friends for over twenty years. How do you account for the extreme personality changes that occurred after the publication of* On The Road?

JOHN CLELLON HOLMES: An irreconcilable division between the private self and the public life. One thing that happened to Jack was that he never understood that he had become *Jack Kerouac,* the Marlon Brando of literature, that he had become a personality, a notoriety. He felt that people were no longer talking to him, but to an image. He knew nothing about that, cared less, and beyond that it seriously bollixed his mind.

INT: *Did the fame affect his accelerated drinking?*

JCH: I think so. Drink sometimes provides the illusion of single-mindedness where all the things around a problem vanish— like blinders on a horse. Of course, Jack always drank a lot, we all did in those days. But I saw him two weeks after *On The Road* came out, after Gilbert Millstein's review, and he had been on television several times, had been interviewed, and he no longer knew who the hell he was supposed to be. He was temporarily discombobu- lated by the image of himself.

INT: *Was it excitement or confusion?*

JCH: When I saw him at that time, Gilbert Millstein was giving a party for him in the Village. He had invited thirty or forty people to meet this new writer. He called me because I was an old friend of Jack's. Well, Jack never showed up. At about 10:30 the phone rang, and it was Joyce Glassman, with whom he was staying then, and she asked me to speak to Jack. In a quivering voice, he said, "I can't come down there. I know you've come into town to see me, and I want to see you, could you come up here?" So I went up there, and he had gone through all these interviews, and all sorts of things like girls trying to lay him, all coming suddenly in the rush of one month.

INT: *After six years of anonymity, rejection and despair.*

JCH: Living like a bum and feeling spiritually wasted. He had been writing things that were unacceptable in the America of that time, things he clearly knew were sensational.

INT: *Like* Visions Of Cody. *It is almost unbelievable that it took so long for that book to be published in its entirety.*

JCH: You can imagine the embitterment felt by anyone who

could write that way and not get it published. He wasn't a primitive, but a very conscious writer.

INT: *That's one of the things that William Burroughs told me that really impressed me, that Kerouac had written over a million words before coming to Columbia. So of course someone like that could talk about spontaneity!*

JCH: He had learned his craft—it certainly shows in *The Town and the City,* which is a sort of Galsworthian family saga.

INT: *When did the physical change begin?*

JCH: You ought to see the kinescope of Jack's appearance with Steve Allen, whom he rather liked. He was still looking good then. He hadn't really hurt himself up to that point. He wasn't bloated or argumentative. The physical change began before he went to Big Sur in 1961. His passion had become muted, and he began to argue with himself in a way that he never had before. The Steve Allen thing was in '59 or early '60, and he still looked as I knew him back in the forties. And theoretically he was supposed to be reading from *On The Road,* but he actually read a few pages of the end of *Visions Of Cody,* which he had put inside a copy of *On The Road.*

SHIRLEY HOLMES: Only you and Allen Ginsberg knew that.

INT: *What can you tell me about the origins of* Visions Of Cody *and how it was related to* On The Road?

JCH: The section about Neal Cassady's boyhood was written before *On The Road,* and on pot. It's a long section that was originally published in *Playboy* about young Neal in the poolhall, and going out and catching the pass. That was intended as part of *On The Road,* written in long incredibly exfoliating sentences of great detail. At that time Sal Paradise's name was Ray Smith. Jack wrote all about his background, his getting prepared for the road, and this material was cut, and has never appeared.

INT: *Wasn't that the kind of naturalistic framework he used in* The Town and The City?

JCH: Exactly. But Jack realized that he couldn't use it in *On The Road*.

INT: *Did you see the original manuscript of* On The Road, *and what were its physical properties?*

JCH: I was the first person to see it, and I read it even before he did. It had no paragraphs, but it was punctuated. The names were not changed, he used the real names. He didn't want to use a conventional structure because he wanted to capture the onrushing flow of his thoughts and impressions.

SHIRLEY HOLMES: I've always contended that Jack had this ability to go with the flow because he was such an incredible typist.

INT: *John, did you visit Jack during the three-week period in which he wrote* On The Road?

JCH: Yes. Recently, I had occasion to examine my journals, which you'll read tomorrow. I have an entry in early April, 1951, of going down to see Jack, who was living in Chelsea with Joan Haverty, and by that day, I think it was the ninth of April, he had written 34,000 words. The long roll of what looked to me like shelf paper was spread out on the floor in front of the typewriter. I found another entry on April 27th when he delivered the book to me. He had finished it two days before, a huge thick roll, and he said he hadn't read it yet. I spent the entire day reading it, and it was almost a third longer than the published version.

INT: *Malcolm Cowley says that he suggested a lot of the trips be eliminated to create greater focus.*

JCH: Jack did a lot of this even before Cowley suggested it. He had a lot of material on the terminal points like New York and San Francisco, and took them out because they didn't relate to the road experience. When Jack typed the novel in pages, he made numerous changes—he always made more changes than he would ever admit to—and submitted it to Harcourt, Brace, and it was rejected. This was quite a blow to him. So I said, let me take it to my agent— he didn't have an agent then, but was working strictly through

Giroux—to M.C.A. and my agent then, Rae Everitt, now Rae Brooks, and she didn't fully appreciate it, but told Jack a few things which he sensibly ignored. Jack was sobered by the rejection though, depressed is not the word. He had to really think about himself and what he wanted to do. He had already had part of this experience in realizing he couldn't write *On The Road* in the way he had done *Town and The City*, that he had to abandon the idea of family structures and just set his characters free in the country. What he started to do almost immediately is what he called sketching; that is, looking in windows, observing the street, and taking it down at the time it was happening.

INT: *Direct notation rather than recalled notation?*

JCH: Rather than trying to *give* a shape, trying to existentially discover it, as in the beginning of *Visions Of Cody*. He told me he never thought of this as being publishable. He was simply trying to catch the flow. He had felt from the beginning that something in Neal had eluded him. Jack had an enormous capacity for saying, "Everything I've done so far is lies." While writing *On The Road* he said he was writing it because *Town and The City* was a lie, a fiction. *On The Road* was to tell the story as it was, but afterwards Jack felt he still hadn't caught the idea of Neal, so he began *Visions Of Cody*, which he didn't conceive as a structured book, but more an expansion of his imaginative conception of Neal.

INT: *So it led to a series of extensions, projections, and games based on Neal which captures him more internally somehow.*

JCH: It's closer to Neal, but ultimately very mythic. I've always thought that the picture of Neal in *On The Road* is dramatically better, but the character is not as monumental as in *Visions Of Cody*. What Jack did was invent a plethora of new techniques for *Visions Of Cody* because he couldn't create the character he wanted if he remained outside him.

INT: Visions Of Cody, *for me, is when Kerouac really comes into his own.* Dr. Sax *also has that sense of inventive leaping, that unique power and freedom of form.*

JCH: Obviously Jack was searching to free himself from all the novelistic necessities as they existed then in order to freely sing, not as in *Town and The City* where the songs were more or less set pieces, recitatives or arias. What he wanted to do was employ the totality of his feeling, sensibility and erudition, and make it part of the flow he was describing. This is why he was always so close to Joyce—a deep passion of his I never particularly shared. He wanted, as Joyce did, simultaneity; Jack not only wanted to describe something—which he did better than anyone I've ever known—but also to embody it with everything about himself and his feelings that he could get into it. And he wanted to find a way in which all of this could flow together. Jack would never have claimed it, but it seems to me that the real engine behind the English in *Cody* is Shakespeare. There are sections in *Cody* which are as eloquent as any prose I've ever read.

INT: It is interesting that Shakespeare, Joyce, and Kerouac are all freed of certain inhibitions of syntax and style and structure, and as a result can perfect a powerful flow, anarchically, freely.

JCH: It happens when the image finds the word or words immediately, and you don't stop to think, Is it working? You just plunge on. That's why there are lines in Kerouac that you must flow with to understand; the moment you stop to conceptualize they break down. But what gets into the line is a whole series of tumultuous impressions and takes that can only be compared to film, and Jack, of course, was very affected by film. Also, Jack spoke French before he spoke English, and like many people who work in a language not their own, he was very sensitive to it. Jack was a word man all the way, and had a veneration for language—which is why he loved Joyce.

INT: He seems, judging from his letters, to have read a lot.

JCH: He was a tremendously well-read man. He read erratically, but deeply, and when he read something he never forgot it.

INT: I've read letters that Jack wrote to Allen Ginsberg when Jack had already left Columbia but was reading as if he were still there, five, seven, ten huge books a week. Not all of them necessarily, parts of Pascal, of the Bible, Moby Dick *in a day or two.*

JCH: He had an amazing memory for what he had read. He would often come here because I had most of Balzac, and I suppose that any writer who is writing a saga thinks of Balzac, as Faulkner did. Jack loved Balzac, and came here because he felt it was quiet enough, and he would pile Balzac next to that chair and read him for a week. Then years later he would make some reference to one of the fifty-odd novels by Balzac that I have. So he read and remembered.

INT: *Do you know whether he read Henry Miller, or ever expressed any attitudes towards Miller's work?*

JCH: Frankly, no. But I had read Miller early, and approved of him as I approved of what I then thought of as good dirty-book writers. I was attracted to Lawrence and Miller in my teens, and managed to read the forbidden Miller in my early twenties. Now Jack loved Lawrence almost despite his reputation, but I never remember him saying anything about Miller until the mid-fifties.

INT: *That's interesting because it seems to me that Miller started something that Jack continued, and that was writing a saga about yourself. Miller, of course, did that remarkable Preface for* The Subterraneans.

JCH: Jack must have been pleased by the effort of an older writer to help him along, and to recognize him, but I know that Jack didn't see Miller even though a meeting was planned. I believe Miller is a great American writer. When anybody really reads what he has done, any idea that he is simply prurient or pornographic is utterly ridiculous. He's in a deep American tradition.

INT: *During the years after the writing of* On The Road, *from 1951 until its publication in 1957, how much of Kerouac did you see?*

JCH: I saw him only intermittently because he was in Mexico and on the West Coast. We saw each other whenever he came back to New York. When he was gone we corresponded, and he sent me all his manuscripts during those years. That is, up to '54–'55 when he went to San Francisco and everything started to happen. They all came back here, Jack, Allen, Peter on their way to North Africa, and they were up here around New Year's of '57. Viking was going to publish *On The Road,* and we spent a whole week up here just getting to know one another again, and Jack was still very much the way he had been before, he'd been on the mountain and written the first half of *Desolation Angels.* He had also written the first part of *Tristessa,* which I read then too.

INT: How had he sent you the other books, like Dr. Sax?

JCH: In the mail. He would send me the originals, and I turned them all over to an agent, or to Allen, or to Carl Solomon. The original of *Dr. Sax* went to Carl who was then working for A.A. Wyn, his uncle, who wouldn't publish it.

INT: The book probably didn't seem commercially feasible to Wyn?

JCH: Carl wanted it published, he was fighting for certain things with Wyn, but they were a very small house. Carl got through that Jaime de Angulo book, *Indian Tales,* which has become a classic, and he got a few others like *Junkie* through. This must have been an enormous source of pressure on Carl. He knew what was good, what would become important, but he was working nine to five. I used to meet him for lunch then. He had his problems anyway, and to fight the publisher's bullshit all the time, when there was no recognition that it was shit anywhere . . . Listen, you couldn't even wrap yourself in the American flag and say, "I'm going down for integrity and how about that, baby!" because the books he wanted to accept were considered filthy—you were considered some kind of fruitcake to believe they were good. But those were awful years. You've treated it so well in that one section of your books that I've read on the fifties.

INT: I was in high school and college at the end of the fifties, and I felt it.

JCH: You must have, because you describe it brilliantly. You felt like you were fighting a hopeless battle against everything. One reason why Jack, and Allen, and the rest of us have not been upset by the new freedom is that we know what it came from. We were serious writers, and we earned every "fuck" we wrote down. Take

Go, for instance. I used no four-letter words except at one point, where I thought it was legitimate. There's a character who is absolutely disgusted with the world, and he comes out onto the street after a party and something has happened—indeed Allen Ginsberg has been arrested—and he says "Fuck You! Fuck You! Fuck You! Fuck You! Fuck You! Fuck You!"—six times. Scribner's lawyer asked me to cut out three of these, and I said, "If I can publish three, I can do six. I'm trying to make a point here: the man is out of control." But that was characteristic of the circumstances under which you worked then. They said, "Can't you change it to 'fug'?" Mailer had done that, but I refused and insisted that it had to be six "Fuck You's"—it had nothing to do with sex, or dirty words, it had to do with despair. But they thought quantitatively then, and that's one reason why *Visions Of Cody* couldn't come out. Now Jack was a very moral, almost puritanical person, but he used the language of eroticism when it seemed right.

INT: That's interesting. I've felt that when Kerouac treats women in his fiction that moral sense creates a false distance making the women less real, more romanticized than he might have realized or intended.

JCH: Well, this was certainly not entirely due to the literary restrictions of the time. He did tend to idealize women.

INT: You can see it in Tristessa, *for example, where you have a woman named Esmeralda in real life—"hope" in Spanish—who is a drug addict and a whore, but whom he transforms into a Mary Magdalene, a saint of the streets. He does capture her desolation, but still there is such a pedestal quality, almost a worship of her suffering.*

JCH: This relates to something larger that Jack intended to idealize. He plunged deeply into the stuff of life in his time, and—it's hard to say whether he was educated by it or disappointed—he had an enormous ability to empathize with human beings. He was a person who stood off from life to a degree that is not recognized. He was not deeply involved, he was not part of the swirl, he was not dancing on the floor or driving the car, he was not swinging.

INT: Ann Charters relates how withdrawn he was at parties, always standing apart.

JCH: To some degree this may be true of artists generally, but it was pronounced in him. I have seen him in the center of things, but this was the exception. This is where drink came in, because it connected him to the outside, but by himself he was serious, grave, not a drag, but hard to engage. He was a man who felt at a distance from most people, and he was aware of this all the time because of his own hunger to cross it, and this is what made him a difficult person for some people to communicate with because he didn't seem to be there all the time. He was a brooding presence. Then he would get drunk or high, and he would be the most gregarious person you ever met, the most charming and attractive, the most imaginative man I've ever known, just a continuous flow of fantasy, ideas, funny nothings and weird images. But he was driven—that is, he was a man who sat completely inside his own consciousness and never, or rarely, got out of that envelope. And he accepted this, and followed it wherever it led, but it was often into things that were debilitating for him. He had a very fatalistic sense of himself, and to me he was a genius, whatever that word means. I've only met one, and I know many people who are extremely talented, and kinetic, and everything else. But ultimately, Jack had a mystery inside him that I never could penetrate at all, and I don't think he ever could either. I think Allen would confirm this.

INT: *And at the heart of him was the energy of his imaginative facility. How would you characterize it?*

JCH: Jack would constantly come up with things: titles, ideas, takes—often he wouldn't follow them up, but the constant spew . . .

INT: *Like the titles for "Howl,"* Naked Lunch, Big Table?

JCH: It was that he would read something and do a take on it, and sometimes it seemed outrageous, mean or bitter, indifferent or too enthusiastic, but it always had some sense to it that often would come out later. About eight years before he died I stopped questioning him—that is, I stopped saying, "Oh Jack you're full of shit!" I would often say it, but I gradually stopped believing it because there was always an odd kind of prophetic logic to the way he thought, even when he was fumed with booze. Like he wrote a thing for *Escapade*—he was something of a right winger, you know—on Khrushchev whom he had seen getting off a plane in Washington, having to stand in the sun during speeches, enduring the passing of the Marine band, a sixty year old man sweating with his hat off, and Jack, who hated Communism, wrote in this tit magazine, "I demand justice for the man Khrushchev." And this was typical of Jack who sympathized with the man, any man undergoing the experience of the moment. He related to that.

INT: Even though Kerouac writes about working-class characters like Neal, exulting, for example, in the power with which Neal could change tires, there doesn't seem to be any sense of class conflict or awareness in his fiction such as you might find in a more political writer like Dos Passos. He goes right to the man because of something central in his subject's experience.

JCH: Still, there was a definite class feeling in Jack, although it was almost always on the surface. Show him the human situation and if it was clear enough to him, that's what he would reach for. That's really what the whole Beat thing was about. It was kind of an American existentialism—it said don't talk to me about essence but show me what's happening.

INT: How does that work in with class though?

JCH: It doesn't, of course. But what I'm trying to say is that Jack, when he was not creatively engaged, thought very much about class—not intelligently, he didn't write much about it, but he was full of class resentment. He who seemed to me to be so brilliant, nevertheless resented people who had more education than he did, more privilege, more money.

INT: Do you think this might have had its origin in the experience of attending Horace Mann, and then Columbia, as a young man from a provincial town without any kind of support?

JCH: Undoubtedly. That must have been a factor. It always seemed to me, knowing Jack, and even more in reading his work, that he always felt separate, he even felt separate from his family and the immediate background which gave him his material. He felt special, isolated, lonely, and this never changed.

INT: *The feeling I have about all of these figures is the spiritual state of exile, not that one has to—like Burroughs—leave the country or expatriate, but in the sense of Stephen Dedaelus' exile which is all the more profound for being within one's own family and country.*

JCH: Well, the Beat thing begins with the feeling of difference.

INT: *And outcast, or self-outcast as a result?*

JCH: Well, at first Jack wanted to be like his father. He started being nostalgic about life in Lowell when he was seventeen, perhaps even earlier. But he never felt part of it. He was like Rimbaud.

INT: *His poem on Rimbaud is probably the best place to begin when looking for what motivated the Beat experience. In* The Town and The City, *when Levinsky first appears, he is carrying a volume of Rimbaud.*

JCH: It is so difficult to speak about it sociologically, but what had happened in the late thirties and early forties was a kind of uprootedness in terms of family relationships, the whole society was changing, and a major event was about to happen, and everybody knew it, particularly young men. And it was also clear that all the ways by which people had understood an event like this in the past were inadequate.

INT: *And isn't what you are attempting to describe exactly the context of* The Town and The City *where both family ties and community allegiance lose their validity in the face of some looming threat? The sense of imminent devastation for young men— almost Hemingway's theme.*

JCH: Right, but what it did with Jack and all of us to some degree was to make more poignant the things that had been lost. You allude to this in one of your essays when you refer to the deep conservative element in all this. It set Jack thinking about families; it set me thinking about marriage, love, cohesiveness, and more than that—continuity. Ginsberg is relentlessly writing about continuity, or its absence, but what nerves all of Allen's work is the broken circuit, and the broken circuit is in Jack's work all the way.

INT: *That's a good image.*

JCH: So we issued out of the war into a cultural scene, the dominant tone of which was irony and craft, Henry James and Auden.

INT: *Containment and form.*

JCH: And caution. Don't spit it out. And this is what made Allen erupt, "I saw the best minds of my generation destroyed by madness . . ." which he has been laughed at for writing, but which is so true, and this is what made Jack write, "The only people for me are the mad ones" in *On The Road*. And what moves both passages is that they were both saying there's a break, there's a terrible break that has occurred: I have known those who have been destroyed by it, I believe in people who are trying to mend. Now these lines were done independently of each other, but they really epitomize what this whole thing was about.

John Clellon Holmes. Old Saybrook, Connecticut, June 4, 1976. Photograph by Arthur Knight.

INT: Last night we were talking about the importance of madness as motivation in Ginsberg's work, and in Kerouac's work, and the fact that from their point of view the madness that they pursued was not madness but the only way to move, to see the society and deal with it, and that stance leading to a whole reinterpretation of the relativity of madness.

JCH: Yes. If you accept the modern world on its terms, and are content with it, then anyone who can't function in it is strange, bent, twisted, etc., but one of the qualities in the Beat movement was the recognition that madness was a kind of retreat for those who wanted to stay privately sane. We understood that madness meant pain, as any withdrawal does, but the idea that there was any way to formulate social sanity was one of the things that we tried to give up, just as we tried to give up Freudianism, Marxism, and all determinisms. And everyone knew people who went mad, or felt themselves going mad sometimes—that is, getting psychically out of step with the world—and all too often it was because of a different standard that the world continually abused. So people broke down because of this dichotomy; in other words, it's early Laing. This was certainly true of Allen who was put in Columbia Psychiatric Institute because of things completely outside him. His apartment was full of stolen goods brought there by Huncke and the two others living there.

INT: Lionel Trilling explained to me that Allen went to P.I. as a result of a deal with the District Attorney, Frank Hogan, who was a Columbia University graduate, and who agreed to allow Allen to serve time in a psychiatric ward rather than a penal ward. Actually, as Laing and Thomas Szasz have argued, it is much the same thing though.

JCH: But what happened with Allen while he was there was interesting—since he ultimately confused the analysts by being saner than they were. He was more honest for one thing, so they said they couldn't do anything for him.

INT: That's another aspect of something Carl Solomon told me—that he felt in his life there was a danger of talking his way into the institution. So honesty is a twisting key itself. But in the culture of the late forties and early fifties, the nature of madness was almost an idea that Norman O. Brown discusses in Life Against Death, *that the greatest madness lies in resisting one's natural inclinations to madness, so that from that point of view you can see the sense of control of a Nixon as being the archetype of madness in our day. Maybe that's what leads to war.*

JCH: Allen would say, and I would agree with him, as Blake said, that anything that comes directly from the inner self is good, it sweats, it's real. Being disembodied is really being mad.

INT: Not being in touch with oneself—what Laing calls "ontological insecurity"?

JCH: Talking like a grammaphone like Nixon talks, simply mouthing things, talking out of a dream, an MGM fantasy.

INT: Yes, like the time he reputedly appeared at the Washington Monument before a peace rally at 5:00 a.m. and addressed a small group as if he were in a trance.

JCH: Certain kinds of cliches are the narcotics of the middle class, and Nixon plays on these automatically. I think he really believes these things so I can't hate him. He's so removed that he is sad to me, not loathsome. But he is everything that we have to recoil from, and I mean spiritually, not just politically.

INT: Was there any general attitude among the Beats towards psychoanalysis? I know Burroughs went through it, and disdains it now. How did Kerouac feel about it?

JCH: Well, Jack had an experience in the Navy where he was discharged, I forget the phrase they used . . .

INT: "Paranoid schizophrenic." In one of his letters, he says they added paranoid to his diagnosis because he was intelligent.

JCH: Well, that about sums it up. In other words, we all felt that psychoanalysis was an inadequate description of human activity. It just couldn't go far enough, the way sociology also failed to include the spirit or mystery, and that's what we were after. It really didn't help to know that you had a father complex or a mother complex. Life amounted to more than that. We felt that this approach was as oversimplified as Marx's understanding of class relations. The Beat attitude, to call it that, was protesting against what we felt was an inadequate conception of the nature of man. In 1945, man was seen as a victim, either of toilet training or his place in society, but he was determined from the outside. That conception of man we all found, quite independently because we all have different backgrounds, to be increasingly inadequate. We felt there had to be something more. Thoreau talks about it, and Emerson, and we found the deepest strain in American politics and poetry to be metaphysical. The American Constitution starts out by enunciating certain inalienable rights; no European had ever conceived of that—that certain rights are innate! When the French began talking about the rights of man it led to the rolling of heads. But we began by defining man as free, and our experiment worked because our variety, our difference, our lack of homogeneity meant that every one of us had to become Americans, which meant becoming new men—it was no birthright, everyone except the Indians came from somewhere else. So primarily we are a passionately political people and politics is our church, the thing that holds us together as both Whitman and Lincoln used to say. Well, we wandered afield a bit.

INT: I'd like to wander in another direction—the importance of jazz music to the Beats. For example, Allen today writing and singing a poetic based on blues, or earlier this afternoon, I was reading in your journals an entry describing a party in 1951 where Allen was singing blues, improvising rhymes to fit the people present at the party. The same interest is certainly evident in Kerouac's work, and in your novel, The Horn. *What do you think caused this general interest?*

JCH: Well, young people in America, at least in the last three generations, have felt music as a very important part of their lives: In the thirties it was swing, in the late forties it was bop, then rock. American music—jazz, blues, it all comes from a black base—has in our century seemed to young people to express all sorts of inexpressible exuberance and energy. Now with Jack and me and Allen and others of that time I suppose jazz meant more than that. Fed up as we were with trite explantions of why things happened, and with an attitude towards the world that seemed inadequate, jazz was a call from the dark, it was the euphoria of joy, dance, let loose. Also, everyone at that time believed that blacks knew something that we didn't know, only because they appeared less surface-worried than we were.

INT: Mailer writes about that in "The White Negro"—about learning a model of experience and the courage to face the world from the black man.

JCH: You can sum it up like this. When Jack wrote about walking in the Denver black section in *On The Road*, James Baldwin said he'd love to hear Jack reading that in the Apollo Theater in New York because Jack would get crucified; less than ten years later, Eldridge Cleaver praised that section as an early sign of a new liberated consciousness. So whether we were deluded or not, what we wanted was that untrammeled swing and style that blacks, undoubtedly as a defense, had created. Also because *we* felt like blacks caught in the square world that wasn't enough for us, and we felt that blacks had more immediate fun than we did.

INT: Do you feel that the Beats had a greater sense of the street than writers have had previously, even the Naturalists? I'm thinking of figures like Huncke or Neal.

JCH: Absolutely. We knew that street knowledge meant functioning in the world, so what writer wouldn't be interested in talking to a man like Huncke. We went to Huncke like you might go to Dostoevski just because of the kind of life he had lived—he was a source—even more, a model of how to survive. That was part of the appeal Neal had for Jack, because Neal had answered questions Jack couldn't answer for himself, or so Jack fancied it. All of Jack's work was motivated by a disappointed idealism, and Neal presented an answer to the break that Jack felt in himself. I once saw Neal look at Jack, and I imagined I saw in Neal's face, "You're not seeing me anymore, you're seeing only your idea," because Neal was a man who had literal day-to-day problems.

INT: So Huncke told me: "He was a nervous cat all the time!"

JCH: Right. He was as hung up with women problems, transportation problems as any of the rest of us, but Jack increasingly saw him as a kind of hero who was being brought down by the necessities of square life. Jack was never unaware of the domestic bullshit in Neal's life.

INT: He had to be aware of it because he lived with Neal and Carolyn several times, and left on one occasion because he could no longer stand Neal's peculiar games. In Big Sur, *however, Kerouac implies that Neal felt exploited, that his life had been used. I mean at the end of the novel when Neal stands in the doorway in a golden light—which for Kerouac signified a moment of annunciation—as Jack unwraps the copies of* On The Road *which have just arrived, and Neal looks away, unable to look into Jack's eyes.*

JCH: I was reasonably close to Neal, and always liked him, and I've often thought about what *On The Road* must have done to him as a man, you know the idea that he had become a myth in his own time, because he wasn't a mythic character—he was simply a fascinating human being. So when Jack gained his recognition after *On The Road*, okay, Jack at least had written a book, but Neal suddenly became a figure quite by happenstance, and it got more and more complicated as Jack's works appeared. Jack was always deadly honest in his work. Not always in his life but always in his work. So that episode near the end of *Big Sur* is revealing, I agree with you.

INT: You said that Neal didn't have a mythic presence, but it is curious to me that after leaving Jack's orbit Neal goes to Kesey, suddenly appears in Kesey's backyard, and that started the friend-ship that led to the Merry Pranksters. But the point is that Neal sought Kesey out as one man of power seeks another.

JCH: Well, Neal liked people who liked him.

INT: Also, to put it vulgarly, he knew where the action was almost instinctively—I think because of that remarkable street sense he had.

JCH: Definitely. Neal was one of the most street-wise men I ever met.

INT: *And sophisticated in certain ways at the same time, and the wonder of it to me—although it fits so perfectly into the American tradition—is that it is all so self-learned.*

JCH: The most sophisticated people are those who have never read books, or gone to school, but just lived their lives intensely. Huncke is one of the most sophisticated men I've ever met. What is sophistication? It's knowing how things work, where things are, keeping all the elements separate and knowing how to handle them.

INT: *That's the way Rojack in Mailer's* An American Dream *defines sanity: keeping in your mind the maximum number of impossible combinations.*

JCH: Neal certainly knew that. Besides, as you say, he wanted action and knew how to get it. But with Kesey everything accelerated, the stakes were higher, the drugs different, like LSD.

INT: *Right. Neal had spent two years in San Quentin for giving two plainclothesmen a marijuana cigarette, and now he was driving a communal-freak bus for Kesey and they all were distributing acid. It is like the magnified end of a cycle beginning maybe when Huncke, Burroughs and Neal drove back from New Waverly to New York City in '47 with a jeep full of marijuana that they had harvested and put in mason jars. And before that Bill Garver's stealing overcoats around Times Square to support his habit, or Huncke hustling, breaking and entry with Little Jack Melody, Neal's reputed theft of over 500 automobiles mostly for joy-rides in the Denver hills when he was still really just a kid. All of which leads to another question: what was the attraction of the underworld and the lifestyle of the criminal? With Burroughs, for example, beginning with a Gidean devotion and fascination. Also his whole notion of the relativity of legality which is expressed in letters to Allen that I've read up at Columbia University where Burroughs comments, for instance, on the wetback situation in Texas where he was farming in '47—how large farmers are allowed to get away with it, while smaller farmers can't, and how anyway the wetbacks are profiting since they could earn three to eight dollars a day instead of fifty cents a day in Mexican fields. Yet at the same time they are treated as slaves, and if they didn't pick cotton, could be shot in the fields, while the U.S. authorities encourage the large growers since there is no other way to harvest. So the whole question of what law is becomes itself in question, or it becomes an economic class determinant more than an ethical determinant.*

JCH: True. It seems that our attraction to criminality, mostly crimes without a victim like drugs, fit in with our feeling that the definition of man's nature was inadequate. And we were interested in excessive experiences, in the extreme, because a man who puts himself outside the law is a man who is putting himself *into* himself—he's said okay, I'll go alone, and we were fascinated with this because then a man has nothing to depend on except what's inside him.

INT: I noticed a picture of Norman Mailer in that group of about thirty pictures of writers in your study. When was that taken?

JCH: Early sixties: it was when he did a thing for *Esquire* about writers and the bitch goddess, and they shot him in a ring with a hand over either rope, and it struck me then as summing up the only Mailer I've ever known, at once aggressive and perceptive.

INT: What was Mailer's relation to the Beat movement?

JCH: He became sympathetic to it starting about 1957. Somewhere around then in his column for the *Village Voice* he got into the conflict between hip and square and predicted that the choice between these positions would be the real problem for Americans for the next twenty-five years. Now when I knew Norman in 1952 or '53, he knew nothing about this and didn't much care. He was a Trotskyite. But the hip/square columns had to do, I think, with something relating to *The Deer Park*, that never quite got into *The Deer Park*. He suddenly had a vision of all this—he hadn't been really paying any attention, and he hadn't been on the street or he would have known. He had found success very young, and had a more or less concretized way of thinking about things.

Shirley Holmes: And he had a very sneering attitude towards the Beat thing at parties.

JCH: Well, not exactly. I remember a party at Vance (Bour-jaily's) right after *On The Road* came out, and Mailer took me into a corner and said, "Tell me everything you know about Kerouac!" And when Norman met Jack, he liked him. But Norman had to run out of all the intellectual disciplines by which he had motivated his work before he came to the dark night of the soul. The inner life broke in on him because everything else ran out.

INT: *Maybe because he was really receptive as well? He did offer* Naked Lunch *its first most significant praise.*

JCH: The thing that makes Mailer for me a very great writer is that he follows his nose wherever it goes. We all know about *Naked and The Dead*. *Barbary Shore* was a really serious attempt to write the first existential novel in America, but what it resulted in was that Norman was rubbed raw. *The Deer Park* was his first attempt to do something where he didn't quite know what he was doing.

INT: *And Sergius O'Shaugnessy, in a subsequent story, "The Time Of Her Time," one of the great sex stories of all time, does finally make that transition from square to hip, from Hemingway's "Lost Generation" consciousness to a glimmer of beatness.*

JCH: But imagine what Norman had to go through to make Sergius do that. He had to be willing to experience it himself first. That is, Norman is the guy who wanted to be like Thomas Wolfe and others—when their books were published people ran right out and bought them. He had the same hope that we all had that the publication of a new book by a certain writer would be an event. We all had to learn that that simply wasn't true anymore. It had nothing to do with money, but whether literature meant anything any longer. So Norman is the only writer I know who made himself into a celebrity by a conscious effort, and enormous sacrifice. To me it has sometimes seemed a waste of energy.

INT: *I wanted to ask you what you thought of Mailer's idea in "The White Negro" that a certain quality of pathology is necessary to heroism in our time, and especially becomes the natural re-sponse to an encroaching totalitarianism, and what did such an attitude have to do with the whole question of rebellion in the Beat movement? You know, the fact that you were not going to accept the given conditions, and you were all seeking another way, of conducting your lives with the kind of joy and illusion of freedom that Mailer attributes to the blacks in "The White Negro." So a kind of craziness, or a pathological response, or what society would have seen as violation of its code of adjustment and acceptance, and therefore termed crazy, which in turn only means that society has the power to intern you in a certain kind of prison.*

JCH: I think we denied the ready-made explanations for human behavior, and we were drawn to aspects of human experience that were ignored by all the sciences or condemned by society.

INT: And apparently, reading the letters describing the parties in the late forties, you were all very drawn to the idea of breaking control and getting out of one's ordinary head, partly for joy, partly for the sake of new perception. In this connection, I wanted to ask you about Jack's friend, Bill Cannastra. What period was that?

JCH: He died in 1950, in a revealing manner. He was on a subway, a local train, somewhere downtown, and as the train pulled out of the stop—the windows were open because it was warm—he tried to get out through the open window, was about halfway out as the train gathered speed and struck a pillar. He was very athletic: he climbed up fire escapes, and dangled over the sides of buildings, and so forth, but he was drunk. The girl he was with claimed that he said, "I'm going to go get a drink." Maybe it was just claustrophobia or boredom.

INT: How would you characterize him? How well did you know him?

JCH: I knew him pretty well. One reason that I put him into *Go* was that he seemed a contrast to Neal, Jack and the rest of us. He was an alcoholic; his motivation was embitteredness, the world's approaching end. His way of playing was self-destructive, it was giving wild parties that went on for days, and which were not chic at all but raunchy—we all dug ugliness then, that is, the worse it was, the more interesting it seemed to be. Cannastra would do anything: humiliate people, usually himself first, you know, take off all his clothes and fart, scream and yell. He seemed to be somebody

playing on the edge, and he appealed to me because I was moving
into a new world which didn't demand that one be a victim as he
was. He thought of himself as having seen the lie of life, and
responded to it like Rochester did—I mean the poet—by saying,
"Anything goes now because it's all rotten anyway." Now I felt like
that then, but I was changing over to the feeling that something in
the streets could be found that was more interesting than this.

INT: Did he work?

JCH: He was a graduate of Harvard Law School who had
abandoned his practice. At that point he was a bisexual drunk who
lived in a loft in Chelsea, and did everyday jobs like working in a
bakery. He couldn't have been more than thirty when he died. He
was an outrageous man, and I liked him because he was out-
rageous. He used to go into bars in Chelsea or near the docks and
give longshoremen big wet tongue kisses, and say, "Buy me a
drink," and they would beat him up, but then buy him drinks
because he wasn't a "pansy," only premature-Camp.

*INT: Did you know Jerry Newman? Allen Ginsberg told me
that he did a radio bit called "The Drunken Newscaster" that
Burroughs heard which may have influenced the idea of the cut-up.*

JCH: I knew him, but nothing about that. When I first met
him he had a record shop off Eighth Street west of Sixth Avenue,
and then he started a record company called Esoteric. Jack had
known him at Horace Mann, and they shared a common passion
for jazz in the early years of World War II. One of the first things he
did was to record that marvelous serenade by Schonberg. It was
just the beginning of LP's. He knew little about Schonberg, but he
had a perfect ear, and he made his performance by editing different
tapes. This is common practice now, but he was one of the first to
get a final product by editing several different versions.

*INT: When did you take courses at the New School for Social
Research with Kerouac?*

JCH: It was in the fall of '49, more than a year after the initial
meeting I describe in *Nothing More To Declare*. Both of us had GI
benefits left, so even though *Town and The City* was coming out we

decided it was ridiculous not to take advantage of the year we were still entitled to, plus they gave you some living money every month and free books.

INT: *What courses did you take?*

JCH: We took some courses in common, like the Meyer Shapiro course about the Impressionists. It was a huge class so there was no real interchange, but he was an inspiring teacher. We both sat in on a course that Alfred Kazin was giving on *Moby Dick*, and he was a brilliant teacher, too. I took a medieval literature course, and a comparative religion course, and we both started a myth course with Harry Slochower but only attented about two classes. He was a bore with a Marxist viewpoint who treated myth like merchandise.

INT: *In* Nothing More To Declare *you mention that Kerouac once tried to screw the earth. That sounds like something that might happen in the excesses of a D. H. Lawrence novel. Was it a literal episode?*

JCH: Yes. It was while he was writing *The Town and The City*. I heard it from him, and read it in his *Journals* of that time. He was trying to write, and he was alone, and horny, and young, and so he thumbed a hole in his backyard, and he fucked the earth. He had lots of Lawrencian feelings anyway.

INT: *We were talking this morning about Jack's humor which has been unappreciated in his work and in his life. Did that exuberance diminish as you got to know him?*

JCH: Seeing the funny side of things comes from a certain distance and an ironical way of looking at life. Jack didn't have this naturally, but he loved good fun. He was terribly amused by his own work sometimes, and as you pointed out when he reads certain things, like some of the poems, he reads them as if they were funny because they were to him. But I wouldn't say that he saw things comedically. He saw things fondly, he loved human folly and silliness, he responded to anything that had a pathetic element in it in a very endearing way.

INT: Like the great flyswatter episode in Visions Of Cody *where Neal, as a child, watches his father and another Bowery wino travel to Nebraska farms selling these ridiculous flyswatters.*

JCH: Well, Jack had a great sense of the absurd.

INT: But isn't that one of the uniquely differentiating qualities about Kerouac as a writer: he is one of the very few who have any warmth left in his sense of humor, as opposed to the way most writers use humor as a devastating social castigation.

JCH: That's why Jack didn't like Lenny Bruce—he couldn't stand anything that appeared to demean human beings. He was a bridge-builder; he felt some wound had occurred in the contemporary soul, and he was trying to suggest how it could be mended. One of the oldest functions of literature, after all.

11

EXILE'S JOURNAL

from the 1960s

John Clellon Holmes

AUTHOR'S NOTE: The journals I kept during the 1960s were primarily work-journals, in which I recorded the day's accretion of new words, sentences (and sometimes whole paragraphs) for the next day, and observations about anything else that seemed worth noting down. None of the fragments I have excerpted here are complete. All of them suggest more than they state about the way I was living then. But together, it is hoped, they may form a kind of lopsided mosaic of that strangely bifurcated decade when American society was in a state of more or less continual upheaval, and Americans themselves were undergoing moral and spiritual changes as profound as any since the 1920s.

For me, the Sixties was a time of self-imposed exile in a drafty, unfinished old house in Connecticut, a time of poverty & the daily scrounge for money, and above all a time of the rigorous work-schedules instituted to get out of an eighteen-month-long drought in my creative life. During those ten years, there were three books—the novel *Get Home Free* (the two sections of which, "Old Man Molineaux" and "Little Orkie," are referred to herein as O.M.M. and L.O.), the essay collection *Nothing More to Declare*, and the travel-memoir *Walking Away from the War*. Also, there was teaching at three universities, and travel around large portions of the United States and Europe.

John Clellon Holmes. Old Saybrook, Connecticut, May 22, 1979. Photograph by Arthur Knight.

The journals from which these extracts were taken numbered over 1,500 pages in length by the time the decade ended, and perhaps more than anything else they mirror the revolution-in-values that characterized the period, and a private list of the casualties—both friends and strangers—who failed to survive that revolution. They may serve, as well, to recall the harder edges of an era whose outlines are already being blurred by the softening mists of nostalgia.

DECEMBER 15, 1960
To write for 2 hours every day, no matter what, to use words *for* something again. And—to pin my life on it.

DECEMBER 29, 1960
In a corner of Connecticut, self-exiled these past years, the fine edge of a quick intelligence dulled, the delicate balance of the nerves upset; a personality, grown reasonably smooth during years

of psychic wear, now roughed up and bent towards ugliness; a reasonably clear, reasonably compassionate eye reddened by idiot-introspection out of all straight focus; a vision that had its small moments of prophetic flair, lacking only, it seems, an essential courage, the bravery to be what I knew I was; but above all capable of hard work, of prevailing over the defeat of my aspirations by the paucity of my equipment so that, on occasion, I did good things by sheer labor—now I sit scribbling in a book, time having slipped from beneath my motionless feet, many talents gone rusty and nerves gone bad, wanting only what I had once, the love of the world that was in me. . . . .

JANUARY 20, 1961
Nearly 2 hrs. in the morning before Inauguration coverage started at 11:00, netting only a trifle more than a page. Shirley was home due to the blizzard, and we ate delectable soup and garlic bread, while watching the ceremonies. And then I had to dig us out—so my work-production remained woefully small. Kennedy's speech strikes me as an eloquent announcement of a new awareness, a new tone, the voice of a fresh generation. I found it graceful and sincere. It was strange to see them riding slowly back to the White House—this strong, rather diffident young man, and this lovely, poised girl, with her remote beauty—both of them the very best this country has to offer—educated, well-bred, handsome, young & vigorous—above all, knowing *who* they are without complication; unafraid to be as intelligent, tasteful and chic as they are, unafraid of appearing brainy and privileged, without either a phony bravado or an equally phony cynicism. I feel *I* have a president for the first time in my lifetime. . . . .

JANUARY 30, 1961
3 good hrs. on O.M.M., close to 3 pages done; break for Kennedy's hard, eloquent, no funny-business State of the Union message via TV . . . Is it possible that JFK could make the loquacious and contentious legislators in Congress act like grown men just by treating them as if they are?

JANUARY 31, 1961
I pick up a copy of *Swank* (Krim's section: Jack, Allen, all the boys), and these are my thoughts. I am not part of that, something shallow and spiteful says I should be; something hungry and

frightened *wants* to be. But my road, my prose, my thought must be my own now. Isn't this one of the lessons of the Great 18 Month Funk? . . . I suddenly realize that I want to vanish so I can work. Well, I am vanished up here, cut off, self-exiled as surely as I would be in Caracas or Butte or Alberta. . . . .

FEB. 3, 1961
We are having Lila & Ray, Charlotte & Bob, for dinner tomorrow and I vowed our exotic soup would cost us no more than 2 dollars. I bought day-old celery (15¢) & beef bones (10¢) at Old Lyme A & P, and stole olive oil & roquefort cheese. Later, we bought boiling beef (53¢), carrots (two huge bunches—29¢), fine pearl barley (17¢), stewing lamb (67¢), a rock-hard turnip (11¢), can of tomato soup (13¢), and a few more items—and I pocketed more olive oil, packet of frozen green beans, garlic salt, devilled ham, and other things. Now, the huge pot is steaming, over three gallons of it, I'd say, enough for tomorrow's dinner, and well into next week. We added onions, potatoes, collard greens, and more things, and the total outlay was $1.95. Such is the ingenuity of poverty, willingly entered into. I also lifted *Reflections in a Golden Eye*. Tomorrow night should cost us considerably under $5.00—two essential social obligations successfully met. If we can do a joint Knollenberg-Stanford evening along the same lines, the decks will be cleared again for us to continue our famous careers as diners-out, with all the attendant savings . . . I feel somehow more honest as an artist-thief than I ever did as a worldly and successful "professional writer". . . . .

FEB. 17, 1961
I should do a piece: Koans on De Sade. All posed questions or enigmatic statements.
—De Sade tied the hands of a serving wench in Marseilles; Robespierre tied the hands of a queen in Paris: it was the mind of Europe, for the next 200 years, that was tied.
—De Sade weeping in Buchenwald because of the saved teeth of Jews.
—De Sade: he did not believe in evil, though he believed in God. Blasphemy as the next-to-last sexual act.
—De Sade saved the last violation for himself, like the last bullet in the pistol when the Indians circle, shrieking, around the wagon train. He ate himself to death. . . . .

MARCH 2, 1961

Up and to work, and two pages fairly easily done, feel good about them, then down to get the car—walking the 2 miles—to be told I couldn't get the key unless I paid cash (we owe them $40 or $50), and they view me with suspicion—that turn-away-of-the-eyes look which signifies that they are talking to a dead-beat—wouldn't even loan me the car so I could get home to get them their lousy eleven bucks. Walked back in a cold fury, knowing why all artists feel themselves outlaws in this society, walked right back down again, paid them in finickily-counted out cash, got a finicky receipt, and left without a word. No angers last long with me anymore—not this kind anyway—but still the work-mood had been broken. . . . .

MARCH 7, 1961

I refuse to quit, to give up, to go down. 35 next weekend, no better off money-wise than I was 10 years ago, aging and tiring, but I *refuse, I refuse!*

MARCH 11, 1961

The violence of the Mailer-wing has taken over; there's hardly a sweet voice left; the blank-face cynicism; the wonder of human life not spoken for; Ferlinghetti, who asked for wonder once, now writes (in *Swank*) a cheap bitter parody of the Lord's Prayer. I want nothing to do with that. One should be able to reject without smirking hate—the hip sneer, as Jack called it years ago.

I am tired—in the bone. I felt the horrible unnatural sensation today—trying to *become* Old Man Molineaux in his mysterious last passion, in his silence, in his abdication. My guts revolted against the willed loss of Self. This is the starkest experience in writing— the bad part, the dangerous part, always the danger of straining something essential more than it can stand.

MARCH 18, 1961

(Apropos Neant: The Last Value—for isn't it rather a search for this last value, rather than a mere debauching of the old ones? . . . Rimbaud burned himself up; I see this happening to many of the feverish young men of my generation—burned-out in their 30s, their nerves overloaded, the mind gone dull, desires having con- sumed all conceivable objects, saying: "I was a bohemian, I was a Red, I was an American chauvinist, I was a hard-bitten professional, I was a Fitzgeraldian drinker in chic places, I was mildly Catholic, I was sex-incensed, I was a Zen idiot, I was beat & beautiful, I was a sad young man, and then prematurely old, all these things together—and I'm the same now—" What else can you say? List the wobbly gods? Joyce, Marx, Kierkegaard, Li Po, Melville, Blake, Lawrence, Dostoyevski, Brecht, Weill, Bird, Picasso, Lester, El Greco, Bach, Yeats, Nietzsche, Spengler, Burkhardt, Auden, Sade—on and on. What do they describe? . . .) Orgasm is the new revolution; this year's religion; this day's Holy Mystery & source of health. I'll go along, but is there something in us that will empty even that? Mustn't we come to humility? Sometimes I know only Gandhi holds out hope for our insatiate lust for certainty. . . . .

MARCH 28, 1961
Finished O.M.M. in 1st rough; tooth aching me for real; slept a little, got up to bourbs & letters, and here I am . . . Won't, as of now, even type up O.M.M., but plunge straight into L.O. Drear, yet warmish March day. River soft milky grey; festoons of hesitant cloud. . . . .

APRIL 6, 1961
Total self-belief—the Work as Secret—the Work as Hobby almost— why must we go through these contortions in America? What is to desire? That each moment be bearable & fecund in *itself.* That our eyes find reality pleasing or interesting. That we become, at times, intoxicated with the keen edge of reality, its waning & its rising notes. That girl's face, that look of attention and excitement barely banked; that hillside suddenly graphic in its lengthening shadows; this melody with its inexpressible perfection of something we did not know we knew until we heard it expressed; the taste of oil, vinegar and roquefort some hours later—that tart-tangy taste that lingers; this moment of strong and tender love for all life that comes on top of the meal, the act of sex, the unaccountable turning of the Cove Road some June morning, the friend's face in all its thwarted gnaw on life—all this, suddenly seen in a complete flash of prescience; this is the preoccupation of sane men.

APRIL 20, 1961
Are we preparing to intervene in Cuba? The day is sunny, April-warm, cloudless—as it so often is when all the news is bad.

APRIL 21, 1961

Mailer's particularly true vision of our age: "Authority & nihilism stalking one another in the orgiastic hollow of this time." The deeper I read *into* his work, and back through it, the more I see & hear. I see where it is going, where it has been always going. Mark it down (as I wrote him on an impulse yesterday): if he can last, he will be a very important writer in this century.

APRIL 25, 1961

Depressed: the world seems particularly grim, the steel filings of several weeks gather to the magnet of my mood. Our crying miscalculation in Cuba—everything but sending the Marines, all done with "ugly American" carelessness and authoritarian superiority—outmaneuvered over Laos—Gargarin spouts dreary Communist cliches upon returning from man's last legitimate adventure—that moment for the human race despoiled by the gutter thinking and pork-chop language of our ghastly politics. . . . .

APRIL 28, 1961

Read Sartre on Cuba, just out. His relatively clear view of Castro and the special character of the Cuban revolution blurs the moment he turns to the U.S. . . . Certainly, I feel that we do not see Cuba clearly, and I deplore our bungling with the anti-Castro invasion. The premise "Castro must go" has idiotically come to dominate all our thinking about Cuba, just as "anti-commnism" has blurred our foreign policy for years, and is the deepest cause of all our failures in Africa & Asia. Certainly, I no longer trust our newspapers when it comes to Cuba—the myopia is endemic—but nevertheless Castro lost me when he started killing people, suspending due process, instituting drumhead courts, and all the rest. "The riders have changed places, but the lash goes on." Can't Sartre ask himself *why* it is that the American revolution is the one revolution of modern times that has *worked*?

MAY 5, 1961

We send a man through space today: I watched it with alarm and concern on TV as it happened. Perfect shot, I gather, all to the good.

MAY 23, 1961

Morning's work for 2 pgs. plus. Apple trees are delicate with Oriental lightness, that fragile white a crude breath withers; smell of mown grass, and freshened air, and early flowers. Want work & health & interests.

Birmingham & Montgomery shame all those who care. Vague flickers of guilt—a feeling of uselessness—of the Real being elsewhere—all this on the edges of my consciousness these days. The pure, open, intent faces of the young; the world has yet to sully them out of their resolve. I might not be capable of their noble abstinence from all violence, and I *do* hate the white riffraff who are doing this—A girl wept hysterically as the rioting went on on Saturday night. Violence is a terrible assault on sanity—this, perhaps the most ghastly thing it does.

"For who can know the despair of being a Southerner, the shame that must find disinterest or cynicism as a mask. . . . etc., etc.—" [First line of a later section of L.O—JCH]

JULY 6, 1961
. . . . And Hemingway is buried today, incoherently with the auspices of the Catholic Church. I never was anymore close to him than 1000s of writers for whom his influence was contagious and irritating, but I learned to temper this with real admiration for his seriousness about the craft, and his real accomplishments, and I'm sorry and shocked that my reality should be suddenly emptied of this elusive & maddening old mandarin. His sense of style (which is stance, consistency of stance) did not fail him. For him, and his maimed values, he died in perspective.

JULY 25, 1961
Reading stray Hemingway short stories. His contagious style has its appeal precisely because it is not a realistic rendering, it is without real verisimilitude, it is an *idealization*. What he has is a perfectly lucid tone, which rarely fails him, but which is extremely narrow—like a one-eyed man's vision, clear but distorted . . . Why do I also feel an almost constant emotional insincerity in this man? All his true feelings never get on the page. In almost every corner of his life some fear lurked, and fear (of himself, his possible cowardice, women, sentiment, what have you) was his goad and spur. Perhaps this is why his range of material is so shockingly limited, his notes so few, his tone so rigorously thin & controlled, his style at once so pure and so thwarted.

JULY 31, 1961
Negroes & whites—how obsessed we all are by this in our time . . .
Guilt? I honestly don't think so. I feel (nor have I ever felt) no guilt
about this problem. Attraction—as if I could lose some hateful habit
of mind—is closer to it. No Southerner can probably ever under-
stand this. And no negro anymore. But to be a washed-up white
man of the bankrupt Middle Class in twilight America is a psychic
experience no negro or Southerner ever feels in quite the same way.
To long for joy, freedom, energy, vigor, song. To want the air to be
vivid again. . . . .

AUGUST 1, 1961
Worked the morning, despite growing depression over the months
ahead, and the frustration over Berlin that is shaping with dire
speed. . . . .
   Curious nightmare: S. and I were making love, though she did
not know me well. I had been horribly burned with acid, my whole
face was gone, badly healed raw meat, something monstrous no
matter the love with which I was viewed. I wore a black sack-like
mask, like an executioner's mask that covered my head & shoul-
ders. Only my eyes & mouth showed through holes. I got up & took
off everything but this, and lay down with passion again, aware, in
horror & anxiety, that she or I might forgetfully tear my mask off in
the throes of nakedness. I anticipated her reaction—it was as if she
did not know I was mutilated, or, even if she did, had never seen it.
Also, I was aware of my own horrified anxiety at the idea of seeing
her reaction, as if I, too, was afraid to see in her eyes what I looked
like.

AUGUST 20, 1961
My New England mythos—the Old Grafton cycle—ever more the
horrors of exacerbated Northern sex obsession & inhibition. The
"charged" verbs of Emily Dickinson. The dark violence in the hay-
barns of remote up country farms. Of Lizzie B. certainly. The
petulant mouth, those cold impenetrable eyes. Sex-obsession is
Northern—Strindberg, Bergman, Munch. Germanic pagan orgies,
Hawthorne-hints. The aim: immorality. Not mere pleasure. Tran-
scendance-by-sin. . . . The sensuality of intelligence.

AUGUST 23, 1961
Put in 3–4 hours, broken here & there, and accrued 2 pages-plus of

the difficult dyke-scene, and the end of the chapter. Have only the last chapter left in this May-tale now. . . . I'm reading *Lady Chatterley* for the umpteenth time, and disagree with almost everyone—it's so clear, so weary, so pure, so good . . . How refreshing to hear Lawrence say "Fuck"; suddenly he becomes less maniacally intense, exacerbated, word-drunk, obscure & overbearing . . . I think of him saying "Fuck" to Frieda, and some of the overblown mystery evaporates. . . . .

SEPT. 1, 1961
The Soviets explode a "nuclear device" right on the heels of their end of cessation-to-testing, and the atmosphere in the world fouls . . . I feel that someone sneezing too near the border in Berlin may precepitate Armageddon. We're all that touchy now. The Knollies are building a fallout shelter—the first of our acquaintances to do so. I think it was yesterday's news that did it. Everyone has their own breaking point.

SEPT. 2, 1961
Desk cleared now, except for Orkie—notebooks & this journal. All extraneous notes & reminders & maps put away at last after almost 5 months of work. And next week I type up O.M.M., having never seen it in type, having never exposed it to Shirley. Now it's been 8 months since I wrote the first words, and not a living soul has seen it.

SEPT. 9, 1961
Typed to within 10 pgs. of end. Some months-old worry, some months-old tension, suddenly snapped—I'm shaky & scared, all my nerves vibrating—I think O.M.. is *good!*

Khrushchev is acting like a man with a terrible secret he is about to spring. These are *final* moves. I can't believe it.

SEPT. 19, 1961
Shirley has read my two tales with satisfactory-enough results. Likes O.M.M. Has serious reservations about L.O. . . . People are butchering each other, all color-lines at last wiped out, in Katanga. Should the idiot-hatreds of Congo, Laos, Tunisia, and all the other boils on the ass of the globe be allowed to lead to nuclear war?

OCT. 4, 1961
Yesterday ended my career as a petty thief. I was caught in Universal with a can of devilled ham, a can of tuna fish, and a ¼ lb. of cheese . . . I was booked, finger-printed, and released on $50 bail. The item, headed "What, no bread?," was in the *Hartford Courant* this morning.

Nov. 6, 1961
"It requires moral courage to grieve; it requires religious courage to rejoice." Kierkegaard. *(Journals)*

JAN. 22, 1962
The *New Yorker* turns down O.M.M. with a funny line about not wanting to publish anything that long about "an old man". . . . Age-old chickens are scurrying relentlessly home to roost: the "new negro," scornful of everything, resolutely proud of being black, and motivated now by a cold, unreasoning hatred of the whites that he can voice at last out loud. The whole world comes more and more to resemble the nightmare politics of the Congo. Everything points to a debacle. The huge, inhuman mechanism of *African Genesis* seems to me (now that I'm into it) only a further indication of the helplessness that is at the bottom of the human will these days.

MARCH 8, 1962
More & more the sexual experience comes to replace the elevated feeling-states of James in our time. I see an entire book in which the complexity of the sexual experience would be used, to the exclusion of everything else, as the symbolic material through which a relationship is illuminated.

MARCH 20, 1962
(just back from NYC) The eyes of the actors in *The Blacks* like so many blow-torches of hate & recrimination burning out at us. The knowledge that Genet has an absolutely free & fearless mind—ugly & true & very French. Lines that bad acting could not obscure . . . The wallpaper of the Albert. Maureen O'Hara on TV—St. Patrick's Day Parade in Julius' for hamburgers & beer. Shirley bought an egg cup in a Jap store outside of which vicious Great Danes took lordly 13th Century pisses on the leashes of long-haired, dark-glassed

Fruits . . . Good scallops in Paris-Brest . . . *Brecht on Brecht* and the surprising lines of sculpted beauty in the face of Viveca Lindfors; George Voskovec and Lotte Lenya knowing everything about Brecht & unafraid; Dane Clark exhausted by America and success. . . . J. weeping quietly at "The German Mother." Chumley's discovered by radar behind its speakeasy door—awash with people, steins of beer, choking smoke, the pointless gaiety of Saturday. Brad Cunningham and his work there. High through the empty streets of the Village . . . Eggs Benedict & bourbon sours, nerves strung high now, J. drunk, *In the Jungle of Cities*: every blessed violation scarring me—unable by then to stop relating to everything around me. Loving what was doing me in. Back to the Albert & nembies. On & on. Conflict of interests. Only what is far-out is interesting anymore. Sex has become an eidolon for all of us, made to carry the burden of these empty times—no mistake—and I'm "stranger" to Shirley, so she says, when we make it. I'm a stranger to myself, going the way the flesh and mind have to go these days. I go into NY to be refueled by the austerity of spirit which never burns so clearly as in the ruins of everything else. . . . New York is now as true and essential and emphatic as Berlin was decades ago. . . . J. a good sport in her black dress & huge empty room without an ashtray. Shirley touching my head in the night of nerves the nembies soon drowned. Young people everywhere, everyone younger than me now. No make-up, duffle coats, pouf hair-dos, & black stockings. Hip children talking with beautiful earnestness about Burroughs. Gabby car-drivers with that NY sense of seige about them. The next move lies in the naked sexual arena, the only territory left. . . . .

JUNE 9, 1962
Sigrid's satiric remark on Eichmann's execution: "Well, at last we're *even*!". . . . The "incurableness" of certain words, as Arthur Adamov says. Words emptied of meaning because they refer to attitudes & emotions from a World of Meanings that has been pulverized.

JULY 6, 1962
Faulkner dead. The end of the oldest American literary theme: the land. Our literature will be urban, international, existentialist from now on, and this protean imagination—perhaps the most inex-haustible imagination of this century—has given us its last as-

tonishing images. A year and a week or so since Hemingway shot himself. . . . He was at home in Oxford, and his heart gave out, and I'm sure he died in bed . . . You felt he wasted nothing; he did his work.

AUGUST 9, 1962
Roethke's line: "I long for the impossible quiet at the heart of form." Handel's World. The symmetries of Bach, in which imbalances are denied. The world ordered to one's fondest, weariest wish.

SEPT. 23, 1962
Poetry: W. C. Williams is most free of the tyranny of the iambic. Pound's mind still moves iambically, he has to keep reminding himself or he slips back into that rhythm. Whitman was free of that, but got stuck on the meter of bardic song. Williams is most free, his ear is the most attuned to "antipoetry," he and Lawrence . . . An anti-rhetorical eye. Scour it down to the hard bones.

OCT. 1, 1962
Genet's "Thief Journal": the raison d'etre of crime as individuation . . . Have we reached a point where the only protest against the lock-step meaninglessness of our time must be lodged in our own flesh?

OCT. 24, 1962
Worked yesterday in the morning, fighting off panics about Cuba, blockade, troops massing, red alerts, and what have you, but couldn't continue in the afternoon. . . . .

OCT. 26, 1962
An assault of orgones against the madness in the Caribbean: black, crotchless garter-belt . . . slow building talk with IPAs . . . first stage carrying us near the pinnacle . . . lapse to have drinks with Burlands . . . then all building again to hours-long fantasies downstairs . . . the same yesterday morning, came down to sheer relieving of sexual energy in tandem, hands & mouths, mirrors and mirroring words . . . until our "Cuban nerves" had, indeed, been quieted, and my dismal panic-on-the-beach of that afternoon (from which I came home palpably shaken & out of control) had passed in a flood of imagery, a storm of sensations . . . all circuits leading to insatiablity, become objects for each other, for the acting out of all

private fantasies . . . The feeling that we had indeed lit a small blaze in the gathering darkness, and now, this morning, some easing of tensions seems to have actually occurred in the world.

Oct. 27, 1962
Hope flares for a moment in the morning at Khrushchev's offer to "trade" bases. Oysters & champagne. Now we have turned down the offer out of hand.

Nov. 11, 1962
Dreamt all night of the girl, Sudie, an indentured servant, stolen out of a frontier jumping-off place (Independence?) in the 1830s, by three drunken mountain men . . . etc., etc.

Dec. 18, 1962
The typing will be done tomorrow morning, and we'll mail the book off in the afternoon. I am of course unsatisfied with a lot of the madcap, 4-day re-write of *The End,* which totals out to something over 53 pages, almost half of which is new stuff, done in that incredible push of last week . . . So—a new regimen, a new year.

Feb. 26, 1963
Evening (till 5-ish) with J. on Sat. Alcohol, music, dancing, straight talk, etc. She stayed over, and the three of us had breakfast, wine and TV in bed on Sunday. The possibility of "a trois"? S. seemed hungoverly willing enough . . . J.? Who can really tell?

In effect, we have talked about everything else, and when, after all, two women lie next to one another in nothing but loose kimonas, and a man lies with them in his shorts, and they talk about the most detailed intimacies, more than mere good fellowship, propinquity, and the spirit of candor, is involved. Or am I being incredibly conventional?

May 6, 1963
Allen G.: sound of a whole man. Warring to the limits of consciousness. He knows more about the spiritual dilemmas of our time—which becomes the crisis of Western Civilization, in deadwall impact with the death of Ideas, swooning back on Undifferentiated Reality—than anyone I know about.

MAY 22, 1963
I cook my brains every day, and eat them every night. I look at the wiser men of my generation—I hear Mailer's coil-spring brain tightening from here. Jack's world grows dimmer & more liquid, towards puttering days and ashen nights. Allen's mendicant eyes will finally have looked on all the dung-heaps. Gregory will pin-wheel too far and simply go into orbit over Athens. Burroughs lumbers like a shadow towards dingier and remoter districts of the huge, unfeeling metropolis of the world. Nelson files his teeth, waiting for the mad, single-minded dogs at the end of the bitter alley. . . . All this occasioned by S. & J. ganging up on me last night.

JUNE 2, 1963
"Revolution Below the Belt" finally clipped & added to & gotten ready for S.'s typing tomorrow . . . Was out walking by 6:45, went all the way to the Town Beach, ugly beach houses, out from the driveways of which huge, new cars backed, full of people off to early Mass, presumably to pray for the dying Pope John.

JUNE 10, 1963
Algren here these past two days . . . There is something spectral about him, severed, cut off—sometimes you'll look up & he has simply vanished. He is as quiet as a lean cat, padding softly up & down the stairs, locking himself into the bathroom, asking for nothing. . . .

JUNE 12, 1963
. . . In Mississippi, the silly thinking results in the back-of-the-back shooting of an NAACP official. The vengeful little-boy-pretending-to-be-heap-big-Forest-Cavalry-Officer-mentality of the Southern trashy-demagogue-unreconciled-to-the-20th-Century PUNK is beginning to seem ever more a luxury that the rest of us can ill afford . . . The South has agitated our national life long enuf. And the Miss. senators blame it on the "liberals," just as if 1860–65 never happened: "You drove us to it, you agitators. You *know* we're stupid, why do you provoke us?"

JUNE 15, 1963
The novel will probably be published by Dutton—hallelujah! I expect nothing in either sales or reviews. But the two years were

not, after all, a total loss, the work will be in print, out there, awakening possibilities. . . . .

JUNE 17, 1963
Talk the other night . . . Finally just came out with it . . . yes, she knew what we meant; yes, she was interested, yes, she, like S., was "curious" . . . Who knows what the reality would arouse in any of us? . . . . .

JUNE 25, 1963
Letter from Vance (Bourjaily) with offer to go to Iowa this coming year; this time I'm sorely tempted . . . we might just save enough to make Europe the autumn after this one for a more leisurely stretch. . . . .

JULY 1, 1963
One of those days when the long hidden smiles of the gods all break thru at the same time. After a muggy three mile walk, the mail brought the novel-contracts, a positive sign that the film-*Horn* contracts will be coming through before too long, and the possibility that *Esquire* would like an expansion of the W. C. Fields section of my movie-chapter. . . . .

JULY 11, 1963
Tuesday night: talk, talk, talk, perhaps heightened by the fact that Vance called from Iowa, wanting a decision, and I said "yes." All of a sudden the moment was there, we were all a little drunk . . . I simply said: "We can't make it any clearer,". . . . Into the bed: everything quite easy & natural. . . .

JULY 16, 1963
Matinee here. . . . Does it all sound cold, licentious, satiate? It isn't really; rather playful, funny, interesting, now & then rousing—the warm upshot: bodies are bodies; only minds vary.

AUGUST 6, 1963
Pendulum swing from the repeated violation of personal integrity. . . . the body's life is, as Artaud describes it, vaguely reptilian, flawed, horrific . . . some temples must not be profaned. . . . quiet, quiet, and in a month . . . Chekhov in broad daylight . . . the day the aphids paid us back . . . ants carry the world away.

Aug. 15, 1963
The revisions in effect done; the book, with luck, finally *done*. Years of it. . . . .

Sept. 16, 1963
Iowa. Our hilltop in working order, ready to go. Cicadas buzz in the twilight, an occasional car whirrs down the obsolete highway to West Branch . . . Shirley coos to a wild kitten that has ventured out of the ramshackle wood behind the house . . . Thelonious makes his arduous explorations on "More Than You Know". . . . .

Sept. 23, 1963
Class in Workshop just now. I'm never much good until I know *who* I'm talking to. I plunged in too much . . . using my current slanting approach to touch the point, but not freeze it. . . . .

Sept. 25, 1963
Introduction meeting of entire Liberal Arts new-faculty. Feeling a hairy beast indeed among all the Masters & Doctors. . . .

Oct. 17, 1963
Just back from our tracking of the Mississippi up into Minnesota . . . thru the old working river-towns, like Bellevue, where fish are in the streets, and the old buildings have wrought-iron filigreed balconies; farther up, in drizzle & mist, to the "lost" German villages—Lunenberg . . . Guttenberg . . . McGregor . . . Marquette. . . .

Nov. 21, 1963
They prophesy snow for tonight; I go about securing the storm-windows; I find a six-inch thirst-maddened rat in the cellar, recently dead under a stiff burlap sack. I consign his corpse to the woods (little fore-paws drawn up under his chin like an alarmed biddy) where snow will bier him later on. . . .

Nov. 25, 1963
The death of the President, and everything that followed it, has made the weekend a nightmare. I was at the oculist's, unarmed, when the initial announcement of the shooting came over a TV set there . . . We went to the Workshop where I had a conference . . . called off the conference, and we sat, stunned, unable to get our

minds to grasp the fact . . . S. and I went out into the rain & started home, but then decided to go have a drink. Kenney's was empty, somber, TV-less. We drank and played the jukebox. I tried to pass the knowledge down into me. . . . the arrest of Oswald, the return of the body, the lying-in-state, the eulogies of yesterday . . . occuring at almost the same time that Oswald, himself, was being attacked and murdered in Dallas. There is something huge & terrible in the air: a feeling of subterranean forces deep down in the national psyche stirring up, breaking thru, in all of us, assuagelessly, dangerously, immensely. . . . America's truly tragic nature, with all its ambiguities, seems to urge itself up *into* events. . . . for here politics are metaphysical, cathartic, purging, disturbing, Athenian. We have gobbled up the best we had to offer; we have turned in despair from the immense change in national style & mood he tried to institute; and no one knows whether the change has *taken* in us. *(Later):* Perhaps his greatest contribution (other than piloting us thru the Cuban crisis, & creating the Peace Corps) was his reinvigoration of our national life on all levels. . . . His relish for risks, his eagerness for times of choice, his courage in situations of anxiety, his self-deprecating and graceful wit; his tact and sense of historical propriety (I think of his presidential statements when Faulkner & Frost died; the state dinners for artists & writers): all of this plus his unfailing poise, the occasional glimpses of his delight in public life—this is what we will miss now. Who can say what this shock will stir up in us? Such events sometimes rouse us, mysteriously, to *become* what we truly are. Meanwhile the last ceremonial acts proceed. . . .

JAN. 11, 1964
Never seem to have time these days—work—another heart panic after a 21 hr. day of teaching, making up MFA exams, dexies and what have you. . . . I've been formally asked back for next year, and privately decided I won't come . . . I've still fish to fry out there in the world, and don't fancy a backwater just yet. . . . .

FEB. 11, 1964
Down in my office, waiting on a tune-up of the car, and NOT SMOKING now these 18 days or so! . . . I walked 3–4 miles this morning—over stubbly fields lightly glazed with frost . . . smelling things mostly, horse-dung, the loam itself loosening in the sun, the *odor of frost.* . . . .

MARCH 14, 1964
Copies of *Get Home Free* arrived today, and I am pleased for the most part . . . In the last week or so, I have missed our house, and New England generally, with an odd keenness. A return of self? Consciousness of self? Next week: the Black Hills. . . . .

JULY 13, 1964 *(Old Saybrook)*
Repub Convention convenes to nominate Goldwater at 1:00. Sorry spectacle of the amateurs-of-history jerking at the reins. . . . The habit of journalizing seems to have left me—at least for now. Won't force.

JULY 23, 1964
The cauldron in NY still bubbles ominously, threatening to erupt into worse rioting: The negro demand now is no longer racial equality, Freedom, 1st class citizenship: it is for nothing less than a revolution in society's treatment of the human person; in this sense they are making an effort to transform America for ALL OF US. . . . Six months crisis in non-smoking. . . .

AUG. 7, 1964
Smoking again, which somehow I register as a failure only on certain fronts. Seven months of a strange absence from myself, subject to a continual, nagging, trivial anxiety, my radarscope of psychic possibilities relentlessly narrowing until I was, in fact, some sort of nervous invalid who could exist quite easily in a cork-lined personality, but who developed all sorts of inner tics & anxieties whenever he ventured out, or the world poked its insolent finger in.

AUG. 8, 1964
Hemingway: his peculiar vision of life became so intensely *ours* that we judged him by his failures of fidelity to it (re-reading *Across the River*).

AUG. 12, 1964
My creative method these years: accretion. I get a node, a happening, more often a setting—and slowly, painstakingly, further things accrete around it.

AUG. 15, 1964
Sleep dominated by the Bonnie Parker/Clyde Barrow saga (sourced in *The Dillinger Days*), first imagined as a raw-grained Kubrick-film—the Kubrick of *The Killing*—and then become a tough, gothic novel of eroticism and viciousness along the lines of *Sanctuary*— *Cast Out The Outcast*. . . . .

SEPT. 11, 1964
Nova Scotia for 10 days. . . . .

OCT. 8, 1964
Ruins: suicide is knowing, without a doubt, what comes next. . . . "He was the sort who would hesitate over his suicide-note, polishing the prose."

OCT. 15, 1964
Reading all the sections of the Warren Report having to do with the life & character of Oswald I have come to some inkling at last as to the psychic process which led him to his "absurd" act. . . . etc., etc., etc.

OCT. 22, 1964
Oswald typed up and sent off to Sterling. . . . Sartre wins the Nobel Prize (overdue in my opinion) and immediately (and perversely, it seems to me) plans to turn it down . . . When it is awarded to worthy people, to uncompromising people, the good sense & taste of the Committee should be encouraged. . . . Refusing is rather school-boyish. He *won* it, after all. . . .

Nov. 4, 1964
(Day after election) Johnson, speaking at 3:00 AM, looking like a dead man, eyes puffy & undeviating, cheeks sagging in a daze . . . Actually, I imagine he is a hungry cat, vain, sensual, intelligent, patient with the shifts & lunges of power, interested in motives more than convictions, something incalculably *feminine* in his nature (I find this is so in many Southern men). . . . .

FEB. 13, 1965
Playboy takes the Oswald piece—olé! $2,000 for 14 pages that took me only 2–3 days to do. I typed up the last words of the 50s (from *Nothing More to Declare*) this morning, and then cleaned my room

from top to bottom in preparation for a new beginning on Monday. . . . .

MARCH 17, 1965
Seymour Krim calls, giving me a chance at a $20,000-a-year, senior editor job on the "new" *Show.* Won't take it of course. That rat-race is not for me. Working with *writers!* Ugh!

JULY 29, 1965
Bad night—writing, writing—the mind would not stop. Bad start this morning, after a feeling that we may be in for another wave of McCarthyism, as the true-blue patriots come out again to flock to Lyndon's standard. For the first time since Korea, I find myself in total opposition to a significant policy-move by the U.S.—not just a minor crisis, a garden-variety blunder, a myopic miscalculation. I am against *every* detail of our newly escalated venture in Viet Nam . . . in six short months the work of two decades has been undone. . . . .

OCT. 1, 1965
The last (of *Nothing More to Declare*) is proofed, and leaves me with a feeling that I "have done with it." Now I go to package it up (382 pgs. of it), and mail it off, and make the 1:00 ferry to Long Island . . . A big gruff autumnal wind rubs an ailanthus branch restlessly against my window frame. And we go towards black water & wet decks & the remote beaches. It's good.

JAN. 16, 1966
And now, meanwhile, and all in a week, we're off to Arkansas. In all the flurries of activity, one has less time to curse Viking, and wonder (about the book). . . . .

JUNE 21, 1966
(Saybrook again) The idea of simply *not* going to Europe now, of taking what money we have (on hand & coming in) and simply staying holed up here. . . . .

JULY 30, 1966
Dire, unwanted feelings today about the state of things. . . . Hate appears everywhere (one choked to see Martin Luther King on TV pleading with negroes to forget "black power," pleading with

whites to remain in the movement, and something in his face revealed the suspicion that non-violence, and the chance it holds out to save America's soul, was relentlessly being abandoned by everyone). . . . Not a little of this, in my opinion, attributable to the worsening Vietnam debacle. It is doing incalculable damage to us here at home. One finds oneself seriously wondering if Johnson is not perhaps going through a slow flip. . . . And I sometimes feel that the only redress we have lies in the streets. An uncomfortable feeling for a modern American. . . . .

SEPT. 16, 1966
Just back from NYC where the book was copy-edited and we saw Allen G. for a late-nite, early-morning visit in darkest East Village. . . . He read us new poems . . . and finally *Wichita Vortex Sutra,* a work that stands with *Howl* and *Kaddish* as a gigantic pier on which his whole accomplishment will rest. . . . finest work on the Vietnam War, a vast diastole of sanity & clarity which might actually bring the world to its senses, if anything still could. We walked through the rain, talking about [young people], what could be done to bring them awake, and Allen said sadly: "But how did *we* know all that almost 20 years ago? Love, touch, the spirit?—it's strange. . . ."

MAY 9, 1967
We're intent on living on no more than $60 a week, which the *Playboy* money will more than account for from now until Sept. 1, so that everything else goes into the Europe stash. If we can amass $1500, I'll borrow a like amount on my still-pending Bowling Green contract, and we'll be off.

JUNE 5, 1967
War in the Middle East . . . Old chickens, old roosts . . . The spring, the sun, the year is soiled, and I can feel little except a private, unpolitical, and ultimately useless anger, and a growing disillusion with the long-range chances—short, of course, of some terrible violence, some sobering mistake, that will shake us all awake.

JULY 25, 1967
Large sections of Detroit in ruins. Violence, burning, looting & sniping in Pontiac, Flint, Rochester, New York, Englewood, Tucson. Insurrection spreads like poison, and all of August yet

ahead. . . . Yoked photographs of bombed-out civilians in Vietnam, and burned-out civilians in Detroit—with American bayonets at the ready on the edges of both pictures—create an indelible image of Imperial America . . . There are those of us here who are sickened. My America is breaking my heart.

[On September 1, 1967, we left for Europe, and stayed away four months—a trip covered in my book, *Walking Away from the War;* see *Collected Non-Fiction,* Vol. One, Univ. of Ark. Press, 1987.— JCH.]

JAN. 28, 1968
Irony: in an exploding world of sexual permissiveness, in the mood of which I have had some little influence, or, at the very least, in which I have been intensely involved for 20 years, I sit here, at dawn, no wife in my bed, nearing 42, utterly frustrated in my flesh and in my imagination, incapable and unwilling to make the sort of extra-marital compromises which got me through my years with [my first wife] . . . Four nights of reading Lawrence (so to the point) result in—*nada.* And I can't even lay hands on myself this bitter dawn.

FEB. 12, 1968—*Bowling Green, Ohio*
First meeting of the seminar over . . . We've been here a week today; in this antiseptic, comfortable apt. since Tues. Small sense of the quality of our life here yet.

MARCH 1, 1968
Letter with "news" of Neal's death from exposure. I've missed him intensely, now & again, in the 15 years since I saw him last: there were moments when no one but Neal would do, and thank God I knew him before he became a legend by which other people proved their "in-ness" . . . Terrible that a man should be thought of as an archetype—Neal's secret contempt for us literary types, including Jack, was that we too often tended to respond to his unique but not-mythic energy & point of view in these terms—but he was a con man; that is, he conned for the best in life, he was not above conning joy, continuance, surcease, and I never saw anything contemptible in that. . . . His consciousness was part of my understanding of my world, and I learned from him (by trying to create him as a character) so many of the things that *didn't, couldn't*

matter. Like the spuriousness of certain styles of grief. Allen will suffer. Jack? Somewhere, below all his current eschewals, Jack will mourn too.

MARCH 7, 1968
Premonition: a decisive swing of power into Asia in the next 20 yrs.; China to become the most important power nucleus in the world; in 1984 one out of every three persons in the world will be Chinese.

MARCH 18, 1968
Bobby Kennedy declares . . . The *issue* is out in the open. . . . .

APRIL 1, 1968
Johnson takes himself out of the race last night, urging "unity" and the "sanctity" of the Presidency. . . . some hint of his personal perception in it—a last chance to get history's good reviews. I do him, I suppose, a disservice . . . His withdrawal from the race adds up to only one thing: he is modifying, and will not personally defend, the policy of the last 3 years. . . . .

APRIL 13, 1968: *(after week in Chicago)*
What to say about King and the disorders following his murder? I took it deeply hard, for my own special reasons. He always ennobled me in his very spirit . . . Dire, habitual thoughts about mad-dog America . . . Urge to apologize to every black on the street. . . . .

JUNE 7, 1968 *(Old Saybrook again)*
Bad two days. Bobby Kennedy shot on Wed. JBB phoned in afternoon, needing the liner notes for his record album, which I'd agreed to do over the phone the last day in Bowling Green. Somehow got down to work. . . . Every once in a while, during the work-haze, a keen pang of real loss came over me, a kind of revulsion against all fatality, a feeling that the people that deeply capture my imagination & allegiance (as a political man) are luckless. I see no talent commensurate to the Kennedys on the horizon. I wasn't sure that Bobby was going to come even close to making it this year, but he was so definitely in all our futures, with all his promise, with that look of brave sadness, the tough fatalistic aura of the luckless younger brother, that I can't get used to the idea that we'll miss all

that those eyes promised. He was not a prince like J.F.K., fortunate, handsome, skilled, quick. He was involuted, more deeply Irish in his hurt, tough soul—serious, even shy, stubborn, brave, reliable, a touch of the puritan in him, and the poet too, but luckless, luckless, a foot soldier. I said to myself in 1964 (after his speech at Atlantic City) that I'd vote for him almost any time he ran. Now that's lost too. We were the same age.

AUG. 1, 1968
A strong premonition that I have gone as far and as deep as I can along the existential road I've been travelling these last years—experiencing my own being, or self, in extreme subjectivities—of sex, of booze, of consciousness expansion. I have come to a dry place, a place of ruins—madness or despair on either side . . . I find myself unarmed before death, no longer brave or self-reliant, and, worst of all, growing ever less capable of loving life for itself. . . . I must get *"outward"* again, see coherence, eschew empty "depths," rebuild resources with which to persevere. God? Some kernel of transcendent faith? I don't know. . . . This strong certainty on this humid, airless August evening.

AUG. 2, 1968
Just back from three good days in Peconic & Greenport. Our welcome-home: the Russians have invaded Czechoslovakia. End of whatever slim hopes there may have been for a Peace plank, a Peace candidate, emerging from the Demo. Conven.

AUG. 28, 1968
The Democrats go down the Administration line on Vietnam, insuring Humphrey's nomination, and Nixon's election. A future abrogated.

JULY 21, 1969
We land on the moon, and, just now, redock with the command ship again. . . . The debate as to the worthwhileness of the project has always seemed to me myopic & silly. . . . Gloria Steinem & Kurt Vonnegut on CBS belittled the flight, carped, were scornfully anti-establishment, embarassing in their bitter lack of insight . . . For myself, I have always believed that the attempt at the moon was inevitable. The idea of liquidating a project that is life-enhancing to cope with life-polluting situations here on earth has never seemed

to me to be sound thinking when there are so many anti-life problems around that should be liquidated first. The enemy of the minorities, the young, and the poor is *Vietnam,* the military, the venality of business—but not space, not the moon.

SEPT. 3, 1969
A decision taken in the rain on my back yard just now. I'll do [finish] *Walking Away from the War* now, no matter whether Dutton will put up money, or *Playboy* takes the Paris section . . . I must turn my creative intelligence to the making [in the four remaining pieces] of a *book.*

OCT. 21, 1969
Jack is dead. I was reading about him in an old journal when S. called out from downstairs, having heard it on the radio. There were the bad, pointless moments waiting for the repeat of the newscast, there were the waves of awareness. . . . etcetera, etcetera, etcetera. . . . .

OCT. 31, 1969
A feeling of *lightness* in me today, of an opening ahead, of my own powers. . . . The result, I suppose, of the catharsis of the last 10 days: the sorrow and horror of the news of Jack's death, which I repressed until I could be alone once we came back from Lowell, my little solitary "toot" the night we did, but above all the catharsis of the incredible siege of work that made the next five days a blur. The stuff poured out—1000s of words, but, more purging, all the emotions. I actually typed away, weeping on the keys of the machine. And the very exhaustiveness of the account, the probing to the depths of what I was feeling, mended me. I wrote out of a kind of need I haven't felt for a long time, rapidly, almost thoughtlessly, prodding my sagging imagination with booze now & then, selfless as a lunatic. At one point, Tuesday, I collapsed and couldn't go on . . . Wednesday was a Sahara . . . But yesterday I rose at 4:30, did 1000 words, walked in the chilly dawn, took S. to work, and did another 1800 to finish. But mainly, something has lifted off me at the moment. Has Jack bequeathed me one more lesson, one more gift? The account, the vast "journal entry," counts out to be something around 16,000 to 20,000 words. Moments of emotional clarity & eloquence in it that made me feel, last night, as if my relationship to almost everything around me had inexplicably changed. As if a

new and decisive *fact* had entered my life. I must see to it that the feeling is prolonged. Reading Troyat's *Tolstoi*.

FEB. 8, 1970
Sunday, three mile walk in winter-air as clear and bracing as ether . . . S. reads in bed, having slept well. Bach's *Clavierübung* plays on my speaker. At $100 a week for everything we can almost reach November with the money I am contracted for at the moment. . . . Spring is coming, and with it our pleasant backyard-porch-balcony life, the garden to do, engrossed mornings at the novel, afternoons with S. at home, outside . . . We are, after all, blessed right now—with luck, and a chance, and closeness to each other. Calm can achieve everything . . . Brave, admirable Shirley, who has endured her gone-bad eye (and its blow to her vanity) like my lovely, strong soldier. I admire her deeply, and love the essence of her spirit. We'll prevail . . . My room hums with good vibes. And neatness. A superflux of saved life. . . . Rosalyn Tureck tip-toes thru the afternoon. I am (amazement!) *happy*.

12
AN INTERVIEW WITH MICHAEL McCLURE

Mick McAllister

I had heard Michael McClure read at the University of New Mexico in 1968, but I didn't meet him until he came to North Dakota for the annual writers conference in 1974. That year's theme was the Beat poets, and the guest list was impressive: Allen Ginsberg and Peter Orlovsky, Gary Snyder, Lawrence Ferlinghetti, Gregory Corso, Kenneth Rexroth, and McClure.

The conference committee had decided to videotape and preserve as much as they could, and to interview each poet. Because I knew McClure's work fairly well and wanted to interview him, that assignment came to me. The interviewers agreed that there should be at least two questioners at each interview, to broaden the discussion and maintain a brisk pace. An English major, Candy Dostert, who was reading McClure for a class and very interested in his work, came to the interview and contributed some good questions and observations.

We talked with Michael in the afternoon, in his hotel room, by the window. We talked for an hour and a half, about his poetry, the prose, the plays, and about *Rare Angel*, only recently published. We centered for the most part on McClure and his work; thus, our interview was quite different from the others collected during the

Hell's Angel Freewheelin' Frank and Michael McClure. San Francisco, California, 1966. Photograph by Larry Keenan.

conference, which dug more deliberately into the history of the Beat movement and its relationship to ecological consciousness.

Transcribing the interview we encountered a minor annoyance—how to abbreviate Michael's name and mine distinguishably. That problem is solved here by a simple expedient; we have used one abbreviation (INT) to indicate either Candy or me, leaving "MM" to stand for McClure himself.

Mick McAllister

INTERVIEWER: *You surprised me last night when you said you were influenced by* The Prelude, *because my understanding of your poem "The Poet's Mind is Body" is that you were criticizing Wordsworth.*

MICHAEL McCLURE: I certainly was. Warren Tallman gave me *The Prelude* when I was visiting at the University of British Columbia at Vancouver in the early 1960s. I was in a very stressed psychic state at the time. I was impressed with the beauty of the idea of doing an autobiography in rhyme. Warren read me some of the most interesting parts of *The Prelude* and I read some of it to Warren. Then I began to compare it with Shelley; that is, I wrote a poem comparing it with Shelley, I haven't seen that poem in years, but I have a pretty clear recollection of it. I couldn't help but weigh Shelley against Wordsworth. [McClure is handed an issue of *Caterpillar* containing his "The Poet's Mind is Body" poem and an old photograph of himself, bearded, on a Harley-Davidson motorcycle] Oh, great—I forgot that that even existed. [Referring to photo] Where's the poem?

INT: *It's right after the picture.*

MM: Yes. The poem was written on the title page of *The Prelude*.

The Poet's Mind is Body
& his Arm is Joy.
SCIENCE
MIND
NATURE
MAN
are toys,

he hurls about like sailboats
with painted wings.
FIRE APRIL FIRE!
FIRE APRIL FIRE!
FIRE APRIL FIRE!
But the deeper blacker being grows from genes
—with sullen eye & laughing yell
and generosity that hurls his senses
into Eternity & Heaven & Hell
like poor mad Shelley
like beautiful mad Shelley
& not this fool!

Well, I went on ahead and decided I needed to be my own kind of fool, and a few years later, not forgetting Wordsworth, and strongly moved by Kerouac's *Mexico City Blues,* I wrote a book that was in 250 stanzas or choruses. They are all about 25 lines apiece and rhymed, and written fast as I could type on an electric typewriter. In the first ten I had not yet discovered, or was only beginning to sense, that they were going to be autobiographical—it was at about the 11th or 12th that they start becoming autobiographical. The poem is named *Fleas,* and it's 250 spontaneously written, rhymed electric typewriter poems about my childhood. They hop from memory to memory like a flea while one image lights up another. So, in a sense, *Fleas* is another long autobiographical poem. In *Fleas* I felt that I was occupying some of the same territory that's occupied by the worst of Lord Byron and the best of Terry-toons. It is like a Sistine doodle. The poem is no more serious than a doodle and yet it's the size of the Sistine Chapel, and as complex as the Sistine Chapel. It proves that childhood is a vision which is what we lose track of so often. When we let the childhood memories slip and slide away, we forget their visionary intensity. I began to recover the visionary intensity of them. And also, fortunately, got some interesting insights, which I'm going to continue to explore, into the way memory works. You see, I didn't plan to write a stanza, saying "now I'll tell about the time I went down to the candy shop"—instead one memory would bring another memory into being. Sometimes memories changed in the middle of a stanza, then I began to sense how one of them would light up another related memory and that memory would light up another and that one would light up another. Then a constellation of those three, having been lit, would light up another one which would be seemingly disparate but was related to the constellation of the three, when they appeared together. But perhaps it was not related to any *individual* one solo. Finally, the ending of the poem is related to the combined constellation of all the 247 preceding ones. The end is a great long stanza, all about mowing lawns in the yards of Heaven.

Here's something slightly related as an aside. When we were traveling in Ethiopia, we had an imaginary character named Flip Flea who joined us on the trip. He joined us at the Grand Ghion Hotel and wrote postcards to all my friends. Later, he sent cards from the Calcutta Airport describing what it was like inside of my boat, what we were all doing, what he could hear us saying, what the weather was like.

Frank Hallman, at the Aloe Press in New York, wanted to do a pamphlet, so I gave him seven of the 250 *Fleas*. To make sure *Fleas* was completely uncensored, I had vowed never to publish it as a book but I published ten stanzas in *Caterpillar* and the pamphlet of seven that Aloe did. I've found that I *do* want people to see them or hear them. I read the last one-third of *Fleas* at a reading for the Poetry Center in San Francisco and they videotaped it. Now they're going to release the tape. The next time they ask me to read, I'm going to read the second third, and the next time they ask me to read, I might read the first third. A videotape of the whole poem would take about five hours.

INT: *The constellation structure of the poem wasn't something that you imposed on the poem while you were writing it?*

MM: I had no choice in that whatsoever. It was an exploration as I went. I began to see how my memory was working, and how one sight would light up another, how they hopped. It all seemed like a pinball machine: one part lights up another part, and then those three make the girl with the fishing rod light up on the boat on the way to Bermuda; and that means we get a free game which means that you get five more balls which light up another bunch of things. If you call that structure then that's structure, I guess. It was a great experience writing it.

INT: *Is the way that* Fleas *came about similar to the way the rest of your poems are written? You talk about spontaneous com-*

position somewhere, that you prepare for days to write a poem, and then you sit down and you write it, and that's the end of the writing—in some cases at least. The place that I'm thinking about is the description of writing The Blossom—*an early play.*

MM: That was specifically in regard to the play. There are no changes in *Fleas* except some spelling errors I corrected. Other errors I kept. The only parts that have ever been retyped are the seventeen that have been published. In those cases, I corrected certain typing errors and changed a bit of the punctuation. I left some spelling errors and mispunctuation because I wanted the stanzas altered as little as possible. The videotape is a good medium for them. If it's a misspelled word and I want to read it a little differently I can read it that way with my voice, and the punctuation doesn't matter a whit.

INT: Then you read them with a pause in between the "Fleas," like in between the jumps, or do you just kind of go like your memory would take you?

MM: I was doing both. It was a lot to ask from the audience to follow me. The audience was sweet—they really went with it. I asked afterwards how many people were able to follow brand names from my childhood, like Wing cigarettes and names of movie actresses like Carmen Miranda. I was sure there's no reaction to those kinds of things—but they said they sensed what they were and they had correspondences of their own and they liked the whole thing. When you're reading something more than an hour long, you tend to gauge it; sometimes you make pauses or you get a good run going, you run with it—I played with it. The reading was a benefit for Chilean refugees. I was to read with Fernando Alegria, who in the meantime had been called away to Mexico City to speak to Mrs. Allende, the widow of the assassinated President of Chile. Alegria left a movie of himself reading. They showed the movie and it had not gone over well because the sound track was bad. The audience had been through an experience they hadn't bargained for, and they didn't know what *Fleas* was for about the first 15 minutes, then it was lovely.

INT: Your poems are set up on the page like pictures generally. Do you have a method for setting up lines? Do you think of a line as

Joanna and Michael McClure and Kit Knight in front of the McClure's house. San Francisco, California, December 29, 1980. Photograph by Arthur Knight.

. . what is it in Rare Angel? *You say the poem tracks vertically on the page like ideograms.*

MM: No. You're mixing what are two issues for me. I have a number of reasons for breaking a line. Once I figured out seven reasons for breaking a line, all of which I do intuitively. I've done it so long that I never think of "why."

Since the poem is symmetrical—since it could be folded down the middle, and it is symmetrical on a vertical axis, it resembles a biological organism. You know, we picture flatworm, human being, mustang, whale—even a five-pointed star—as symmetrical. The stanzas (a stanza being a cluster of lines without a break) are subbeings of the organism, of the whole poem organism. A poem can be an overall organism, the direct extension of our biological selves in the sense that Jackson Pollock or Franz Kline imagined abstract expressionism to be a spiritual autobiography—an extension of their arm's energy leaving a trail of paint. I picture poems as being the same kind of extension. Projective verse, as Charles Olson conceived it, is a related form.

INT: It seemed to me, when I was reading Rare Angel, *that it would have been natural to make the page in the book four inches longer because every single stanza is conceived for a large page. . . .*

MM: I think John Martin [Black Sparrow Press] would have given me a book of that size. Then John and I both would have spent our time hoping that ten bookstores in the country would sell a book that size. I wanted people to read the poem, and if we had made smaller type it would have been unreadable. I prefer to have a book available. In the case of *Rare Angel* I was sure readers could go with the turn of the page. And so far everybody has said that they understood the poem.

INT: The mechanics of making a poem symmetrical—the printer can make any poem symmetrical by simply counting the letters. . . .

MM: It was a style of printing in the nineteenth century. Dylan Thomas did it a lot, Herbert did it a lot, and I do it consistently. My centering the poems though, you know, is not mechanical. That I center is not a mechanical choice on my part. When I write poems they are centered . . . they come out centered, and I seldom write any other way because I picture it as an organism as it happens. Here's a manuscript. You can see how centered it is, and it was written, you know, waking out of a sound sleep—I just woke up and wrote this out. Gregory Corso streaked us at the reading that Allen Ginsberg and I gave in New York last week at St. Mark's Church. I woke up the next morning and reached for a pen and wrote this. I gave Corso a copy of it on the plane.

FIRST POETRY STREAK
GREGORY CORSO
your naked
torso
is not a bore.
So
here you are
streaking
at St. Marx!
(You're even in good shape.)
We're larks
of prestige.
We're grapes
speeding past
at 50,000 miles per hour
with our noses
in the press.
The stars forget to dress
and they run naked
as an ape
or cherub
through all the old
cathedrals.
Death to doldrums!
There goes mooning,
beamy
Corso!

[Publ: Poetry Project Newsletter #14
1 April 1974]

*INT: Did they turn out that way when you started writing?
Was it a conscious choice to make them centered like that?*

MM: It was a definite shift in my feeling; I remember with my
body when it happened, I have the body remembrance of every-
thing shifting over to the middle.

Oh, I remember. It *may* have happened this way. I wrote a
poem called "For the Death of 100 Whales" in 1954. First I wrote it
as a traditional ballad with 3–4–3–4 meter and with A–B–C–B

rhymes. Then I destroyed it like a cubist poem. Then, in the new shape it slid over to the middle and centered. In my first book everything except one poem called "Night Words: The Ravishing," which *should* stand out differently, was centered. It may have started with the whale poem. I never thought specifically when it happened, but that's the way it seems at this moment.

INT: Were you doing free verse then, when you wrote "For the Death of 100 Whales"?

MM: Yes. I wrote free verse in high school, and then in 1954 I took Robert Duncan's poetry workshop at San Francisco State College. Helen Adam was there, Jack Gilbert was there, Spicer visited it. Duncan was bothered because I was writing Petrarchan sonnets in the style of Milton. And he was so majestic and wise and elderly (ten or fifteen years older) that I didn't know how to tell him that I had always written free verse, and that I was just on an experimental tour of writing villanelles and sestinas and sonnets. He couldn't understand why an intelligent young man would be writing sonnets, but he liked them, although he'd lecture me about it. Then, I brought in older pieces and said, "Look, I used to write these." And then we got to be good friends.

INT: Was the movement back to the symmetrical form the point at which you moved back into free verse?

MM: No, it's not that simple. There were other things in between, and I may have had other earlier poems centered, but I think it was with "For the Death of 100 Whales" that I felt the shift to the center as being something other than a convention. I love the beautiful way that Williams's late poems look on the page. I've never liked endless amounts of poetry going down the page. I open those books, and all the lines are the same length and they all go down the page with the same margin. It seems unnatural. I suppose some people look at my poems and say, "This can't be real." But it's uncreaturely to have those rigid endless right and left margins. They fill up whole pages mercilessly.

INT: Do you revise your poems?

MM: Lots of poems are spontaneous and unchanged; some are

heavily revised and some are revised a shade, trying to get them to do what I feel would be the original impulse.

INT: And there were no revisions on the "Ghost Tantras"?

MM: I can't remember any.

INT: After you did the poems in beast language, the "Ghost Tantras," it became part of the vocabulary of your poetry—the language of those poems. When you use beast language in your poetry after the "Tantras," are you using it as a conscious addition to your language, or are you using it because of this same kind of spontaneous . . . what?—the description you gave in "Ghost Tantras" sounds like possession.

MM No, it's almost as though they startle themselves out of me after that. I didn't really care to pursue it any further, but "Ghost Tantras" are like a war—you can't completely end all of a sudden. Everybody thinks, Now we've ended the Vietnamese War—it's not true. It's going to take 20 years to end it. Everybody should have known that. The "Ghost Tantras" are like that, an intense and involved commitment, although I didn't know it when I was doing it. Not that it was done in frivolity, but I didn't know that it was going to be something that would fill me that much. And then afterwards, they did keep coming out. I did things like starting to translate Rimbaud's *A Season in Hell* into beast language, and I wrote a short story in the form of a long roar in beast language, it's about 17 pages. One roar. Earlier in about 1960 I wrote my play *The Feast* in beast language. I've written a lot of small things in beast language but I don't have copies of them. They were poems for people, valentines, things like that.

INT: Posters for The Beard—*there's a poster in the Coyote edition of* The Beard.

MM: You don't know the story of that?

INT: No.

MM: Well, it's a good story. Before I wrote *The Beard*—in 1965—I was flying to Los Angeles and I had a copy of a boxing

magazine called *Ring* with me. As I was looking through the magazine I found a reproduction of an extremely beautiful boxing poster reproduced in full page. Then flashing over my head, as in a comic strip, was a poster with Billy the Kid on it, and the text was in beast language. (This was several years after I'd written "Ghost Tantras.") I did my business in Los Angeles and flew back to San Francisco, got off at the airport and got in a cab, and as the cab went by a liquor store, I saw a boxing poster. I stopped the cab and I looked on the poster and it said Telegraph Press. I woke up the next morning and phoned Telegraph Press and said, "You make boxing posters, right?" and he said, "Yeah." I said, "Would you make a poem poster?" He said, "Polo poster? Sure, we'll make polo posters." I said "Poem Poster." He said, "Well, bring it in—we'll make it." So I did a mock-up of the poster and got the photo of the Kid and Harlow; wrote all the letters on it in the right size. The poster is 22 × 30, standard boxing poster size. I got the dimensions and mocked it up; got the type sizes and mocked them up, and wrote it all out in beast language. Then I took it down to the print shop. An old guy was chewing his cigar, the walls of the basement shop were covered with boxing posters. All they ever printed was boxing posters, except for one thing, which was a Rolling Stones concert poster. I showed the mock-up to him—he was chewing his cigar. "Hrrmmph hrrmmph hrrmph," he grumbles. He reads it. Chews his cigar . . . His name's Les Jelinsky. He looks at me and says, "I won't print it." I say, "Why?" He said, "You punks are all the same; you kids. You think you know what Jean Harlow looks like. Look at that, look at that dumb photo. Her neck's ugly there. You picked a bad photograph." I looked at it and said, "You're right." I went out and spent a couple more days looking at pictures of Jean Harlow and I found another one that I liked. I showed it to him and he says, "O.K., come back in two days and pick up the poster." I waited. In two days the assistant phoned me. He said, "Come on down, you gotta proof it." O.K., and I went down: "Just beautiful, print it! Just perfect. I want it," I said and went home. The phone rings, it's Jelinsky, not his assistant. Jelinsky says, "You gotta come down here." I said, "Look, I'm very busy. Just print it, it's beautiful, I want it. Do it now." He says, "Nope, you gotta come down here. Come down, or we don't print it." I went down. He said, "I want to check this through, line by line." He reads it, "'Love, Lion, Lioness,' right?"—chews on his cigar. "Right." "'Gahr thy rooh graheer'—two o's, two e's, right?" "Right." "O.K., 'Grah ord (O-R-D) gleem (G-L-E-E-M) claw,' right?" "Right." We go all the way down to the bottom, we get past the "fleck boot mercury vapor grahhh." He says, "Grahhh with three h's?" I say, "Right." He reads further. He says, "Grahhhh with four h's?" I say, "Right." Then he stops and he turns to me and says, "What is this shit anyway?" Total paradox! I said, "It's poetry and it's beast language." And then he started telling me about a poet he knew in the WPA. I brought him a copy of "Ghost Tantras." And he printed the poster and he did an incredibly beautiful job of it. Jelinsky wanted to print 5000 more of them so that he could sell them to a guy who would use them for souvenirs in Alaska. I nixed that. The edition was about 200 copies.

I took the posters around and I put them in liquor store windows. I went to one liquor store and the owner said, "I won't put it up." He didn't even look at it. He said, "No." I said, "Why?" He said, "You don't give comp tickets. I should put it in my window and you don't even give comps?" So I said, "O.K., wait." And I went down and had Jelinsky print up complimentary tickets in beast language, and I took them back to the guy's shop and I handed him the tickets and I said, "Now can I put it in the window?" He says, "Go ahead." I don't know what he thought, man; I never went back. It was in his window for months. I don't know what he did with the comps. I gave one poster to Kenneth Anger, another to Kenneth Rexroth, and to everybody I knew. I put one on the wall behind my desk, and it focused Billy the Kid and Jean Harlow onto the back of my head as I typed. And then, within a day or so they were there and they started doing *The Beard* in my consciousness. I typed it as they went. They'd come for a few minutes each day. Then I'd get very wrought up about what I was doing—what was this? The poster came first and then *The Beard* happened.

INT: *"The Sermons of Jean Harlow and The Curses of Billy the Kid" is later, isn't it?*

MM: It's later. I thought I was through with Billy the Kid and Jean Harlow, and then they'd come back in the middle of the night, and they wouldn't go away until I'd write. It was almost against my will.

INT: *The first thing about Harlow is the "Meat Science" essay, and the first thing on Billy the Kid is your play, "Blossom."*

MM: Yeah.

INT: *Of all the possible people to pick, how did you wind up with Billy the Kid?*

MM: Well, if I tell you in the framework that I see him, you'll understand. In the play "The Blossom" the Kid is a prophet of death; he's a mystic of death. It's as if he sees over the edge of the nineteenth century into this century and sees the rapine here; it's as if he's the tiniest hint then of what's to come now. There's still some honor and some meaning in what he's doing because it's revenge slaying, you know, for a friend's honor. But the manner of it and the brutality of it and the numbers killed, and the style, is like a preview of the twentieth century. What he's doing is still beautiful, still is auric. That makes him like a visionary for the future. I think maybe we, meaning people like Allen and myself and Gary, were in a visionary position in '56 and '57, seeing into the now. I'm not very surprised, you know, by anything that's happened. I guess looking at the Korean War (I grew up with World War II and Korea happening) none of this surprises me a bit. What we're going through is a natural outgrowth of Korea as much as Korea was an outgrowth of what preceded it. All of us may have had the same relation to the present that Billy the Kid had to the twentieth century. We may have felt like we were looking over the horizon with rather visionary eyes. Also we wanted to liberate ourselves and to escape. The Kid's great at that. Some of Kid's great acts were escapes. He made one particular jailbreak that was incredible. He did some amazing things—he was a physical genius.

INT: The one where he killed Bell . . . I don't think they've ever figured out how he did that one.

MM: Have you kept up on this at all? Has anybody ever printed or released the third photo of the Kid?

INT: I don't know.

MM: There's a third one, and I don't know who has it, and it's not going to be released until they die or sell it. Be an interesting thing to see.

INT: I guess the thing that makes Billy the Kid seem so strange is that you, and you've added Ginsberg and Snyder now, the bunch of you seem like such gentle people. The two times I've heard you read, I hear people muttering, "That can't be Michael McClure." They expect a wild man. And with Billy the Kid again— this gentleness and the terrible violence of the poems.

MM: I can only say to you what I said about Allen once before. Somebody said, "Allen is so nice." I said, "Man, it's only been about five years that Allen's been so nice." And I guess I would say that again, only now it's about two years later. I could say, "Well, it's only been about seven years since Allen has been so nice." Oh, and they said, "You're pleasant, too." And I said, "Yeah, and I've been pleasant two years less than Allen." We've had acceptance, and acceptance helps.

INT: I guess what I'm getting at though is not that you and Ginsberg and Snyder are mellow people or anything like that but that there seems to be a schism of some kind between your—I'll say ethics for the time being—your ethic of poetry, and the ethic you seem to be living by.

MM: I've changed quite a bit.

INT: Well, the violence in Rare Angel *is in the killing of the giant ground sloth . . .*

MM: The killing of the giant ground sloth was interesting to me. It was something I had no control over. I felt it was developed too poorly. I said this has got to be clear, this has got to come forward in some big straight and clear rosy scene where it's understood that this is a thread in the poem. I took *Rare Angel* to Robert Duncan. He said, "You can't determine the laws of that poem, it's got its own laws." And I said, "You're absolutely right. I brought it over here to hear that."

We live in the midst of incredible violence. I don't feel any need for it myself anymore. I felt a great desire for liberation which I confused with violence, and I'm more liberated now. With the liberation a lot of desire for violence dissipated. As I saw my own liberation grow in an entirely different way. The scales of my reason weighted out what was going on in an entirely different way. I think my life is an interesting life historically—as any of our lives would be interesting historically—because of the transition that takes place. From the disintegrated personality seeking violence as liberation, to the need for violence dissipating, while the violence around one grows so abundantly. Sometimes it's practically incandescent. It doesn't look very incandescent out there in the snow [Pointing to the window], I'll admit. But the civilization we're living in is incandescent and *that's* what I'm saying in *Rare Angel*. I realized just the other day that *Rare Angel* is not just passively recounting a vision to you. *Rare Angel* is getting out there and smearing itself all over everything to show you what the vision is in case you missed it . . . *Rare Angel* is a vision projector.

INT: Would you like to talk about the difference between a theatrical event and a poetry reading event? You see them as different things just as poetry and theater are different things?

MM: Theater is a play. A play is a special kind of organism. A play is an organism in which the author is the DNA, the director is the RNA, the actors are the proteins and the limits of the play form the cell membrane, and what goes on within makes the endoplasmic reticulum of the play, and the streaming of the cytoplasm within it. A poetry reading is a man standing up repeating for an audience the organic extensions of himself, which have very subtle and beautiful interplays within themselves, but do not form a single coherent organism for the same purpose as theater.

INT: When you write your poems do you see them as visual experiences?

MM: Yes, as well as audial.

INT: Do you think you're likely to do poems simply as oral things rather than written things? Have you ever experimented with that?

MM: I have. I tried composing poetry into a tape machine and it didn't work for me. I didn't pursue it very far. Allen has done it. I think that if I wanted to spend the time involving myself in it I would probably have success. I don't feel alien to it but I've not gone in that direction. I have gone in directions that have more desirable payload for me. I've learned the autoharp so that I could find more music and get more rhymes into my poetry, more of a song quality into what I was doing. I don't think if I composed directly by sound or tape that it would be much different from what I do with a pen or typewriter. And so there's not very much challenge to explore in that direction. My very style is to use all the styles I can invent, and that way I can express given muscular feelings that I call thoughts in as many ways as possible.

INT: How did The Blossom *come to be dedicated to singer Jim Morrison?*

MM: I flew to London to bring *The Beard* and *The Blossom* to a film producer who wanted to use Jim in them. We all had terrible hangovers. I had brought a copy of my new novel, *The Adept.* I said, "I got a great idea, Jim. We'll do a movie of *The Adept.*" He said, "O.K., great. I'll play the lead." So then we worked on a screenplay of that, but I still felt that Jim should have done *The Blossom.* Jim wanted to get a theater in L.A.; several times he negotiated for one. He gave financial aid to the Living Theater when they were in trouble down there. Jim was involved with the theater, and had gone to see The Living Theater a number of times. In a play like *The Blossom* you have a kind of compressed Elizabethan revenge tragedy—yet also something like Noh. When writing it, I was trying to formulate a play in which the real sensation of Yūgen was emanated. So it was only right that we dedicated it to Jim. Jim had Yūgen.

INT: Do you want to talk about Rare Angel *now?*

MM: Yes, you asked me about tracking vertically . . .

INT: Yeah, the line in the introduction to the poem is something like . . . "the poem tracks vertically on the page." What I wanted to ask you is how do you determine the lines, and what you mean by tracking?

MM: Oh. I have to cut back a little bit before that so I can give you the answer to those. The poem started with my understanding that many biologists believe that we think with body sensations. Einstein also believed he thought with bodily sensations. So I thought, Ah, now if I write a poem directly from these sensations, if I write with the body sensations without trying to give them pre-destined subject matter, but try and write only what my body sensations immediately become as I type, then that will be new. And then I thought, And I'll make the stanza a full 8½ × 11 inch page so that there won't be any side issue of determining the length of the stanza. I'll just go from the top to the bottom of the page and write out words as my body sensations create them. Of course it

Michael McClure. San Francisco, California, 1972. Photograph by Gerard Malanga.

does begin to form its own tracks. Nothing's perfect—one can't just have an abstract poem; it begins to make its own laws, demand and create stories, and they repeat and recur, and take on a being of their own from their own selves. So the poem begins to come out of the substrate of itself, forming the giant-ground-sloth murder, and shaping the Dantean imagery near the end—travelling on escalators through the heavenly cities while the topology of the universe interwinds upon itself—with the island of Okinawa floating over all. You have the substrate of the body, the substrate of the poem, creating its own material and surfaces; but I remain true to the idea of writing from muscle sensation. *Rare Angel* seems really Oriental, not anything in subject matter of appearance, but *linguistically*.

INT: The physical act of the reading?

MM: Right. It's a projected vision . . . It projected what was inside of me outside on to everything around me. I don't think I've ever written anything like it—I don't think I'll write anything like it again.

13

JACK & NEAL IN GROSSE POINTE

FROM *YOU'LL BE OKAY*

Frankie Edith Kerouac Parker

Jack and Neal came to visit me in September, 1947, following their first road trip. They stayed with me and my girlfriend Virginia Tyson at her parents' home in Grosse Pointe. The Tysons were out of town, visiting Nova Scotia.

Virginia's father, Ty Tyson, was Detroit's Number One radio announcer, famous for his Detroit Tigers baseball broadcasts and popular interview shows. Jack loved the grand piano in Virginia's sunken living room, and Neal was attracted to Virginia.

Ed White, who was staying in Dearborn that summer, had received a letter from Jack telling him to advise me of his pending visit! The two lane roads were quite primitive then, like the Mexican roads today, and the boys needed a rest. Of course I would put them up, but I could not do it at my house due to my mother.

Virginia planned a big party with the Tigers because the house was hers. Her brother Bill was at home, but he was no problem; he had his own crazy group of friends. Virginia decided to have the party catered, so we went shopping and spent everything on booze

*Frankie Edith Kerouac Parker
(Kerouac's first wife). Columbia
University, New York City, 1943.
Courtesy Frankie Edith Kerouac
Parker.*

and big roasts. Thank God for her charges, or Virginia would have dined on cookies for the next two months (the house was stocked with all her father's advertising products, including beer).

Jack and Neal were coming from Denver; Jack's letter to Ed White had come from Marin City, California, where he had stayed with Henri Cru. Jack and I had not conventionally "split up" in our own minds anyway; in a manner of thinking, we never really did. We were just caught up in the "excitement" of our lives, of what we were doing from day to day, enjoying the freedom of finally having become "adults." Our parents left us pretty much alone, as they had during the war, our living together, Jack's shipping out, and getting married.

My mother was pleased that I was back in Grosse Pointe, out of New York for good, and thought that Jack was out of our lives. She could not have been further from the truth. We met whenever we could, and this was one of the times in the late '40s and early '50s.

This time, Jack and Neal arrived by Greyhound, coming from Chicago in the middle of the day. We stuck their canvas luggage in the trunk and off we went, Neal in the driver's seat with his blond, and Jack and I holding hands tightly in the back seat. We loved each other, and I could see he has happy traveling. "Go!" as John Clellon Holmes' book says. The top was down on the big white Lincoln convertible, the radio was blaring, and we were all talking at the same time. The wind was in our sails, whoo-whee!

We stopped at the Rustic Cabin Saloon for drinks. Virginia drank V.O. and ginger ale so we all did. It was thirty-five cents per drink, and we had a tough time rounding it up between us. Funny thing about Grosse Pointers: the people have everything except cash! Jack got up and went to the men's room, then came back grinning. He ordered another round, and came up with a rumpled "ten spot." Neal was shocked. "Where did you get that gold?" he asked. Jack never answered. Neal didn't know Jack as well as I did. He gave Neal a quarter for the "great" juke box. Pete Ouelette, the "French Canuck" owner, loved Frank Sinatra. He played six of Frank's songs for two bits and we had to sit through all of them.

We got to Virginia's about four; Billy was playing baseball in their big front yard. Jack and Neal joined right in with the gang; Neal pitching, Jack catching. Bob Jackson, a friend of Billy's, came over and helped Virginia and I with the luggage. Neal was in the room with the double bed, and Jack in the twin-bedded master bedroom. The house had four bedrooms with four huge bathrooms. The grand piano was downstairs, the real reason Jack wanted to stay here, instead of the Saverine Hotel with the Detroit Tigers. When they wanted to stay at the Saverine, Virginia got them in with food and lodging for a very low price, which she and I later split.

Virginia and I unpacked their luggage for her maid Maggie to do the laundry. Maggie and her daughter were downstairs in the kitchen, preparing dinner. Some great smells were drifting through the house. Hams, turkeys, potato salad, and garlic meat sauce for spaghetti!

The Tysons had a tradition of "silver and candle light sit-down dinners," served at 7:00 PM in the dining room by Maggie. Jack was expecting this as we had the same custom at my mother's house. Suddenly the piano came alive, and Jack was playing loud jazz music. Neal wanted a beer, which was through the kitchen and outside. As I showed him the "ins and outs" of the house, he beamed at all the young, tanned help. They were great, and lived in the house. I was concerned about their welfare around "jail educated" Neal. The cupboards were full of Altes beer, Wheaties, cookies, and "Chuckles."

Ty Tyson had a live broadcast, "Man Of The Street," where he talked to people "and pronto!" in front of the Michigan Central Railroad Station every day at noon, five days a week, for station WWJ. He eventually became president of the station. Ty always wore a black French "tam," which was placed on his casket at Verheyden Funeral Home when he died; even his pallbearers wore them. And I also wore one—as a hostess—for that memorable event. All the Detroit sports and political "big shots" came to the house for Ty's wake, the same kind of wonderful party we gave for Jack and Neal.

Virginia was nervous so she kept the silver locked away in drawers. She need not have worried, for Neal never would have done anything to discredit Jack. If Neal had been alone, however, she would have had more than silver to worry about! As seven o'clock approached, Jack went upstairs to take his customary shower and shave. He came back downstairs wearing one of Billy's clean white shirts, no tie. Jack scowled at Neal, so he went to wash up and comb his hair.

We went in for dinner and the phone started ringing. Virginia took it off the hook, and we started passing the dishes for our feast. Maggie and her daughter ate in the kitchen, where we brought our plates after dinner, rinsing them and setting them in the sink. Then Virginia served coffee, apple pie, and Sander's vanilla ice cream. This was Jack's favorite dessert, and he was pleased. Neal wanted to know whose birthday it was! He was always making corny remarks.

We got up and went into the living room, with Jack and I on the floor, stretched out by the fire. He wanted to know who was coming to the party we had planned for the next day. We said we didn't know what to do about the music, either to play the radio or our own records on the Victrola. Jack and Neal said to leave it to them. Then we all went to bed, after a long day. Jack and I were anxious to be together again behind closed doors.

The next day flew. Jack, Billy, and Neal went out for fresh bread and to the Saverine to see about a band. I was so excited about Jack's return that I started drinking too much, too soon. When the guests arrived I was well on my way.

We held the party in the Tyson's rathskeller, a finished basement with a bar serving Altes tap beer. We had a large assortment of food on a covered ping-pong table. Jack and Neal had found a black, three-piece band, where I'll never know. They were great, with Jack and Neal taking turns on the drums. There was an upright piano which they also took turns playing. We drank and danced until very late in the night; it was wonderful. But I'd had it about midnight, and went to bed. I woke up once to hear the party still going, and Jack finally came to bed when it was light. He crawled into my twin bed, I heard the musicians laughing and leaving in a cab, and I fell back to sleep.

I got up before the rest of the crowd, and put on my pajamas. I went to the bathroom, flushed the toilet, and it started to gurgle! I was too sleepy to give it any thought, so I started cleaning up, picking up glasses as I worked my way downstairs. The Tyson's wonderful old school clock in the kitchen said 6:00 AM. The place was half picked up, so I made coffee. They had so much coffee, I wondered if they got that free, too. I took my coffee into the living room, which was filled with sleeping bodies! I started the fire up, and sat down to enjoy my thoughts of Jack's visit. I should have had a hangover but I felt pretty good. I was still in love with Jack, which kept my adrenalin flowing.

One of the guests, a nurse, got up with her boyfriend as she had to go to work. He reported that the toilets were stopped up! So I phoned the plumber for emergency repairs. I woke Jack up at 7:00 AM; I was never happier to be with him, then or ever. The plumbers arrived in two trucks, I suspect to partake of the party! They were all over the house with electric snakes and all their paraphernalia. It took a half day to discover the problem; they reminded me of doctors. They were continuously consulting about the four bathrooms. There was a blockage of some kind in the pipes, and they decided they would have to dig up the lawn outside. In the meantime, some of the guests were still partying, particularly Neal. I wondered who he'd slept with. I woke up Virginia and told her about the plumbing situation; she put me in charge and went right back to sleep.

The plumbers dug up the front yard and several of us stood around the hole, watching. This took at least an hour. It looked like they were digging a grave; the hole was big enough for a casket! Then one of the plumbers jumped in with his hip boots on and pulled the pipes apart. Out floated, with you-know-what, a pair of men's shorts! The plumber, Dean, grabbed them, rinsed them with dirty water, and put them on display on the grass. We were spellbound; they were white with big red polka dots! We became hysterical with laughter. Fortunately, no one claimed them.

The plumbers mended everything just as before except for the new "bump" in the lawn, looking like someone was buried there. When Virginia got the bill for the damages, it was more than the cost of the entire party, and boy! was she furious, wanting to know whose shorts they were. She was hoping someone would help pay.

Well, the party went on for another three days, then everything ran out: beer, food, patience, hospitality. Jack and Neal moved to the Saverine, and later, in a lost letter, Jack told me the shorts belonged to Neal. He had recognized them, but never let on. They really didn't have any money anyway. So they enjoyed the rest of their stay with the Tigers at the Saverine, with fun players like Roy Cullenbine, Barney Markowsky, and Dick Wakefield.

Jack and Neal later visited my friend Lee Donnelly's future husband Clotaire DeMueleemeister's bar on the eastside of Detroit. Clot's mother Emma was always there. Clot was John Wayne's tall double. At Emma's house, there was always plenty to eat, and the basement bar had a walk-in refrigerator. Their bars were fully stocked, with beer on tap, pool tables, rifle range games, and "one-arm bandits," which were legal then and I loved to play them, in our homes and other far away places. The speakeasy atmosphere of the twenties and early thirties still hung around such places, with a hint of illegality and gangsters. We were all drinking and driving at the age of 14, and no one enforced the laws in Grosse Pointe society.

Emma, Clot's mother, was something else. Clot had his bar on the same avenue as his father, up till the late 1970s, and Emma worked with him to "get the kid ahead in the bar business." It was across from Motor Products. Clot had married Lee while in the service. One late night, two hold-up "artists" came in (the bar cashed checks, so was known to have a lot of money), stuck big guns in Emma's neck, and told her to open the register. Emma snapped back, "the hell I will, you'll have to shoot me to get it." These boys were astonished! They ran out of the bar, but were arrested, one of whom turned out to be a future Detroit Tiger's player. He was discovered when they sent him to Jackson Prison.

But Clot said he wouldn't endanger his family and closed the bar, and Motor Products followed. The whole eastside of Detroit was by then in depression, and could not cope with the growing crime, taxes, city government, and unions; moving their business south and out of the country.

Lee lived on Mount Vernon Street in Grosse Pointe. Her mother Marie and her husband Kelly also lived there, and her Aunt Jean. Clot's Uncle Tyne, a poor relation, lived in Emma's large home on Jefferson beyond Grosse Pointe, as did a number of Belgian immigrants. Uncle Tyne maintained a large bathtub in the backyard, which was continually running over with water supplied by an ugly black hose. He kept an assortment of fish in it, ready for the frying pan; he had fresh trout for every lunch.

Emma's huge mansion was covered with ankle-deep oriental rugs, silk upholstery, the most expensive glass, and porcelains, with Belgian masterpiece paintings on the walls. There was a huge American flag on the wall over the couch, as the focal point of the living room, where the double Tiffany glass doors were always locked, and all you could do was peek into this exquisite gallery. Never being allowed in made it even more extraordinary.

Jack and Neal visited this house one afternoon. They were drinking beer, and then we started to have Courvoisier brandy; this is when Lee and I discovered "Manhattans" made with this brandy. Boy! it was delicious. Then Clot, Neal, Jack, Tyne, and a few others started playing baseball, this time with Jack as right fielder, Neal as pitcher, Clot on 2nd base, Tyne as catcher, Lee on third, and me on first! It was hilarious, none of us "feeling any pain," and the game did not last long. Then Tyne said "Let's eat," and we ate on Emma's wonderful porch, looking out on beautiful Lake St. Clair. Jack wrote about this, but his editor Malcolm Cowley cut out most of his Detroit visits, changing Lake St. Clair to Lake Michigan, clear across the state from Grosse Pointe!

14 AN INTERVIEW WITH ALLEN GINSBERG

James McKenzie

The following interview took place at Dan Eades' home on the last day of the 5th Annual Writers Conference at the University of North Dakota, March 1974. The scene before the interview began was a miniature of the week-long City Lights Conference of which it was one of the concluding parts. Gregory Corso and Kenneth Rexroth had taken turns noisily walking off a fractious, sometimes stormy marathon Open Mike discussion, each protesting loudly the other's words and conduct. Each time it was Ginsberg who patiently reknit the ragged threads of the panel discussion: "Now Kenneth, come on. The problem is that what we're dealing with here is only a sample of the difficulties that we have in America in getting a dialogue going, Kenneth, in which we have to deal with all sorts of aggressions, and control our own aggressions in order to come to some resolutions where we act in the community." Allen's entreaties prevailed and Rexroth and Corso rejoined the panel, the discussion proceeding with only a little less anarchy.

With just a few hours between this final Open Mike session and the Ginsberg-Orlovsky reading that night, there was not much time for the interview, and a similar chaos reigned: technicians tested sound equipment, people wondered where we could all get

Allen Ginsberg. By Jules Feiffer.

lunch, Peter continued his seamless web of exhortations against smoking and drinking, urging everyone to begin organic gardening and explaining how properly to chew peyote. Again it was Ginsberg who focused the activities. Without a word he began foraging through Eades' kitchen as though thoroughly familiar with it, opening drawers, rummaging through the refrigerator, clattering around until he had collected the ingredients for an enormous chef's salad, which he then assembled and served us all. Someone turned on the tape recorder as we ate, and the talk gradually crossed whatever the theoretical boundary is between conversation and interview.

James McKenzie

JAMES MCKENZIE: *In our conversation on Tuesday, Gary spoke about how he was being influenced by you again and saw both a personal and—the way he put it—a movement-wide reinvigoration of the Beats that was related to your recent serious study and turn towards the East, though he did go as far back as when you were with him in India. And I wondered how you would respond to that.*

ALLEN GINSBERG: Well, of course, I have always had Gary in mind so partly I'm taking a formal Buddhist meditation discipline in order to please Gary, and make him feel secure. That's sort of a minor shrewd extra reason—to keep the scene together and to continue the scene. I mean, all of us have an esthetic and dramatic, even melodramatic, view of ourselves as history, and what we've done as history; and we want it to come out all right. We always *did* want it to come out all right.

JM: He talked, too, about his influence on you earlier to give up graduate studies, which I think Kerouac alludes to in Dharma Bums. *Snyder has for a long time been someone that you said you wanted to "please."*

AG: Yeah, I learned from him a great deal. I learned mountain climbing from him, love of nature from him. When we went through India, he already was experienced in Buddhist iconography, and place histories, so that the two months we were there together at the beginning of my visit with Peter, we were able to take advantage of his Buddhist knowledge to go around to Sanchi, Ajanta and Elbra; and I think the first time I heard the Prajnaparamita ("Highest Perfect Wisdom") Sutra chanted was in a cave at Elbra, I believe, or Ajanta, where Gary sat down on a rock in the middle of a cave and chanted it the Sino-Japanese style. Before that Kerouac had laid Buddhism on me because he had studied that and was really quite a deep Buddhist and quite an adept Buddhist intellectual, according to Gary and according to other people who are expert. He was the one that turned me on to the Three Refuges in Buddha, the first person I ever heard that from in the Sanskrit form: "Buddha, saranam gochami, Dharma saranam gochami, Sangha saranam gochami," which he used to croon, sort of like Frank Sinatra (Here AG croons the Refuges), which I think he was singing in '54 or '53 or maybe even earlier; I remember him singing in Berkeley when we were all living together in a cottage. Gary was always sitting, already back then.

JM: Sitting?

AG: Meditating, sitting is the technical word in Zen for meditating. Jack did some sitting at that time also, and has recorded his experience of a sort of satori he had in a text called "The Scripture of the Golden Eternity." But when we went to India, we went to the historical places of Buddhism that Gary knew . . . we went to see Lama Govinda, and went to see the Dalai Lama, and so we touched certain Buddhist home bases that he knew about that I didn't know about. And then when I left India I went to see Gary in Kyoto where he lived near his temple, and I did some sitting there in his temple. I took part in a four-day sesshin with him. So Gary got me sitting in Kyoto. Then I did a lot of other experimenting with different forms of Hindu mantra chanting from the time I left India and left Gary and spent in the United States from '63 to '68 or so. I did all sorts of Hindu mantra chanting, and developed that—vocalization and concentration and finally got a good Hindu teacher who gave me a mantra for sitting—around November, 1970. And then finally we met a Tibetan teacher, Chogyam Trungpa, in 1971, after about a year of steady sitting. And then sat with the mantra that *he* gave me; and finally last fall went to a Buddhist academy and did long sesshin—about ten hours a day—25 days, as part of the seminary studies that we were doing, so that by the time I got out of there I was more familiar with what Gary had been talking about all along. So that now that I've been doing that I'm more able to transmit that than I was before, because I was transmitting mantra and ideology of Buddhism before and Hinduism, and now, sitting, I'm able to be like a little firmer and quieter and securer in what I'm proposing to students in audience or in poetry. And lately I've been including sitting sometimes as part of poetry reading. In other words, doing some mantra chanting, bringing it down to a low slow breath, and then maybe doing a ten-minute meditation with the audience.

JM: You've talked about Gary's spiritual influence on you over the years; I wonder if you'd care to comment on any influence his poetics have had on your poetry?

AG: We still haven't covered like the mutual thing in the Beat Generation in relation to the acid freak-out and the acid illumination in relation to meditation, which is what he was concerned with.

JM: And Gary's sense of responsibility—O.K.

AG: Yeah . . . well, we all had that sense of responsibility that way; we'd gone out and shot our mouths off and made public manifestation of our own private lives, which included acid and acid friendships as with Leary, for myself at any rate, or peyote, and all felt that since we had broken through early, and had experience from the early '50s with peyote, that we should be able to share that experience with any younger people that were turned on by our own behavior or articulations or symbols or poetries or dramas or public theory. And that got increasingly hard as police state closed down, particularly in the drug area, and as the regular respectable professors refused to deal with that area—well, doctors and psychiatrists gave it over into the hands of the police, or the police grabbed it out of their hands. So it was left to some extent to the poets to formulate some sort of public knowledge, to transmit granny wisdom about those things. Gary always knew all along, and I slowly came to realize that the safest way of preparing mind, people's minds or young kids' minds for psychedelic experiences is training in meditation to give them firm ground and firm balance and firm awareness of mind, clear mind. No trip, to cut down the horror tripping as well as the celestial tripping. The teacher I'm working with now, Chogyam Trungpa, is very strong on this particular point, not as a put-down of acid but as, you know, like finding an equilibrium.

JM: When you say, "no tripping," is that related to what you were saying on the panel about clutching after something, either good or bad, holding on to it?

AG: Yeah. A choice statement that Dudjom Rinpoche, the head of the Nyingmapa branch of Tibetan Meditation Study, told me when I went to visit him in India bringing with me a tale of all sorts of LSD horrors, you know, bum trips. And he said, "If you see anything horrible, don't cling to it; if you see anything beautiful, don't cling to it," which is a straight Buddhist position, Manjusri's sword of intelligence cutting right through the mental knot. So we all felt that dramatic and historical responsibility for what we let loose, to the extent that we were responsible for letting anything loose on America, in terms of opening of consciousness. I mean, nobody knows whether we were catalysts, or invented something, or just the froth riding on a wave of its own. We were all three, I suppose—froth on the wave of biological consciousness consequent on the over-crowding and the over-industrialization.

JM: Is that something you've come to think about recently?

AG: No, we knew that back in 1948–49. You see, Gary and I and others, by '48 had had some kind of a psychedelic breakthrough without drugs—that is psychedelic mind manifestation—which I've talked about at great length at other places, [see *Paris Review* interview, 1965, and Preface to *Jail Notes* by Timothy Leary, Douglas Books NY, 1970—JM.] so no need to go through that here. There already was that; and by '58, around the time when the media began coming around really heavily, exploring what we were having to say and distorting it and projecting a Frankenstein vision of it all over America, by that time—I remember there was one night I lay in my bed, in the middle of the night, realizing that if all those people were coming around, we must have touched some nerve, and if what we were saying had any truth to it . . . and then I shuddered in bed, realizing that America was going to take some awful fall and go through some great transmogrification and change because if other people's minds were going to be opened as ours were, or they were going to glimpse some of the nightmare of Moloch, of the money bank capitalist earth-eating monster realization that we already had, that everybody was going to go through a funny change. Like it took me to go through a bughouse to get adjusted to it, so I realized that in a sense we had an awesome responsibility that we had sort of intuited but hadn't asked for, but which I took very seriously, and realized it as a sort of national shiver around 1958—that it was really serious—that what we were talking about, though it seemed light and funny and, you know, beatnik humor and angels in the valleys and "High on the peak top, bats! and down in the valley the lamb," though it was all poetical, that there was strange penitrant awareness that we had been gifted with or latched on to.

JM: Can you say what made you see that then?

AG: We'd already had, by '48, some sort of alteration of our own private consciousness; by '55 we made some kind of public articulation of it; by '58 it had spread sufficiently so that the mass media were coming around for information, and by that time I realized that if our private fancies, our private poetries, were so serious that they absorbed the attention of the big, serious military generals who write for *Time* magazine, there must be something strange going on.

JM: You're speaking of the discovery of the Beats, and that made you know that it was. . . .

AG: No, I'm speaking of the *exploitation* of the Beats—the Beat discovery is '52 or something. I'm talking about the mass media spread and exploitation, actually, in the stereotype characterization, the Frankenstein image that they put down. See, and as I saw Frankenstein image being laid down by everything from Congress for Cultural Freedom, *Encounter* magazine, through *Partisan Review,* through *Time* magazine, through the *New York Daily News,* you know, sort of like a yellow press image of what was

Allen Ginsberg. California, Pennsylvania, June 1980. Photograph by Robert Turney.

originally a sort of ethereal and angelic perception of America, and the world, and the nature of the mind, I realized early that if they were going to do that to us who were relatively innocent—just a bunch of poets—if they were going to make *us* out to be the monsters, then they must have been making the whole universe out to be a monster all along, like from the Communists to the radicals to anarchists to the Human Being in America; so then I began reflecting back that what we were doing had some kinship with what Whitman was doing in announcing large magnanimous full-consciousness of American Person. Then I began digging Whitman's use of the word "Person" and linking our own struggle back to the tradition that was immediately contractible in the Populist good heart of William Carlos Williams, with whom we were in direct contact; and that linked us up, both by study and personal contact and letter, with Pound and his struggle with America; and through Williams to a great extent with Alfred Steichen and the Bohemians of the '20s and An American Place Gallery; and forgotten figures like John Herrmann of 1932 who won a literary prize with Thomas Wolfe for a proletarian novel; and Sherwood Anderson for his examination of the beating heart of lonely souls in Winesburg, Ohio; and the strange, cranky privacy of Melville in his old age writing love stories to Billy Budd, the handsome sailor; and Thoreau pondering in the woods about the overgrowth of competitive materialism in his own time as distinct from solitary study of minute particular detail of nature of which he accomplished by himself; and Thoreau going to jail not to pay war taxes for the Mexican War. So when the mass media began creating a hallucinatory image of the poetry activity that we were involved with and took that as sort of like something to mock and make an enemy of, then I realized that the whole country had a false mentality built up which was almost on the scale of mass hallucination. And so in 1958, Independence Day, I wrote an essay ("Poetry, Violence, and the Trembling Lambs," see *A Casebook on the Beat,* Thomas Parkinson, Ed., Crowell, N.Y., 1961] saying that America was going to have a nervous breakdown, and that part of the cause of it could be located in that year's 30 billion dollar military budget and the growth of military police state; that one aspect of it was the persecution of the junkies and the drug people who were basically sensitives who may or may not have been fucked up but needed compassion and medical care rather than Swastika-like police agencies chasing them down with guns, calling them "fiends," which is a terrible violation of the human spirit to create a class of people in America called "fiends"—I mean it's diabolical . . . once you realize that you've got a class of armed police calling another group "fiends," you've really got a situation so surrealistic and hallucinatory and violent that there could be no outcome but some massive nervous breakdown in America when people find out that they've not only been lied to but drawn into a dream of reality which is not only false but painful and bitter and murderous. So I began seeing very clearly a line of transmission, gnostic insight—I think I picked up the gnostic aspect of it very early from Raymond Weaver at Columbia, who was a friend of Kerouac's and mine, who suggested Kerouac read the Egyptian gnostics. I never explored it until maybe '67, and picked up on the actual tradition, except through Blake as of '48 and Blake was also a gnostic, and I had some direct transmission there. But I was seeing the transmission, in America, as a transmission of person, the concept of person, the feeling of person, as a breakthrough, a *reasonable* breakthrough, beyond the purely conceptual mind that had gone mad with the fake conceptions of thinking head cut off from the body and cut off from affective feeling. So when I was lying in bed one night in 1958 I shuddered, realizing that America was taking a fall, was going to have to take a big fall.

JM: That's before the July 4th essay?

AG: Probably around the same time, you know . . . yeah, the July 4th essay was written in McClure's house in San Francisco. We had said relatively the same thing before. There's an early interview in the first City Lights *Journal for the Protection of all Beings* talking about . . . I wrote a whole bunch of essays around that time, one was for the *London Times,* one was published in *Evergreen* and also *San Francisco Chronicle,* and one was in the *Journal*—which were pretty good statements, prophetical—sort of summaries of what I felt it had been all about, that is our poetic activity, and the breakthrough into public consciousness of that; why I felt it was almost inevitable and historically charming and real and why it had some significance and what it represented. In other words, I think I was able to figure it out early, and I think everybody knew pretty much what it was all about. Rexroth certainly did. Gary did very clearly, in much finer detail than myself because he was already into not only realization of natural man as distinct from capitalist, or police-state man, but he also had a realization of birds, beasts and nature. He already was into nature and so was McClure. It took me a long time to catch up to that; not till '67 did I really get into ecological perspective as Gary already had.

JM: What did it in '67? Was there something?

AG: Yeah, I went to London to a Dialectics of Liberation and there I met Gregory Bateson and R. D. Laing, and a whole bunch of people; and Bateson gave a great lecture on ecological mind and perspectives, and just presented the information that Gary and McClure were talking about with our discourses on the Club of Rome about *Limits to Growth*. And Bateson said, you keep the heat up the way you're keeping it up and the fog gathers up, and pretty soon you have a cloud over the sky and you have the greenhouse effect and the earth will heat up and melt the poles and the poles will melt and drown the cities with 200 feet of water. I mean he was just pointing out the natural consequences of over-activity and thoughtless feedback. Of course Kerouac has a lot of statements like that, and essays like that in *Lonesome Traveler*; he's got quite a few social statements which are really good. His realization of the fact that something really hard and terrible was coming to America was the realization that the road was no longer open for the wandering hobo saint. In its place you find police cars prowling up and down in strange shark-like science fiction faces and policemen with steely glint of murder in their eyes, stopping people and feeling them up. So Kerouac had a very clear and direct picture of that hard military police-state that was descending on America. The machinery is so big now that it's built that it would be impossible to uproot, just because of the drag of inertia, and the fact that there's so many people whose paychecks are dependent on their work as police or police aids, now—secret police. It's an industry worth several billion dollars now, and if you put on top of that the dope bureaucracy, it's a billion dollars—750 million dollars in the dope bureaucracy now just for the social workers and the police and so forth, the cost this year for suppression of dope. That's just the dope aspect. Then there's billions of dollars that go to Army Intelligence, Navy Intelligence, FBI, National Security Agency, and CIA and what other agencies we don't know. It's an economic interest now, like a cancer—and to cut it out might be a rather violent operation. Nobody's yet X-rayed the government to see how large the cancer is and how fast and far apart into all the nodes of the body the metastasis has spread.

JM: Where's the X-ray machine for that?

AG: Well, the X-ray machine is you have to get access to all the computer material, find out who's on the computers and see everybody's files. I have a solution for the problem actually, I think rather than attempting to destroy the computers and files, there should be a move to make all that information public, to open up the libraries of dossiers on everybody so that anybody can see anybody's dossier, which means that not only can Nixon read my dossier, but I can read his. (Laughing)

JM: Is that what Gregory means by talking about truth in the 70s?

AG: Yeah. In other words, the only way to confront this technological monstrosity is to make it all open and make everybody's head transparent. Just like Watergate disillusions everybody and brings them back to reality, so if everybody's dossier was available with all of the raw data and all of the gossip, fine, sure. As far as I'm concerned I got nothing to lose. But anybody that's got something . . . some secrets (laughing) they are the ones who started all this secret collecting and now let them take the karmic consequences of it—that is, the police agencies themselves. So, that's one way that, I would think, would be working with the negativity of the computerized police state, working *with* that negativity, and making it an asset instead of a liability by bringing all that information out.

JM: You have that essay in Naked Poetry *in which you trace the development of your poetic—it's only about a page—and I wondered if there's any. . . .*

AG: Changes since?

JM: Yeah, or if Snyder has any influence . . . you know you were tracing Snyder's influence on your thinking; how about on your poetics?

Gregory Corso and Paul Krassner. Boulder, Colorado, July 25, 1982. Photograph by Arthur Knight.

AG: No, not too much because I relied more on "spontaneous mind" that I got from Kerouac. From Snyder I got the sense of "riprap," or just hard, tough facts, and some idea of Chinese poetry which was useful to supplement what I had gotten out of Pound's Fenollosa essays. From Snyder it's more like a life-influence, you know, like climbing or sitting or taking Refuge and working with Buddhism. Now I've been wondering, I don't know where I brought that up to in that *Naked Poetry* essay, probably up to mantra chanting . . . O.K., so by then, from mantra chanting then I began doing like devotional homage to my guru, Blake, by putting his words to music. And that's an outgrowth of long experience with monochordal music in the mantra chanting, and then extended to "The Lamb" in Blake or other poems which just required one or two chords, one chord, at first; and then I did about 20 songs on one chord. And then I discovered a second chord, from C to F. Then about 1970 I got much more influenced by Dylan, and then as a result of working with the musicians recording the first Blake album that I did, which was '68, '69, '70. I discovered a third chord; and then by '71 ran into Dylan and he gave me some more information about three chords, and encouraged me to do improvisation. So he and I worked together and made an album and did a lot of recordings together. I started doing my first complete improvised poems on that occasion. And so I got then into studying blues and blues forms as a proper modern ministrelsy, and from that went into ballads and rhymed verse for singing. And from experience with Dylan, who was interested in Peter's gift and mine for improvising, there was a reinforcement from Chogyam Trungpa, who said that what I ought to do was be able to make up poetry on the spot, like the great poets—like Milarepa and his tradition, rather than depending on a piece of paper—that I should be able to trust my natural mind to provide the language and the ideas. In other words, it was just natural mind—and finally came, with him, to another apothegm as good as an earlier one that Kerouac and I had worked out, which was "Mind is shapely, art is shapely" . . . this is an early thing that Kerouac and I figured out; and with Chogyam Trungpa came to "First thought, best thought"—first thought is best thought. That was last year. So, you know, it was a combination of Buddhist influences and jazz influences and there were Kerouac influences.

To continue what I was talking about in the development of poetics in that *Naked Poetry* thing, what I've been doing lately is songs and blues as well as regular writings (regular open page poetry), songs and blues and ballads and then improvisations. So I took *some* instruction from Dylan, as I took instructions from Kerouac, as I took instructions from Chogyam. So it's really nice because it's a feedback from a younger generation, feedback from people who learned from us, then feeding back to us. Even Peter's picking up on the banjo now—doing banjo songs and improvisations on his guitar.

The point of *Howl* that Rexroth made at one time or another, that was historically interesting, was that it was a return to the vocalization of the poem, a return from the page to the voice in which everybody was interested—Olson, Creeley, Williams, all the Black Mountain Poets, Snyder, Whalen—actual voice. With *Howl* it was from voice, to spoken conversation voice, to chant, or to long breath chant, tending to the bardic-chanting direction, the ecstatic direction, and then from chanting it actually moves to song with Dylan in the next generation; and then returns to us as song.

JM: You're talking about your poetry getting this new input from your influence and the return of your poetry from the printed page to voice; have you talked anywhere else about using a tape recorder? I think I heard you say today or yesterday that you've abandoned that now.

AG: Well, Dylan gave me $400 to buy a Uher tape recorder in 1965 as a Christmas present, as he gave Peter enough money to buy his first guitar and. . . .

PETER ORLOVSKY: Amplifier—$40 for an amplifier.

AG: No guitar?

PO: No, no. No. The guitar I bought for $20; amplifier I bought for $40.

AG: Amplifier, yeah—and McClure, enough money to buy McClure an autoharp. And he told me I should learn an instrument. So I bought a Uher tape machine and I used it for like talking into it to make up the poetry like "Wichita Vortex" and the travel poems in *The Fall of America* are taken from the tape machine, transcribed, edited quite a bit (not a great amount, the main body is just as given but blue-penciled for repetition), stitched together somewhat, as are interruptions in conversations—the "Wichita Vortex Sutra" itself is almost intact, except one problem with the tape machine is that at the climax of "Wichita Vortex Sutra," the calling on all of the gods, in that part, the battery went dead while I was dictating that, and I had to reconstruct it later on. (Laughing)

JM: Oh—how awful!

AG: No, it gave me a chance to reconstruct it stronger. But the original one had a funny kind of force that I don't know if the second version has. So from about '65 to about 1970 I had a tape recorder around; it wasn't the only way I wrote poetry, I wrote a lot of nice poems on it like the "Elegy for Frank O'Hara," the "Elegy for Neal Cassady," most of the "Auto Poesy," the traveling things; everything except the stuff in airplanes. But then, well, it was just too much to carry around—notebooks are easier, and sometimes the batteries fail; not as reliable as writing it down. There was one time I went into the field, laid down in a meadow with the tape recorder in Cherry Valley and wrote this exquisite long pastoral poem, cricket chirps and star twinkles or something, you know, it had everything together. I was laying there in the fields and assembling all the sounds and describing them and putting them together. Then I came home and I found out that the machine hadn't been turned on properly and the whole poem was gone. And I said, "Well, fuck this. From now on I'm not going to depend on that machine anymore." It's too much. But it gave me some confidence in improvisation. You realize that if you can talk it, why not just write it; you just talk slowly, you know, talk one line at a time, just like you wrote one line at a time. It's no different, except there's more work transcribing. But then I got to be very artful at transcribing and doing that. But then it's too much trouble carrying it around. And also my Uher got ripped off in 1970 or so. A friend of mine was living at my house in New York, and a couple of guys with knives came in and ripped out the telephone wires and tied him up with telephone wire and stole the Uher and a good Sony I had, ripped off all the tape machine equipment, which was like a real blow because I was just *then* getting into working with Dylan and I needed all the equipment. I had to find cheaper replacements but they've never been satisfactory. So I haven't been using tape anyway, lately. But now I'm in an interesting situation where a lot of the material I do, write, compose, the only *exact* extant manuscripts are chance tape recordings of poetry readings I improvise. So almost every poetry reading I do some improvisation, you know, at one point or another—sometimes extended, sometimes generally rhymed blues form or ballad form, and I'm just slowly verging toward trying to improvise without music, you know, and do my regular forms like *Howl* or "Sunflower" or something like that, but without the crutch of music, or rhyme. Haven't gotten to that yet. Almost did the other day, though, because I went to a lecture of Chogyam Trungpa, and he said, "When we finish with the Refuge Ceremony, would you improvise a poem?" And I figured out, let's see now, (semi-chanting) "Krishna has left the light bulbs, but the illumination shines by itself. Allah is gone out of the Holland Tunnel . . ." And I figured out four or five lines to begin with—then he forgot to call me up (Laughing) after the ceremony. But it made me think of how to do it without music, you know, just thinking fast; I had to—for that situation, to improvise sensible Buddhist imagery, on the subject of there being no god but our own empty mind.

DAN EADES: *Have you yet transcribed any of those, or do you plan to transcribe the ones that you have improvised?*

AG: Yeah, a couple of things. But I've been so busy that I haven't had a chance. I have like maybe several hours of un-transcribed verses on tapes and a lot more that other people have that I haven't ever gathered together. So now I have to make more effort to gather my tapes together in an archive, but it's an awful lot of work; unless there's a reason, I don't think I'll do it. But I'm digging that as a form and I'm discovering that's a most classical form of poetry, the bardic improvisation. That was the oldest form. And it's one that's almost fallen in complete disrepair, and disuse. And it really shows the differences between the rigidification of mind in poetry in, say, the '40s when we came on the scene—which was totally a question of scratching and rewriting and rewriting and rewriting—that is presenting a poem for just a page, as against no more fear of embarrassment at the possibility of simply even forgetting to leave a record behind, but just simply giving forth inspiration into the air. It's a whole transformed attitude, and it's more neolithic. (Chuckling) The latter one is more neolithic—and may ecologically be absolutely necessary when we run out of paper, then people will. . . .

JM: *But you are still concerned with leaving a record behind, surely?*

AG: Not enough to make sufficient effort to gather all the tapes I've made and transcribe them. I'm more interested in being able to compose spontaneously. If I felt that I were just able to do it all the time with no check or hindrance, then I think I'd just forget about the whole problem of books and just go around being a minstrel. And I think it would be an exemplary thing to do, actually, insofar as I could fill out my life from here on out, working toward that— that's the next stage of exemplary poetical activity. There's one thing I did try and do once I realized I was going to be famous and that *Howl* was fixed—I thought it would be nice to really present the persona of a poet "without death as a consequence" (a phrase of Apollinaire), without fuck-up as a consequence, with a really good. . . .

JM: As a consequence of the persona?

AG: No, without death as a consequence of high poetics, as the old Dylan Thomas, Hart Crane, Baudelaire, Rimbaud tradition was. It would be nice to do something else, without death as a consequence, without fuck-up as a consequence, with just increasing spread of consciousness, and increasing powers of a gentle nature that didn't require mass murder, violence, war or anger or aggression. And to really open up some territory that would be usable by other people, but to set a good example. I figured that was one of the best things I could do with the powers that I was given in terms of fame and poetic inspiration. I figured, well, you know, why fuck it up. I've got my health, why not do something nice—like answer every letter, and go around and read free for a long while and develop that into music, or develop it into improvisation if necessary. But that also meant cutting the ground from under myself a lot, like reconciling myself to my father in rhyme again, taking lessons from younger kids like Dylan, and not coming on like a haughty old dog-father, avoiding some of the corniness of dignity and fame, and just developing into something that would be encouraging, rather than a blank wall or a death trap. I'm referring back now to what Gary was thinking of in terms of like what we could do since we were given a Movement, so to speak; it was a *donne*, a gift.

JM: I was just going to ask you if you see Gary as part of that?

AG: Oh sure, Gary is conscious of it too. I don't think it's a question of being too conscious of our roles, in fame or history, because that's just part of the general reverberations of eternal consciousness which is much larger; it's part of the understanding of life as a dream or an illusion or a play, and it's not quite a corny matter of making a good act. It's more involved with Bodhisattva's vow in Buddhism, which is "sentient beings are numberless, vow to illuminate all; attachments are inexhaustible, vow to liberate all; nature gates, Dharma gates are countless, vow to enter every one; Buddha path limitless, endless, vow to follow through." And there's a certain natural impulse towards that, which then becomes more conscious as you study Dharma and meditate, but that Bodhisattvic compassion aspect was something that was very clear very early in Kerouac, and was really the basis of my feeling of love for him; and his tenderness to me was the realization that we were going to die, that we're here a very brief time, and that the body, the situation we were in, the houses we were in were all full of tears of mortality. And with Kerouac, the realization of the existence of suffering was very strong; and the briefness of it, the mortal clouds over it, the skies brooding over the pitiful lonely short brief man vanity puppet-doll sense in his prose, that was really clear in his person and his prose. That perception in Kerouac, which he awakened in me, is very similar to the substance of the Bodhisattva vow. Then there's the problem that if you calculate too much esthetically in terms of careers and in role-playing, you obviously can make mistakes . . . you obviously automatically *will* make mistakes if it's all calculated like that. So it then comes back to dependence on spontaneous mind for inspiration and trust in the heart as the teacher, as the guru, poetically and cosmo-socially, and playing it by ear. I mean both the public activity in imagery—which is a poem, the public role is a poem for everybody, not just the poet, everybody invents their existence and their theater except poets are aware of doing it, sometimes—and maybe are even able to cut through it and show the backstage of the theater; in other words, show that it is theater rather than try to hypnotize other people. And Gregory certainly does that, you know, like really shows the back of his theater and breaks the spell that he makes all the time, and breaks anybody else's spell who's trying to hypnotize you. So he's very valuable that way, painful as it is—it cuts deeply, exposes the raw nerves, the suffering that he goes through, and that you go through to bear with him, and to bear with yourself.

JM: Before we started this tape, you were expressing, understandably, your concern about the chaos of some of the things that are happening in the conference, but on the other hand, Gregory is functioning that way [AG: Yeah.] and it's been important for me, I guess.

AG: Yeah. (Pause) It's funny, it's both repulsive and at the same time absolutely necessary that there be somebody completely mad, as they used to say, but completely sane also, in a funny way. It's the old question of, you know, don't commit god-slight, if the god is Dionysius. Do you know that little canto of Pound's where they commit god-slight? All the sailors mock the young god Dionysius

Allen Ginsberg, Michael Hogan, and Alex Harvey. COSMEP Conference, California, Pennsylvania, June 1980. Photograph by Arthur Knight.

who is there in disguise and he turns them all into leopards and the vines grow over the scuppers.

JM: Yeah, that Second Canto.

AG: (To Peter) So from what we're all saying, do you have anything you want to lay out?

PO: To grow your own food, to start your own orchards: I'd like to, as soon as I can, start growing apple orchards—write away to the government to get some information on how to grow apples and fruits and nuts and grapes and rose hips. I want to grow a lot of rose hips. They're very easy to grow, they're very easy to harvest, and they're very easy to dry in the sun, they're very easy to store for the winter, and they're full of natural Vitamin C. And they probably stop you from getting colds so they are very, very good for you. So I'd like to do that. And Gary was saying that up where he lives at Kitkitdizze it's so hot up there in the summertime that they've got a lot of dried fruit stored away, and that he harvested 300 pounds of wild apples.

AG: They also have acorns there; he knows a lot about acorns. I'll come back in a few minutes. Why don't you ask Peter some historical . . .

PO: Let me say, to finish this. So Gary harvested 300 pounds of apples, then cut them up and dried them all, and he's got a couple of big jars when he's got all the dried apples in them. It's good. He says he doesn't go into the garden though; his wife does the growing of the food. Gary does the hunting. Well, I'd like to try to be a vegetarian, you know. I don't hunt animals; I don't hunt deer. Gary believes in hunting deer with a bow and arrow; I don't think that's fair. If you're going to hunt a deer, you got to do it with your hands, not with a bow and arrow—that's not quite fair; you know what I mean. So in that sense I would be a little worried about Gary; but then again, I've broken my own rules, I've been eating meat lately, meat and chicken and stuff. But I'm planning to get back to vegetarianism, you know. It takes a little while but it's good to be a vegetarian—you're supposed to live longer, I think. You live longer and it's probably more healthy for you. It makes your shit smell clearer and better. And I think also it's probably better for your stomach to be a vegetarian, it's easier on your stomach. That greasy stuff, you know, takes your stomach and ties it up into knots. And stuff like that, you know what I mean? But you ever tried being a vegetarian?

JM: No, I haven't.

PO: Have you, Dan?

DE: No, except for very brief lengths of time.

AG: Don't you have any historical . . . because Peter was in on most every scene. Peter knows lots of detail.

PO: I was with Neal Cassady at the Six Gallery reading, and Neal Cassady said to me, "Come over here, Peter, come stand next to me." I said, "Why? Why, Neal?" And he said, "Well, I don't know anybody here." So I was standing next to Neal but then I moved over and stood next to someone else because, you know, I was a little embarrassed. I was very, very bashful and embarrassed—very self-conscious, you know, in those days. And Neal was there, dressed in his brakeman's uniform. He had his vest on—his watch and his vest.

AG: He was very proud.

PO: He was very proud, smiling, very happy—he was very happy, full of smiles and bowing . . .

JM: *About what was going on?*

AG: Yeah; he came up to me and he said, "Allen, my boy, I'm proud of you." (Laughter) It was really nice—it was the nicest thing I heard that night. It was completely, unabashedly, friendly, happy approval.

JM: *For a historical question, I'd like to know how you first got to San Francisco.*

PO: The Army—the Army sent me over. I was in Letterman Army Hospital, military hospital, in San Francisco as a medic. And I got to meet Robert LaVigne, an artist in San Francisco. And then I was LaVigne's boyfriend for a year, and then Allen saw a painting of me, naked Cleopatra-type painting of me, with a bottle of wine on the painting couch, and fell in love with me through the painting, [AG: Right.] and wanted to come up and meet me right away. And so Allen stole me away from Robert LaVigne. I looked at Allen and said, "My God, he's very smart—he talks very nice, he knows about the world and everything. Boy, it's so good to hear Allen talk." So I really felt intrigued by listening to Allen talk all the time. So I went and lived with Allen; we made love and played with each other. And then we all went to Mexico together—with Allen, Gregory, Jack and . . .

AG: To meet Jack. We were on our way to Mexico and we wanted to give a reading there on the way. We figured . . . let's see, Gary and I had gone up and given readings in Portland and Seattle already and spread the poetry up there, and then I came down. Gary went to Japan and Peter and I and Gregory took off for the south to visit Kerouac who was living in Burroughs' old flat (Burroughs was gone) in 210 Orizaba Street in Mexico.

DE: *What was Kerouac writing then?*

PO: Kerouac was writing then? I think he was writing a poem everyday.

AG: He may have been working on *Desolation Angels* already.

DE: *How accurate do you see Kerouac's characterizations of yourself and other people and your friends?*

AG: I see myself somewhat caricatured, but very tenderly so, and sometimes very penetratingly, critically right, in a way. His criticism of my vanity and egotism was really right, I think. It was a good view—and my general superficiality, actually, as a person. He didn't have a very comprehensive or sympathetic eye on my cock and my love life, or anything like that. He was very reticent about our own relationship sexually, or any sexual relationships that weren't idealizable in his own terms, so that he never really wrote in depth about my relationship with Neal or Peter or himself or anything that involved like a heart-throb sexuality, tenderness, or Gay Lib, so to speak—what it would be called now. So there was a whole area left out there that would fill things out and make me more sensible. As it was, he had me as a sort of thin, nervous heterosexual, I seem to remember, basically. He knew more than that.

DE: *What about Cassady?*

AG: I think his portrait of Cassady is very full and very genuine and really solid. There were three or four people that he was always completely good on, people that he really respected and loved and idolized. One was Burroughs, he's got really good pictures of Burroughs; one was Cassady; one was Herb Huncke; and a couple of others, probably; Gary. . . .

JM: *Yeah, Gary in* Dharma Bums?

AG: Yeah, Gary; it's really a good picture. That's right. Then there are the minor characters, the secondary characters who are not the heroic ones in his books, which includes myself and Peter Orlovsky—well, many many others—John Montgomery—in which he saw the slight crazy vanity within us; and so that was the main tone. But I didn't mind it; I still think it was nice. I once wrote a letter saying: "Why ain't I a hero?" but I said, "What you do with your heroes is that you really get them full, and with us less ignu characters, you have a thinner characterization, more cartoon-like."

JM: To continue with the history, I was wondering if you care to say anything more about Anne Charters' biography than you did in that little introduction. Are you pleased with that?

AG: Well, I wrote that little introduction only on the basis of reading a couple of chapters of the manuscript which had not turned out to be the final manuscript. She had a better version before it was edited and there were a lot of troubles. One main trouble was, of course, that there were a lot of little tiny mistakes, which she has corrected in the paperback. But one problem was Kerouac's estate did not cooperate with her and wouldn't let her see many necessary documents, including the original manuscript of *On The Road*, so she's got the whole *On The Road* story upside down because *On The Road* really is mainly first draft.

JM: It's mainly first draft, not revised, as she told it?

AG: Not as she tells it. It's revised slightly, you know, tacking a couple of trips together, and weaving and looping a few things in together. But the kind of extensive revision that she described, she describes on the basis of his letters to his publisher, which were letters to keep the publisher busy and make the publisher think that Kerouac was working hard because they wouldn't know the difference. And they thought that if you did a lot of work, it would make it nicer. So he just wrote them letters saying, "I'm working on it, I'm working on it, I'm working on it." But I read the original, in the original, and I've also read the final version, and I know they're not very different. It's divided into paragraphs and sentences instead of one long continuous sentence—that's different, of course. But she has it as enormous revisions, you know, stage after stage of superimpositions just like a regular novel—and it's not so. And also she wasn't allowed to quote directly from most of his published texts, which were owned by the estate, because they had another biography—official—scheduled by somebody else.

JM: Do you know who that is, or how reliable it's going to be?

AG: What's his name? Oh, Aaron Latham, who is an editor of *New York Magazine,* who has written a biography of Fitzgerald; and they had gotten an expensive contract with Random House or Scribners, much of which went to the Kerouac family, or a percentage of which went to the widow. So the contract said that they couldn't cooperate with any other biographer until that one was published, and Charters had already started working on her biography sometime before, a year before; so they shut her out from access to materials and letters. And they wouldn't even allow her to quote from Jack's letters to me which *I* gave her to read from my archives. So the direct quote in nine-tenths of the cases has had to be paraphrased, was paraphrased. And she was having a baby at the time when the news came through that there were no reprint rights allowed, no quote rights allowed, so the Straight Arrow Press assigned some secretaires to do the paraphrases. And so they've come out like all botched and messy; so they don't realize that she is quoting Kerouac's own intelligence on himself, his own language and attitudes on himself. It sounds like she, the lady biographer, is kvetching about his neuroticism, his failures and stupidities, when it's *Kerouac* ruefully commenting on his own foibles. In many, many cases you get a really gross view of Kerouac, when it's Kerouac's own view, which makes it a very refined view, actually, and you know, self-critical. You think it's the biographer being critical rather than the author including that insight—the most striking passage that I remember is when she's describing his return from Big Sur, and he got out on the highway where all he could see were middle-class housewives staring straight ahead into their cars and didn't notice the bum on the road. Well, it's actually Kerouac saying, "Then, I got up on the highway and all I saw was a bunch of middle-class housewives looking through their car windows and wouldn't even look at me cause I was just an old bum on the road." Well, from the prose point of view of the present biography, it sounds like Kerouac was limited as some sort of jerky beatnik that got out on this big highway and all he could see was middle-class housewives staring through the windows of cars; whereas when *he* says it, it means something different and much funnier and much more ample, much more Spenglerian, much more aristocratic almost, you know, it's more elegant; whereas it sounds very inelegant—like he's just got some kind of cruddy beatnik view of all the human beings in the cars. And unless you know it's a quote, you really think, Oh, this is sort of a drag; this guy, you know, he gets out on the highway and all he can see is middle-class housewives, and he's got all these prejudices. So it's the thrust of the whole book and it brings it down; it doesn't credit Kerouac his own intelligence, is what it boils down to. So I regret that little blurb I wrote, because I wrote it on the basis of the original manuscript and quotations, and only on a few chapters that I'd seen rather than the whole book.

JM: That's really helpful to know.

DE: Yes, it is. Would you care to comment on one of the implications of her book, that is that Neal Cassady's letters were the start, in a way, for Kerouac, who . . .

AG: Kerouac always said that. I mean, there's no implication. Neal wrote Jack a long, long, long letter which I lost.

JM: Oh, that 40-page letter?

AG: Yeah, well, I loaned it. See, there was a time when I was carrying all this literature in San Francisco when I got there, which was what is now published as *Visions of Cody*—in '53, my own poetry, pieces of Burroughs' *Naked Lunch, Yage Letters,* Neal's letter, and some other poetry. And I brought it around to Rexroth and other people, and Duncan, so that everybody could read it, and I loaned it to various people in Mill Valley, and having less sense, and not having xeroxing in those days, I didn't have copies; so when one batch of all the stuff was returned, Neal's letter was missing—and it's never been found since, except I think it will turn up ultimately, but . . . I noticed it was gone immediately and went back . . . it was in somebody's car trunk on Montgomery Street up where we lived, and went back to ask about it and they said "Oh, what? What? I don't remember." So it's still lost. The guy is still lying—and I keep blaming him for it and he keeps saying, "But I don't remember." Jack kept blaming me for it. Anyway, there was this long letter, part of which was recopied and is the *The First Third:* the description of making it with a girl and then squeezing out the bathroom window when her mother comes in. That's from that letter.

Neal had read Proust at great length and was very good at Proust and could read him aloud because it was very similar to his own mind, that is operating in long lines of simultaneous free-association in Proust, while contained and balanced in a sort of mobile of long sentences with subordinate clauses. So he was really good at reading Proust because it fitted his own mind and tongue. And so his own prose was sort of American-Denver talk, but with Proustian detail. And so he wrote Jack this long buddy-buddy letter, beginning how he was going to tell Jack all about his first flushes of consciousness in adolescence, the first time he got laid, and his first discovery of the universe and his first discovery of consciousness, basically, which is probably something he wrote over the weekend, or in two days, or maybe a week of writing a little bit every night—forty-thousand words, I think. He sent it to Jack just as Jack was trying to write a book about Neal. So the portion of the book about Neal that Jack was writing is now embedded in *Visions of Cody* as that long scene ending with Cody . . . did you read that at all? *Visions of Cody?* It's Kerouac's greatest work, I think, written right after *On the Road.* Well, anyway, there is a scene in *Visions of Cody* in which Cody Pomeray, in a business suit, does a flying tackle on the field outside the high school just at sunset when his old teacher is in the schoolroom slamming his desk shut with a grieving heart, car speeding by with some friends going to a party on the other side of the road, near the football field. It's all sort of like a flash photo in the dying red sunset with Neal, flying forward, and then the tackle. Well, Kerouac had completed that passage which was done in sort of Proustian-Wolfean prose, sentences and all—in the last gasp of a style he had done in *The Town and The City,* his first novel. Then he got this long letter from Neal in which was all this excited talk with all that kind of simultaneous information but done as if he were talking in one long endless sentence without commas, but with dashes for interruptions, and it turned Jack on to the fact that he could just use his natural spontaneous mind, recalling everything he remembered all at once, in the order of memory. So he called the book *Visions of Cody,* meaning his illuminations or visions of the hero, not in chronological order, not in story order but in terms of the most intense flashes of recollection. Like if you have a friend, a close friend, you don't remember your relation to them as a story, you remember it as the most intense moments—you know, and they come up, outside of chronological order but linked together with a structure, the development of feelings between you. So what he did was *visions* of Cody. . . .

JM: Almost to say, poetry, not fiction.

AG: Well, *On the Road* was not fiction either—it's simply . . . I mean, you could tell a chronological story and it not be fiction but poetical or autobiographical. But this was non-chronological, spiritual autobiography; non-chronological in the sense that it just dealt with the most intense moments, moving back and forth in time. And the most intense moment, I think the two of them were taking a piss together in some bar after knowing each other five years, and they were both sort of hating each other—you know, ragged and tired—and Neal was like completely beat out and sort of vulnerable, and suddenly looked over at Jack and said, "You know, Jack, I really love you." And Kerouac was so surprised that he had opened up. So, well—read the book. Oh, he handled it nicely, I

**Gregory Corso and George Plimpton. New York Book Fair, May 14, 1983.
Photograph by Arthur Knight.**

mean, that was like an intense moment when the whole facade of their personalities cracked open and they had . . . so it's *visions* of Cody and there are a lot of other . . . maybe the next chapter would be something that happened five years earlier, some similar re-collection five years earlier, that linked up to that moment. So it was non-chronological, right? But the story, anyway, in terms of flashes. That was his idea. And I think he was turned on to that by Cassady's letter.

JM: You described that vision of the flying tackle in the sunset and it reminded me very much of a poem of your own, and that's the "Sunflower Sutra," because of the sun going down. . . .

AG: Well, I got most of my style from him, from Kerouac; that long line style is from him. That's Kerouac's development of Cas-sady's eager, excited, high fraternal talk.

JM: So there is a direct connection?

AG: We were all influencing each other, I mean everybody influences everybody; you get close to people spiritually and phys-ically and mentally and pick up their habits of mind and you begin to see things through their eyes. I mean, is there anybody in whose eyes you see things? You know, like when you see something you say, "Wow, what would X think of that if he were here, what would he say?" So we were doing that about each other all the time. Kerouac was always saying, "What would Allen think of this way?" I was thinking, "What would Neal say if I told him this? What would Kerouac think of this?"

JM: The other poem that I was thinking about when I asked you about "Sunflower Sutra" in connection with Kerouac's inter-pretation of Cassady's experience, is "Crossing Brooklyn Ferry" because of the sun going down in that poem too, and the stream of associations that are going on there.

AG: Well, I read Whitman in high school, but I wasn't thinking of him when I wrote *Howl*, too much. But then *after* I wrote *Howl*, but before I wrote "Sunflower Sutra" and a lot of other poems, I laid down in bed for a week in Berkeley in a little cottage that we all lived in, and I read all through Whitman from beginning to end, all of *Democratic Vistas*, and the whole of *Leaves of Grass*, and really got turned on—totally turned on, because it was like a complete revelation of the same consciousness cutting underneath the culture and every once in a while with a full dazzling breath and body and basic common sense—basic humor and common sense and natural mind. That really turned me on because, in other words, I'd written *Howl*, and then I went and read through Whitman and just went on to "Sunflower" and all the other poems of that period—"Whitman in the Supermarket," and things like that. I realized that what we were into was right, and it was right in the very basic rightness of attitude that we were into—mood and content.

DE: *Jim has mentioned before that in many ways he thinks that you have become almost the persona that Whitman was projecting, that actually in your travels and in the sense that you really encompass most of the world, it seems like, and bring it together in your poetry. . . .*

AG: Well, I was working consciously to do some of that, but it was more like the natural thing, like we've got airplanes now so it is inevitable. I was working consciously out of the Whitmanic tradition once I read him, thinking, now what did he do that needs to be fulfilled and what did he prophesy that would be useful to do, that would be *sensible* to do, and did he make any prophesies that made common sense that would be useful, you know, to continue a tradition of, without getting too heavily into it because I had other . . . I mean there were a lot of other things to do, but it would be nice to fill out the blank areas.

JM: *You made the "Passage to India" that he said.*

AG: Mmmm, yeah. But I wasn't thinking of him when I went. I mean, esthetically speaking I *might* have been doing it; but at that time I just wasn't. Kerouac was mad at Whitman for saying "Older, wiser Brahma; younger and tender Buddha," "indeed . . . That stupid Whitman faggot." (Laughing)

JM: *What was he objecting to?*

AG: Oh, Buddha is immeasurably older than Brahma, or something. (Laughing) Buddha is much more important than Brahma, and Whitman was making Brahma older and wiser and Buddha younger and tenderer, and Kerouac thought that showed how little Whitman understood real Oriental stuff.

DE: When I read The Fall of America, *and I read it very closely after reading* On the Road, *it almost seemed that it was an updating in time through a different consciousness of much the same things that had happened in* On the Road *and that* On the Road *was almost a celebration of a kind of dying part of America [AG: Yes.] and your poem is almost a lament for the death of what had happened and I wondered how conscious. . . .*

AG: Yeah. Right, but I wouldn't say for the death of what had happened, but the death of the hope that we were all . . . but which is not our hope but the old Whitmanic hope for America, so it's like a recognition that that hope—at least in the form that it was proposed—was now frustrated and the whole situation might be turning sour; that if the hope was ever to be accomplished it would require the fall of America as a nation.

DE: Did you consciously structure The Fall of America *in any way?*

AG: If you notice, it's just absolutely exactly chronological. It's just all the poems I wrote during that time. It isn't really one single book or epic or anything like that; it's just fragments of funning around on the road with a tape machine, then interspersed with just poems I wrote sitting at a desk. I tried to separate out all the material, but there was so much cross-reference, like a lot of stuff on the road—you know, the travel poetry with sometimes elegies for Neal, or sitting at home poem with sometimes references to Kerouac or Neal; or references to the megalopolitan industrial machineries, so that finally I just put everything exactly chronologically, divided into sections covering different eras of time and travel. So in a way it's a little bit of a deceptive title. But it's one that I was sort of cherishing as a title for years, but I never wanted to use it because it seemed like too much of a curse, but seemed final and inevitable after awhile. There's still more of that around, I still have more to publish of that—several conclusions to it. And more— but I just keep adding on to it like a tapeworm. My original conception was that it would go on as long as the Vietnam War went on, and when it was over that would be the determining thing.

JM: In the first part of The Fall of America, *are you consciously thinking of Gary Snyder's* Mountains and Rivers Without End? *Where you start down from Oroville?*

AG: Mmmm. I guess that's a little bit, too. Yeah. I mean the idea of the long scroll poem. But then also I was thinking of the *Cantos* and *Paterson*—but also I was thinking of just the tape machine.

JM: The reason I say Snyder is because of the situation—your coming down through the Northwest is like the second or third poem in Mountains and Rivers Without End *in which you are a character. . . .*

AG: Oh, that's the same trip! No, no, no. That's not the same trip. We made two trips: there was a trip—a hitchhiking trip north and back that we made in 1956. And then in 1965, after the Berkeley Poetry Conference, we took the Volkswagen and drove up to Canada and back down through the desert and Pendleton on the other side of the Cascade mountains, the western side, down through Pyramid Lake, back to San Francisco. I think Gary's poem refers to the first trip; and my poem actually begins and was written during the second trip coming down. But he may have pieces of both. He mixes it up in time, see.

I think some of the anecdotal material involving me is from the first hitchhiking—anything involving hitchhiking would be the first trip; anything that involves driving a Volkswagen or a white Volkswagen coming down would be the second trip. I began mine on the second trip. But I wasn't thinking of *Mountains and Rivers*, no, because I wasn't really aware that it covered that territory.

There was another poem I wrote on that first trip which is, I guess, in *Reality Sandwiches* and called "Afternoon, Seattle," which is a description of the first trip, going to the Wobbly Hall with Gary, and that was in Seattle—the Wobbly Hall in Seattle on Yessler Street. But my influence from Gary was much less really, basically, than my influence both in terms of Buddhism and spontaneous mind; the big influence, the soulful moving thing was Kerouac's heart. Because I was in love with him, I was just sort of romantically in love with him for about six years when we first knew each other, or longer . . . '45 through '55, or so, at least. It was sort of a direct, regular crush, so I was taking instruction from a lover so to speak, from someone I loved at any rate. But it was a very frustrating love affair in *that* sense, because it was a love affair on my part. He loved me in a different way; he was very tender. But it wasn't a physical thing with him except every once in a while we made it. (Long pause) He was very shy about that—more than, I guess, what people are now. There seems to be more of an open scene, now. Maybe partly because of our constant imagery propaganda.

JM: Partly because of your propaganda?

AG: Yeah, a little bit, I think.

JM: Well, Beat poetry had propaganda effects on us all. Just to connect that with Corso's reading—the reason I had Gregory Corso's "Bomb" when he needed a copy, you know, was because that was the first book of poetry I ever bought. It just happened that I had never bought poetry before and the first one I saw was that, and I knew there was something there for me. I did not see Howl *at the time because my reading was still very accidental. In Dan's case, I believe* Howl *was the first book. . . .*

PO: Getting back to City Lights, I knew Neal before he died, you know. I saw him . . . he came to New York City before he died. Sad—he was taking a lot of amphetamines and stuff, you know, but he was very bad. Then Jack was worried, calling us "Communists" . . . Jack was always calling us "Communists," you know, and stuff, in 1969 or '68 or '67, or something . . . '67 . . . '66, because we were going on demonstrations and stuff, you know, being arrested. He was always saying, "Well, I'll be up in my tree with a gun and shoot you Communists—shoot you Commies when I see you riding by."

JM: What do you think caused that in Jack?

PO: What I think caused it is him staying around his mother and looking at TV and the radio and the news, though he was writing a lot then, he developed like a very persistent on-path attitude, which was "Commies, I'll be up in the tree with a gun waiting for you."

AG: Later on he began writing for his mother's ear rather than for Burroughs'.

DE: Did his mother actually dislike as many of his friends as Charters reports in the biography, and especially you?

AG: Well, no, I think the key was that his . . . the story I once heard from Jack was that his father, on his deathbed, made his mother promise to protect Jack from the evil influence of me and Burroughs and maybe Cassady—I don't know about Cassady. So that was like a really heavy paternal instruction, you know, so that really gets internalized—so he internalized that family view. You know, but he also had an inspiration, like Dylan and other people, which is really necessary, which is to include the redneck, hard-hat view. And there's a real view there too.

JM: We're running short. I wonder if . . . would you be interested in talking about your own father at all. Or have you done that elsewhere? You mentioned. . . .

AG: My father has a book out, which I wrote a preface to. And it's pretty much there. My father was relatively friendly to people. Though at first all the parents were offended by their children's friends. Mrs. Kerouac was apparently bugged by us, and my father was bugged by Kerouac, and Lucien Carr and Bill Burroughs, and everybody was misunderstanding everything. That was another instruction for us because we were all such close friends, and our parents all thought we were all monsters seducing their sons, or leading their sons into iniquitous ways and unwholesome influences. That lasted ten years, but then they got over it. I finally had a reconciliation with Mrs. Kerouac after Jack's death. I went to see her in her sickbed in Florida, and sang her Blake's "Lamb." She cried. So did I. And that was the end of our. . . .

JM: That's nice.

AG: Yeah, it was nice to resolve that ghost. It also turned out that she was afraid of my beard. I went to see her at a time I had shaved. I happened to have shaved at the suggestion of Chogyam Trungpa, the lama, who said he wanted to see what I looked like without a mask . . . wanted to see my face. He said he loved me, he

Allen Ginsberg and Bruce Elder. Boulder, Colorado, August 14, 1981. Photograph by Arthur Knight.

wanted to see my face. So I shaved my beard that night, in a big drunken conversation, because he reminded me of Kerouac. And maybe a month later, I was in Florida and saw his mother and I didn't grow a beard. Apparently she was phobic about beards on account of some German uncle.

SELECTED BIBLIOGRAPHY

BOOKS

Cassady, Carolyn. *Heart Beat: My Life with Jack & Neal*. Berkeley: Creative Arts Book Company, 1976.
 Autobiographical account of her life with her husband Neal (the basis for Dean Moriarty in *On the Road*) and with Jack Kerouac.

Challis, Chris. *Quest for Kerouac*. London: Faber and Faber, 1984.
 An account of a trip across the United States by a British writer who rediscovers some of the locations mentioned by Kerouac. Challis also meets many of the "real life" characters from Kerouac's novels.

Charters, Ann, ed. *The Beats: Literary Bohemians in Postwar America*. vol. 16 of *Dictionary of Literary Biography*. Detroit: Gale, 1984.
 This is really an encyclopedia. There are biographical chapters on virtually every figure in the Beat Movement along with critical commentary on their works.

Charters, Ann, ed. *Kerouac: a Biography*. San Francisco: Straight Arrow, 1973.
 The first biography of Kerouac to be published.

Clark, Tom. *Jack Kerouac*. San Diego: Harcourt Brace Jovanovich, 1984.
 The lay person's biography of Kerouac. Sometimes innacurate due to Clark's tendency to treat Kerouac's novels as sheer autobiography, but otherwise helpful.

Gifford, Barry and Lawrence Lee. *Jack's Book: An Oral Biography of Jack Kerouac*. New York: St. Martin's Press, 1978.
 The people who knew Kerouac talk about him in a series of statements linked together with narrative provided by the authors.

Ginsberg, Allen and Neal Cassady. *As Ever: The Collected Correspondence of Allen Ginsberg and Neal Cassady*. Edited by Barry Gifford. Berkeley: Creative Arts Book Co., 1977.
 Letters from the 1940s through the 1960s.

Holmes, John Clellon. *Nothing More to Declare*. New York: Dutton, 1967.
 Splendidly written pieces by one of the foremost essayists of our time.

Holmes, John Clellon. *Interior Geographies: An Interview With John Clellon Holmes by Arthur and Kit Knight*. Warren, OH: the Literary Denim, 1981.
 Signed, limited edition.

Holmes, John Clellon. *Visitor: Jack Kerouac in Old Saybrook*. California, PA: *the unspeakable visions of the individual*, 1981.
 Autobiographical account of Kerouac's various visits to Old Saybrook, CT to see Holmes. This also provides a vivid account of Kerouac's descent into alcoholism.

Holmes, John Clellon. *Gone in October: Last Reflections on Jack Kerouac*. Haley, ID: Limberlost Press, 1985.
 Four essays about Kerouac.

Hunt, Tim. *Kerouac's Crooked Road: Development of a Fiction.* Hamden, CT: Archon Books, 1981.
> Myth-shattering scholarship. Hunt provides solid evidence that there were several versions of *On the Road.*

Johnson, Joyce. *Minor Characters.* Boston: Houghton Mifflin, 1983.
> Autobiographical account of a woman who dated Kerouac at the time *On the Road* was published.

McNally, Dennis. *Desolate Angel: Jack Kerouac, the Beats, and America.* New York: Random House, 1979.
> This biography of Kerouac also provides a broad social picture of the times.

Nicosia, Gerald. *Memory Babe: A Critical Biography of Jack Kerouac.*
> The most researched and detailed account of Kerouac's life accompanied by critical chapters devoted to Kerouac's major works.

Tytell, John. *Naked Angels: The Lives and Literature of the Beat Generation.* New York: McGraw-Hill, 1976.
> Pioneering study of the lives and work of Kerouac, Ginsberg and Burroughs.

ANTHOLOGIES

Bartlett, Lee, ed. *The Beats: Essays in Criticism.* Jefferson, NC: McFarland, 1981.
> Academic but often helpful pieces on the "mainstream" beats plus pieces on lesser known figures such as Bob Kaufman and Brother Antoninus (William Everson).

Donaldson, Scott, ed. *On the Road: Text and Criticism.* New York: Penguin Books, Viking Critical Library, 1987.
> The first half consists of the corrected text of the novel; the latter half consists of writings, both pro and con, about the book.

Knight, Arthur and Kit. *the unspeakable visions of the individual* (series). California, PA.
> Titles include *The Beat Diary* (1977), *The Beat Journey* (1978), 10th anniversary edition of *the unspeakable visions of the individual* (1980), *Beat Angels* (1982) and *The Beat Road* (1984). An invaluable series of books about the Beat Generation. Each volume consists of previously unpublished primary source material by such writers as Kerouac, Burroughs and Ginsberg. Profusely illustrated with previously unpublished photographs.

Knight, Arthur and Kit. *The Beat Vision.* New York: Paragon House Publishers, 1987.
> The "best" of *the unspeakable visions of the individual.*

Parkinson, Thomas. *A Casebook on the Beat.* New York: Crowell, 1961.
> This was the first book to treat the Beat writers seriously. Rather than dismissing them as popular culture figures, it provides an often academic look at their writings.

MAGAZINES

The Kerouac Connection. Edited by Dave Moore, 19 Worthing Road, Patchway, Bristol, England BS12 5HY.
> A quarterly publication that is virtually indispensable for anyone with an interest in Kerouac or the Beats.

Moody Street Irregulars: A Jack Kerouac Newsletter. Edited by Joy Walsh, P.O. Box 157, Clarence Center, NY 14032.

An irregular publication devoted to articles about Kerouac and other Beat Generation figures. Several issues are devoted to special themes.

PLAYS

Duberman, Martin. *Visions of Kerouac, A Play.* Boston: Little, Brown, 1977.

The first play devoted to the life of Jack Kerouac. It was first performed in New York in 1976.

Knight, Arthur Winfield. *King of the Beatniks.* Sudbury, MA: Water Row Press, 1986.

The play is about John Duhon, Jack Kerouac's fictional alter ego. Knight searches for a "poetic" reality rather than a biographical one. The first of the three acts was performed at the Shropshire Drama Festival in England where it won an award in March 1985, but it was banned in Wales.

INDEX